CHICAGO TENANTS' HANDBOOK

Ed Sacks

Illustrations by Juanita Giles

Published in San Francisco by

Harper & Row, Publishers

New York / Hagerstown / San Francisco / London

Dedication

To the struggle for dignity everywhere.

FIRST EDITION

Designed by Hal Hershey/Fifth Street Design Associates

Library of Congress Cataloging in Publication Data

Sacks, Ed.
    Chicago tenants' handbook.

    Includes index.
    1. Apartment   houses—Illinois—Chicago.   2. Landlord   and   tenant—
Illinois—Chicago.   I. Title.
HD7287.6.U5S23   333.5'3   77-20455
ISBN 0-06-067023-1

78 79 80 81 82 10 9 8 7 6 5 4 3 2 1

Contents

Part Five: Is There Really a Santa Claus?

Part Six: Putting It All Together and Making It Work

Appendixes

How It All Began
and Other Required Reading

The realization started several years ago, as they say, when my wife and I discovered that we were paying part of our landlord's electrical bill. There had been some fights about parking cars, and skirmishes about blown circuit breakers. We decided we wanted out. We trudged the cold city streets until we found our "dream apartment."

The place was to be completely rehabilitated. (That's something done to prisoners, political hacks, and old apartments.) New kitchen, new bathrooms. The wood was going to be stripped, and the floors reconditioned. The place was going to be rewired: no more blown fuses. And parking, there would be a real parking lot, no more hassles.

The entire "six-flat" was being "done over" from top to bottom, inside and outside. And to top it all, we could actually afford the rent and, miracle of miracles, the heat was included! Wow!

The management agent was very nice. He promised the apartment would be ready on the first of May, about two months hence. The timing was great. We took it, signed on the dotted line, made a list of things to be done, attached it to the lease, and went on our happy way.

We booked a moving van and started to plan and pack. Occasionally I would call the landlord and ask how the work was progressing. "Fine. Great. No hitches. Right on schedule." He kept on saying that until I stopped by the new place a week before moving day. I was horrified to see the apartment in shambles. A drunken bull elephant crazed by a mouse in the middle of a tornado blitz could not have created such a disaster.

I panicked home as fast as I could. I told my wife. We analyzed the situation. The apartment would not be ready for months. Our current landlord would gladly set poisonous snakes in our bed if we overstayed the lease and we didn't have time to find another apartment. After a minute of calm deliberation I found the ideal solution: suicide. After another minute I thought it might be more advantageous—and certainly more pleasant—to throttle the jerk that rented us the apartment and made all those phoney promises. Instead, I made a phone call and my heart was melted by his honeyed words. The landlord made an absolute "I-swear-to-God-on-a-stack-of-Bibles" promise that the place would be ready on the first of June, four weeks from now when our current lease expired. I said, "OK, so be it."

As trusting lambs, my wife and I went gently on our merry way packing and planning. Occasionally I would call the landlord who would report all was good in heaven. And I believed him. One week before move in, I again inspected the premises. The same wild elephant and mouse had done another number on our new place, or had the landlord lied?

Another "if-words-were-lightning-then-you'd-be-electrocuted-before-you-could-say-hello" phone call. The landlord claimed he was a sober, God-fearing man and knew nothing about my elephants. I was in a corner with no real way out.

We couldn't possibly find a place in a week. The landlord continued to promise. This time he swore on a stack of Chicago Real Estate Board procedures and advisories. I should have known better, but I was raised to trust people; force of habit, I suppose.

When we arrived with the moving van at the new place, there was chaos. No working bathrooms, the floors were still wet from varnishing, windows were missing, no light fixtures, no kitchen sink, the place was half painted, and the wood trim and all interior doors were missing. The closets had neither shelves nor clothes bars. The place smelled of leaking gas. The landlord "forgot" we were coming so he "forgot" to open up the storage room in the basement. Boxes and assorted junk littered the apartment until it was useless to live in.

What was supposed to be a well-planned move from point A to point B turned out to be a rout. It was at this point, looking towards the light from my bottomless pit, that I suddenly understood that the word *militant* was not political rhetoric. It denoted an act of desperation for survival.

The apartment was untenable for the next ten days. One could not shower or cook. The place was littered with boxes of clothing and utensils that could not be put away. My wife couldn't stand the place. She moved out leaving me alone in hell. I spent my days watching over the workmen who seemingly would do nothing without me prompting them. I also guarded our possessions. The front door "didn't quite lock," and the landlord had not put in the new lock, so God-knows-who could come around to rip us off.

This went on for six weeks. Just me, one or two workmen, the landlord on the phone, and the roaches. What the roaches saw in my place was beyond me—just elephant dung, not even any food. Eventually my wife returned and other tenants in the six-flat made themselves known. They all complained of unfinished apartments, leaking roofs, gas leaks, roaches, clogged pipes, no heat, the usual. We joined together as a group and made a formal written complaint. It took thousands of dollars, court orders, rent withholdings, letters, and confrontations, but our mighty band succeeded in getting our building more livable and justice done.

During the course of this horror tale I decided I should share what happened to me and the other tenants in our building with other renters. I hope that I can protect some of you from being ripped off and help show other tenants how to fight back. My story is not isolated or unique. These things are happening all the time in Chicago and I surmise almost everywhere there are landlord wolves setting traps for sweet lamb tenants.

Read on my friends and keep strong.

The Chicago Tenants' Handbook is designed as a resource tool for the apartment dweller and details the entire realm of apartment living (except decorating, partying, raising pets, and plants).

Keep this book handy—it is your bible to survival in the apartment jungle. Browse through the entire book once to get the feel of it. Then dive right into the parts of the book that specifically concern you. Skip chapters that contain information you do not need at the time. Check out the appendixes. The phone numbers alone are worth their weight in gold if you need the garbage picked up or if your power has been shut off.

The *Handbook* is written by an apartment dweller, a tenant, an occupant, a lessee of the first part. I am not a lawyer. Discussions about the courts and the laws are my own observations and interpretations. The *Handbook* is not a legal advisory service. It is a practical guide to apartment survival. Affront the law and confront the landlord at your own risk. Be gutsy and be prepared.

A brief comment: in apartment struggles the economically disadvantaged can turn to public and community organizations for advice and legal aid, the rich can buy their way out of the situation, but the vast majority of us—the so-called middle class—cannot afford the private lawyers, the time off our jobs, or the money to move to a better apartment. We are stuck in the middle. The *Handbook* offers alternatives. Take them and use them.

Ed Sacks
Chicago, Illinois

Acknowledgments

I wish to thank, and make special note of the following people and institutions who have contributed in one way or the other to *The Chicago Tenants' Handbook:* David deVries, Jerry Smeltzer, Humberto Correa, Steven Smeltzer, Marie Kurgan and her son Kenny, Francisco Martinez and his parents, brother, and sisters, Hélène Rozenberg and Judith Diaz (who started the ball rolling). These people are the Fremont Tenants' Association—strong individuals who demand dignity and fairness and are not afraid to fight for their rights.

Thanks also to Anne Wilmot for manuscript assistance; Peggy Harrison, Avena Ward, and Janice Murphy for manuscript preparation; Terry Russell, Matt Piers, Joan Topping Russell, and G. Pat Gloor for legal advice; Howard Ryder of the Chicago Real Estate Board; Beverly Dordick of the Institute of Real Estate Management; Judge Eugene Wachowski, retired, First District, Cook County Courts; Dennis Gurgone, Administrator, Building Department Complaint Bureau; Frank Sulewski, Assistant Corporation Council; and, Fred Deters and Katherine Smith, Department of Development and Planning (all from the city of Chicago). I would further like to thank W. Donald Sally, Vice President, Baird and Warner Management Company; Bob Roemer, Commonwealth Edison Company; John Oddy, Illinois Bell Telephone Company; Jim Green, Hull House Tenants' Union; and, Lauren Poole, Jane Addams Center.

And, finally, thanks to David and Sue Herman for their continued encouragement and love during this long struggle. Also my regular clients who had the patience to put up with my usual gruff and still understand.

To all of you I say *merci.*

E.M.S.

A Tenant's Education

by Helen Shiller

A tenant's education often takes longer than a doctor's or a lawyer's, and it is more expensive, because the rent must be paid every month. The first grade of the tenant's school is the ice on the inside of the windows in January, the busted water pipes, the cold water, the peeling paint that causes lead poisoning, the doors with locks that fall open, the pop-a-top again mailboxes, and more and more likely, the taste of smoke, the sight of flames, and the sounds of screams on a cold, dark night.

The tenant's school teaches fear, frustration, anger, and heartbreak. But we admit that it gives knowledge. When the tenant begins to fight back, it is like peeling an onion. Layer after layer of lies and corruption and concealment are revealed. A system becomes clear, based on the suffering of tenants.

The small landlord may make life miserable, but usually because his own life is being made miserable. The tenant learns, when he fights the small landlord, that he is really fighting the banks. When the tenant tries to use the city housing departments, he finds they are already in use: the slumlords have them busy being bought off and the speculators and developers are using them to harass the small landlord out of business. When the small landlord is driven out, the "businessmen" come in.

The tenant learns in fighting the larger landlords that they are just small-time muggers, taking advantage of dark and unprotected places in the road. They buy a building cheap, collect rents, do no repairs, pay no bills until the building is near death. If called into court, they sell it for a dollar to one of their associates and get another year from the court to milk the building. When the building is almost gone, then they burn it, collect the insurance, and sell

*This editorial originally appeared in *Keep Strong Magazine*, 2, no. 8 (March 1977), and is reprinted here with permission of the magazine.

the land. When the tenant finds out who bought the land, he has earned his high school diploma.

Behind the small-time speculators and slumlord rip-offs are banks and multinational corporations that own half the resources of the world. The men at the top of these corporations and banks are the ones who have decided that the tenants of the city—those who are poor and working people, who are Black, Latino and poor White—should be driven from the city. They brought us here in search of jobs, now they are finished with us. They have made the decision to let our neighborhoods self-destruct, to let our schools go out of business, to let our children go hungry.

When the tenant learns that it is possible to fight these giants, step by step, one piece at a time, the tenant has earned a Ph.D. Tenants can go from busted pipes and burning buildings to people's power, fighting to learn and to win every step of the way. It is not the most pleasant way to live life, but there is no real alternative, and we owe it to the next generation to take the knowledge we gain and use it to fight the enemy.

PART ONE

The Stalk
and the Chase

1

Apartments in Chicago
—What Are They Like?

Apartment hunting is a frustrating, time-consuming activity that most people would rather avoid. And because of the bother, choosing an apartment can become a haphazard activity guaranteed to haunt us with our mistake until the end of the lease.

If we are going to live in an apartment for several years, we owe it to ourselves to select a place and a landlord we can survive with for the time spent together.

Put simply, if care is not taken with the initial selection of an apartment, the problems inherited with the lease can destroy much of the peace and pleasure to which every man, woman, and child are entitled when an apartment is rented. From noise to roaches, to lack of essential services, to leaking roofs, broken windows, and peeling paint, and the many things in between, if you choose the wrong place there will be hell to pay. Sometimes moving out is the only answer; other times, court battles hassle everyone involved. Doing it right the first time is the best advice.

Before hitting the streets, a brief discussion of the kinds of apartment houses that are available might be helpful for first-timers.

There are many types of buildings available in Chicago. The most common types are *three-flats, six-flats, courtyards, low-rises, four-plus-ones, townhouses,* and *high-rises.*

Most of Chicago's apartments, about 65%, are found in low rise buildings from small two-, three-, four- and six-flats to twelve-, twenty-five-, and thirty-two-flat complexes. Sixty-seven percent of all apartments in the city were built before 1940, so they are old.

Three-flats were built around the turn of the century. These are usually three-story buildings containing three apartments (hence the name). They are white stone front or brick walk-ups with five to seven rooms. The bedrooms are small, the kitchen, dining room, and living room are moderate in size. Usually there is a gas fireplace (but not necessarily a working fireplace). Typically, there is one cramped bathroom. There may be two or three small closets, probably not enough room for most people's requirements. These flats are laid out lengthwise and are affectionately referred to as *railroad apartments:* long and narrow with all the rooms coming off a main hallway.

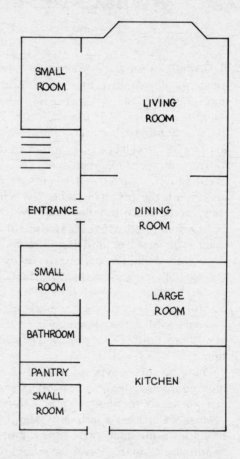

Typical layout of a two- or three-bedroom "railroad" apartment in a Chicago three-flat, circa 1890.

In the older, nonrehabilitated three-flats, steam heat is normally supplied as part of the rent so the flats are usually warm in the winter. But because these buildings were constructed before widespread use of electical lighting, wiring is barely adequate. Normally only two circuits are provided for an entire apartment, and window air conditioners are out of the question. These buildings, though structurally sound, are a bit "fragile." The walls, of plaster and wooden lathing, are cracked, the wiring is old and of small gauge, the plumbing is probably undercapacitied and over-worked. Sometimes the beautiful wood trim, hardwood floors, and doors have been painted a dozen times. Notwithstanding the foregoing, these three-flats are great places to live. They are the closest thing an apartment dweller will find to a single-family home. They are quiet, secure, and friendly.

The rehabilitated three-flats are even nicer. Usually the front room is enlarged, closets are added, walls and floors are redone, plumbing and wiring are revamped. There has also been a trend toward installing central forced air heating and air conditioning

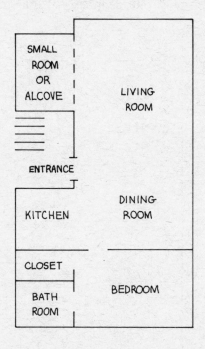

Typical layout of a converted one- or two-bedroom apartment in an old three-flat.

systems for each apartment. A new hot water heater may also be part of the same package. These rehabilitated apartments rent at higher rates and, because all the utilities and heating are extra, operating expenses will also be higher. If there is any storage space, it will be in the basement.

Two-flats are similar in type to the three-flats, but they tend to be smaller. Typically, the two-flat will be owned by the occupant of the first floor. The chances of living with the landlord in a three-flat are more remote because three-flats are more likely investment properties, while two-flats are homes for the owners.

A word of advice: avoid living with the landlord or owner. In taking a proprietory interest in their property, they sometimes go overboard in herding after the tenants. A landlord living in the same building can become a haunting tyrant, swooping down at the first sound of a picture hook going into a wall, or at the first sniff of paint. Lectures on excessive toilet flushing are not uncommon. Forewarned is forearmed.

Six-flats or *eight-flats* are three- or four-story buildings of brick construction with brick or white stone fronts. They are walk-ups.

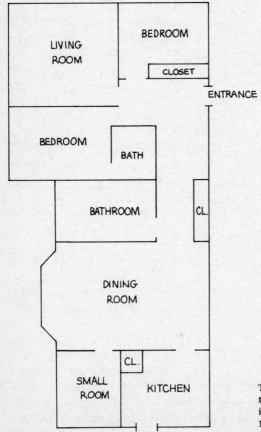

Typical layout of a two- or three-bedroom apartment in a six- or eight-flat, circa 1910-1920.

Essentially these buildings are two three-flats joined at the middle with a common entrance and stairway to each side of the building. The layout and rehabilitation potential for these buildings is the same as for the three-flats. They seem to be a bit larger, however, but the same warnings about walls, electricity, and plumbing apply. When maintained in good condition, these apartments are the next best things to a real house.

Unfortunately, many of these beautiful buildings have been converted into three-room apartments, splitting up the spacious old flats. Crowding in these converted buildings is a problem, and maintenance is a real crisis. The plumbing and wiring cannot adequately support the added apartment load and the management of these buildings is usually more interested in the bottom line than with decent living conditions. If a small three-room apartment is needed, find it in a larger building designed to sustain the heavier loads of higher density living.

In a six-flat there is probably storage space available, and maybe a coin-operated washer and dryer. There may also be a greater chance of renting a parking space or garage than in the smaller flats.

Courtyard buildings are "newer" buildings constructed in the first thirty years of this century. Three- or four-stories high, they are usually a series of small buildings with four to eight apartments in each building. These buildings share common side walls and present one unified façade with many doors (one set for each small building). The courtyard building forms a *U*-shape on a large deep lot. The courtyard is the central open area. The apartments are one- or two-bedroom units, laid out in a square (as opposed to the railroad effects of three- and six-flats).

The courtyard apartments are the type one expects an apartment to be. They tend to be small and in need of a good face-lifting. They are most often walk-ups. Steam heat is supplied. The wiring is almost adequate and the plumbing fixtures are old. The place has that "lived-in look," not necessarily an affirmative commendation.

There may be a janitor or maintenance man on the premises. The residents are probably long-term. Parking will no doubt be on the streets. The construction of the walls is plaster and lathe, the floors are wooden.

Unfortunately, many of these buildings have not been well cared for. Some are beautiful, with lawns and gardens, decent (but not stunning) interiors, and unchipped, nonleaking plumbing; however, most are slipping.

The *low-rise*, noncourtyard buildings are about the same as the courtyard apartments. They are getting old and tend to have smaller rooms and apartments than the three- and six-flats. They can contain anywhere from twelve units to one hundred; there are a lot of thirty-two-unit buildings. Sometimes there will be a small lobby, sometimes not. Occasionally there will be an elevator, but usually the building will be a three-or four-story walk-up. These buildings tend to be the dingiest and saddest when neglected. There may be a janitor and perhaps a manager on the premises. If there is no one from the building on the premises, this should be a good indication of how serious the management is about keeping the building up. Beware and stay away.

These typical older apartment complexes, when left to ruin, are the seeds of blight and slums. When shopping for an apartment in the low-rises, take care to pick a building that is not sending the manager to Majorca and the tenants to hell. Many of the better buildings are being converted to condominiums, thus these reconditioned buildings are lost to renters.

Quite obviously there are other configurations among these older style buildings. A bit of looking may reveal some elegant examples of an older Chicago. There are also many wooden *balloon frame* houses. Chances are they are the worse for wear when compared to brick buildings of the same age.

Of the newer buildings are the *high-rises*. Most of them are less than thirty years old. The older high-rises are brick, the newer ones are constructed from cement, steel, and glass. Most new high-rises are dedicated to condominium sales, and most of the newer buildings are being converted to "condos."

High-rises offer many conveniences: a large lobby, usually decorated; a doorman; 24-hour security with TV monitors; two or three sets of doors to get into the building; parking in the building; four or five full-time maintenance men; elevators; an office-of-the-building to receive packages or big pieces of mail; fire-fighting equipment on each floor; front and back door buzzer/intercom system; and a large self-service coin-operated laundry. In addition, there may be a food shop, a snack bar or restaurant, a dry cleaner's station, a tailor, a drug store or cigarette shop. Some even have meeting rooms, swimming pools, club rooms, and a small children's nursery.

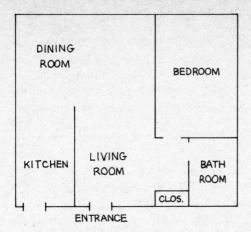

Typical layout of a one-bedroom apartment in a relatively new high-rise building.

The high-rises are centrally heated with steam or hot water and usually have central air cooling via the same system. Floors are usually tile or carpet over cement. Walls are plaster veneer over lathe, or just plain old dry wall (plasterboard). The condition of the apartments is mostly acceptable. The plumbing system works, the wiring is adequate. Ventilation in the apartment may be a problem, however. Window openings to the outside are restricted. Sometimes this can cause the entire floor to share the scent of a neighbor's sauerkraut and cigars.

The amount of ambient noise is dependent upon the type of flooring (carpeting on the apartment upstairs makes it quieter downstairs) and whether the walls are dry wall or real plaster and lathing. Generally, the older high-rises are more soundproof than the new buildings. A friend who lives in a new high-rise once claimed that his walls were so thin that he could read the newspaper of the man in the next apartment through the wall. I doubt it, still, sound is one of the major drawbacks to a high-rise. The steel and cement are excellent transmitters of noise. The thin wall construction is a very poor insulator. The result can be instant cacophony.

High-rises also tend to be like dormitory living. They act as large protective structures which shield the dweller from the outside. They are also very "cold" places where people see others only in the elevators or laundry room. Neighbors don't know or speak to each other. There is a strong feeling of isolation. And if there are strangers in a building (and there are, you know) there is nobody to identify the intruder and call for help. The high-rise is for individuals not wanting a lot of adventure and with a desire for a trouble-free, if colorless, apartment existence.

Many first-time apartment dwellers seek out a type of building known as the *four-plus-one*. This is a five-story building with a ground floor parking lot. They have 85 to 100 studio (one room) and one-bedroom units. Elevator, gas, hot water, hotwater

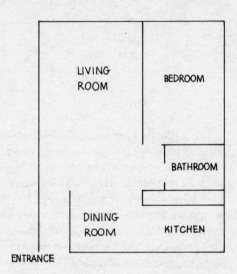

Typical layout of a one-bedroom apartment in a "four-plus-one."

baseboard heating, and a window unit air conditioner are usually all provided. Mostly singles or roommates live in four-plus-ones. The construction is "economical" (to be generous). The building is a brick façade over insulation. The main supports are steel but the building is essentially a five-story, wood-framed structure with plywood decking. They are only five stories high because the Chicago building codes require stringent fireproofing, safety precautions, and parking spaces for buildings above five stories.

The interior walls are of the thin, dry wall, sound-passing type. Floors are either wooden planks (classic floors), parquette tiles, or carpeted. The room layouts are square. There is usually a janitor nearby. The buildings are run by management firms who usually underbudget for maintenance. If a problem crops up for which parts are needed, a long wait may be in store. Four-plus-ones have no real lobby. They usually provide a small, overworked coin-op laundry facility. Storage may be available on a first-come, first-served basis. This storage, unfortunately, is open for pilferage and not recommended for anything that can be resold such as bikes, tools, or suitcases.

Parking for about half the tenants of the building is available underneath the structure. Tenant turnover in a four-plus-one is fairly high. In three years time there is probably an entire turnover of residents. Rumor has it that four-plus-ones are not expected to last much more than fifteen years before they require demolition. Because of Chicago City Council action, few new four-plus-ones will ever be built. The main restriction to building is that more parking be provided on a better ratio of occupants to spaces.

The newest trend in apartment living is toward the *townhouse.* These are usually two- or three-story single-family dwellings sharing common exterior walls. They are also called *row houses.* Townhouses can be built with as many as six levels, staggered front and rear, or simply two or three levels. In concept, they give every person a castle, with the freedom of renting. Many townhouses are also sold as condominiums.

Townhouse construction is similar to the four-plus-one: economical! The layout is "squarish." There is sometimes a balcony or open, wrought-iron spiral staircase. No utilities or heat are provided in the rent. Because there are fewer people housed with this row house concept, the noise may not be as bad. There will be a central courtyard or plaza for three to ten of these units where one might find gas grills, a garden or grassy area, and some paved or bricked walkways. Many of the townhouses are built on urban renewal lands. Some can be found tucked in between older buildings on residential streets.

There are obviously a number of buildings not covered here. In a sense every apartment house is different. It is possible to find friendly, quiet high-rises and also well-kept low-rises. Sometimes, when a building is rehabilitated, innovative work is done and the building becomes a real find. What type of building you choose will depend on your taste and your pocketbook.

2

Finding an Apartment: How and Where to Look and Look and Look

Deciding Where to Live

The first question to ask yourself in deciding to find a new apartment is: In what part of town do I want to live?

Chicago is divided into well over 100 small areas and ethnic communities. The part of town selected may well be influenced by race, religion, family background, job location, schools, public transportation, parking, cost of rent, current residents, population trends, types of rental units, safety in the area.

If you are new to the city, you should understand that we are not homogenous. We are a marble cake of peoples. Each block has a character and ethnicity of its own. There are pockets of Eastern Europeans in the heart of the Latin Quarter of Chicago. The Italians cling to a piece of the West Side. Take a walk down Taylor Street, or up Milwaukee at Ashland and Division, or Clark just north of Belmont. You would think you were in a different world. This is really Chicago—bunches of peoples. This is what gives the city its particular personality.

The real estate types have hyped the North Side along the lake and Hyde Park as THE place to move or buy. Subsequently, these parts of town have become posh, expensive, and although of mixed ethnic groups, predominantly waspish. The neighborhood strength and ethos are diluted because the high rents push out the more "native" residents for high-ticket interlopers.

Even though I will discuss where the heavier apartment traffic is located, and even though these areas are perceived by us as "popular," they are not necessarily the most desirable or friendly.

It is in the best interest of the real estate holders to promote those parts of town where they have control, and where they can

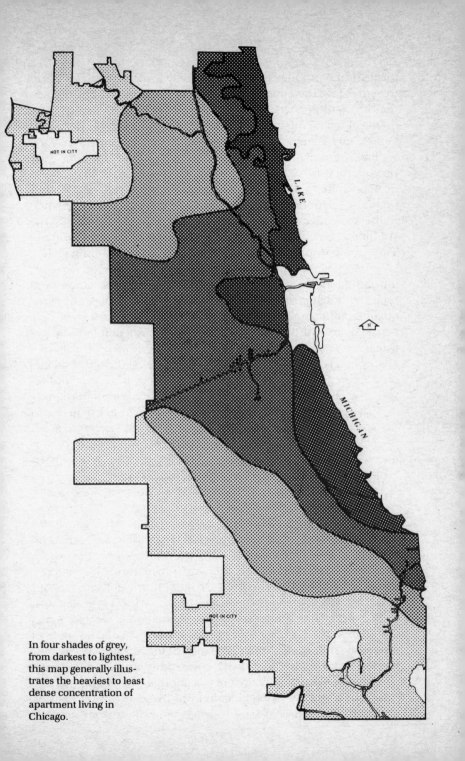

NOT IN CITY

LAKE

MICHIGAN

N

NOT IN CITY

In four shades of grey, from darkest to lightest, this map generally illustrates the heaviest to least dense concentration of apartment living in Chicago.

make the most money. If you would like to live in an area more akin to a small town neighborhood with reasonable rents, shop outside the high rent districts.

One of the many small wars being waged by neighborhood and community groups is to stop the developers from putting the redline squeeze on bank loans and fire insurance rates for their neighborhoods. This squeeze stops almost all rehabilitation and promotes blight. Redlining is a tactic whereby the loan institutions and insurance companies draw a red line on a map and then refuse to loan money or issue insurance to people inside the "redlined" area. The money people call such areas HIGH RISK. The people living inside the red lines call the area strangulated! When the neighborhoods begin to crumble, the panic sellers move out and slumlords move in (sometimes with arson gangs) and rape the housing stock. After the collapse is complete, the area qualifies for federally funded improvement monies that redlining banks share with the ticky-tac developers and slumlording real estate interests.

The area is "revitalized." This really means all the old residents have been forced out and a new set of well-paying "out-of-towners" crash the neighborhood. Everybody loses but the banks.

My suggestion: If you are new to Chicago, plan to live in one of the so-called popular areas just long enough to learn the rest of the city. Then pick a nice, real neighborhood and act as the grass on a hillside—put down roots, hold the soil in place, and stop the rent and apartment erosion of the big money boys.

The accompanying Model Cities map shows 76 major community areas or names of parts of Chicago.

Younger people tend to congregate along Lake Michigan, north of the Loop. On the north side, just west of this lake shore belt and north to Division will be blacks. Latinos, mostly Puerto Ricans, are in a heavy concentration in the west town Humbolt Park area, north to Howard. From Irving Park Road north to Evanston, Appalachian whites will also be located. From Wilson Avenue north to Howard a large American Indian population is located. Along Clark Street north of Belmont there is a sizeable concentration of Japanese and some Koreans. Around the Lawrence/Lincoln/Western area is the new Greek community and an old Jewish community. West along Lawrence is another Latino community.

Germans still live along Lincoln from Diversey north to Foster. The Polish community, formerly living along Milwaukee Avenue, is now dispersed. Other Spanish-speaking communities occupy an area from about Ohio Street on the south to Fullerton Avenue on the north, Elston/Ashland on the East to Pulaski on the west. Heavy industry, and now predominately poor blacks occupy the area south of Fullerton and, making a crescent sweep south, east along Kostner and Cicero Avenue to south of the Stevenson Expressway. Between Kedzie and Lawndale along 16th Street is Little Village, a Mexican community. Along South Ashland at 18th Street is Pilsen, another Mexican community.

There are two Chinese areas of town, one on the near South Side at Wentworth and Cermac (Chinatown) and a new area north in the Edgewater area of Uptown around Bryn Mawr and Broadway. The Swedes claim Andersonville, north on Clark Street near Foster, as a Scandinavian enclave. The Italian communities have somewhat dispersed but there is a concentration just west of the University of Illinois Circle Campus along Taylor Street.

There are still several Jewish communities in the city: in the areas along Wilson/Lawrence/Foster from Kedzie west to Pulaski called Albany Park and West Albany Park. Also west on Howard Street in the West Rogers Park area and east along Rogers in Rogers Park. There is also a shrinking Jewish population south of 88th Street near the Lake in the South Shore community. On the outer southwest and northwest edges of the city the population is mostly white, Protestant or Catholic, working, and middle class.

Areas that seem to be popular for apartment dwellers are: the **Hyde Park** neighborhood near the University of Chicago on the south side (in the middle of a poor black ghetto); the **Gold Coast,** from Lake Shore Drive west to LaSalle, and from Division north to North Avenue (in the middle of the rich, white ghetto); **Old Town,** Clark street west to Larabee, North Avenue north to Armitage; **Lincoln Park,** Armitage north to Diversey, Lincoln Park West and Lakeview west to Halsted; **Park West/Sheffield/De Paul,** Larabee west to Racine, Willow north to Wrightwood; **Lakeview,** Diversey north to Irving Park Road, Lake Shore Drive/Sheridan Road west to Clark Street/Sheffield/Sheridan Road; **Uptown,** Irving Park North to Hollywood, Marine Drive west to Kenmore/Ashland; **Lake Shore,** Hollywood north to Devon Avenue, Sheridan Road west to Broadway; **Loyola,** Devon Avenue north to Touhy Avenue, the Lake west to Western Avenue; and **East Rogers Park,** Touhy Avenue north to Evanston, the Lake west to Western Avenue.

There are also some good places away from the Lake. **Jefferson**

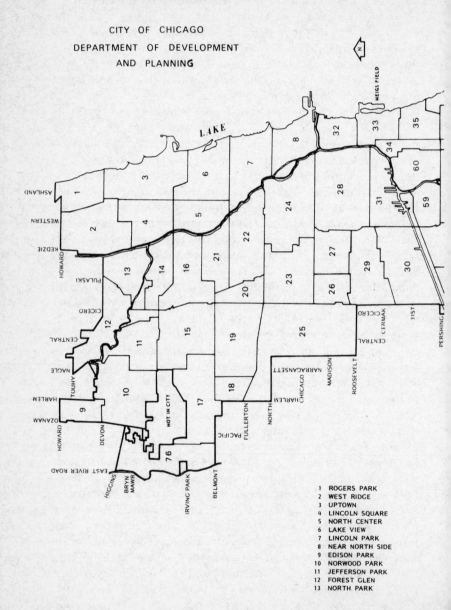

CHICAGO
COMMUNITY AREAS

CITY OF CHICAGO
DEPARTMENT OF DEVELOPMENT
AND PLANNING

1 ROGERS PARK
2 WEST RIDGE
3 UPTOWN
4 LINCOLN SQUARE
5 NORTH CENTER
6 LAKE VIEW
7 LINCOLN PARK
8 NEAR NORTH SIDE
9 EDISON PARK
10 NORWOOD PARK
11 JEFFERSON PARK
12 FOREST GLEN
13 NORTH PARK

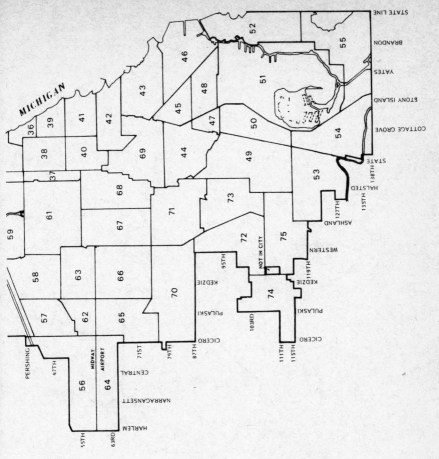

		31	LOWER WEST SIDE	52	EAST SIDE
14	ALBANY PARK	32	LOOP	53	WEST PULLMAN
15	PORTAGE PARK	33	NEAR SOUTH SIDE	54	RIVERDALE
16	IRVING PARK	34	ARMOUR SQUARE	55	HEGEWISCH
17	DUNNING	35	DOUGLAS	56	GARFIELD RIDGE
18	MONTCLARE	36	OAKLAND	57	ARCHER HEIGHTS
19	BELMONT CRAGIN	37	FULLER PARK	58	BRIGHTON PARK
20	HERMOSA	38	GRAND BOULEVARD	59	MCKINLEY PARK
21	AVONDALE	39	KENWOOD	60	BRIDGEPORT
22	LOGAN SQUARE	40	WASHINGTON PARK	61	NEW CITY
23	HUMBOLDT PARK	41	HYDE PARK	62	WEST ELSDON
24	WEST TOWN	42	SOUTH SHORE	63	GAGE PARK
25	AUSTIN	43	SOUTH SHORE	64	CLEARING
26	WEST GARFIELD PARK	44	CHATHAM	65	WEST LAWN
27	EAST GARFIELD PARK	45	AVALON PARK	66	CHICAGO LAWN
28	NEAR WEST SIDE	46	SOUTH CHICAGO	67	WEST ENGLEWOOD
29	NORTH LAWNDALE	47	BURNSIDE	68	ENGLEWOOD
30	SOUTH LAWNDALE	48	CALUMET HEIGHTS	69	GREATER GRAND CROSSING
		49	ROSELAND	70	ASHBURN
		50	PULLMAN	71	AUBURN GRESHAM
		51	SOUTH DEERING	72	BEVERLY
				73	WASHINGTON HEIGHTS
				74	MOUNT GREENWOOD
				75	MORGAN PARK

17

Chicago is a city of many cultures and ethnic groups. It is also a city of neighborhoods. In a general way, we try to identify the predominant flavor of some of those parts of town:

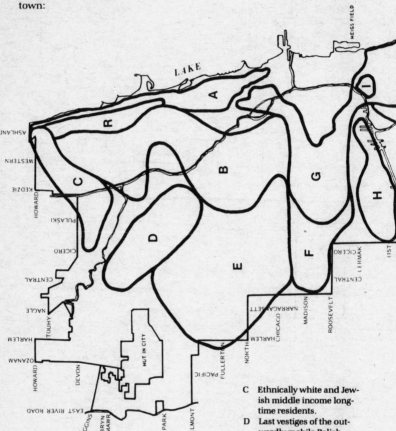

A   Lakeshore peoples, predominantly white, ethnically purged, middle and upper income.
B   A mixture of long standing European ethnics with a substantial Latin, mostly Puerto Rican, flavor; middle and moderate incomes.

C   Ethnically white and Jewish middle income longtime residents.
D   Last vestiges of the outwardly mobile Polish and German population concentrations, middle income.
E   Nondenominational whites of middle income status.
F   Polish and other European ethnic groups of moderate income.
G   Predominanantly black and lower moderate incomes.

18

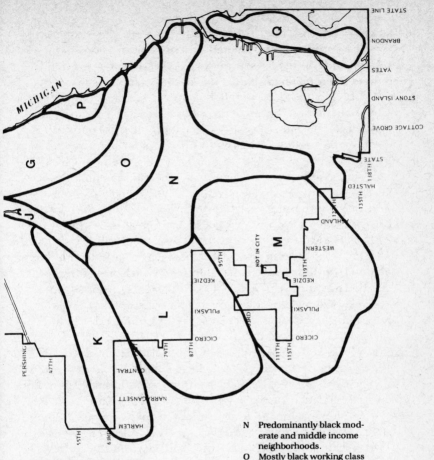

H Predominantly Mexican
   with moderate income
   status.

I Chinatown, mostly Chinese
   with middle to upper
   incomes.

J "Back of the Yards" working
   class moderate income
   whites.

K Eastern European and
   Irish ethnic working class
   area of moderate to middle
   income status.

L White working middle
   class with Eastern European heritage.

M White middle to upper
   middle class income levels
   from Eastern Europe and
   Ireland.

N Predominantly black moderate and middle income
   neighborhoods.

O Mostly black working class
   moderate income area.

P Hyde Park: Bastion of the
   University of Chicago and
   mixture with emphasis on
   whites, with middle and
   upper level incomes.

Q Solidly working class,
   Eastern European middle
   income area.

R Uptown: port of entry for
   newly arrived, be it from
   another country or part of
   this country. Not really a
   melting pot, but a mixing
   bowl: Chicanos, Latinos,
   Blacks, Chinese, Indians
   (American, East, and Sub-
   continental), Appala-
   chians, students, even
   Russians.

Park is northwest along the Kennedy Expressway at Foster and Central. **North Central** is located west of Lakeview along Western and Addison. On the far southwest side is **Morgan Park** and far south is **Beverly. Logan Square** is in the middle northwest.

In addition to these rental hot spots, housing is available throughout most of the city. It probably will cost less, but may also be less desirable either because of location, size, or condition.

Before starting the long trek to find an apartment, "let your fingers do the walking." Get a good map of the city of Chicago. Maps can be purchased from the Chicago Tribune Public Service Office, 435 North Michigan Avenue ($2.10 by mail), or from the Rand McNally Map Store at 39 South LaSalle. The Blue pages of the Chicago Redbook (Yellow Pages) also list each street by its north/south –east/west location. Together these tools will save hours when the actual search begins. And if you are new to the city, the maps will provide good directions and keep you from getting lost.

By the way, Chicago addresses are designated north/south – east/west. The dividing lines are State Street and Madison Street. All locations north of Madison on streets running parallel to the lake are prefixed *north* and those south of Madison are prefixed *south*. The lateral streets (those running east and west) are divided at State Street. The layout is quite logical and Chicago is an easy town to learn. The tricky streets are the diagonal streets. These all have interesting histories. They were the first paths into the city—some were Indian Trails, some toll roads or pikes, some cattle paths, and some interconnecting routes from the outside world. Because they cut across the city diagonally, the addresses can be confusing. When traveling these streets for the first time, be sure and take that map.

Organizing Your Search

Drive, walk, public transit, or bike to several areas in that part of town that appeals to you. Check out the general condition of the buildings along the way, find where the shopping areas are located, note proximity to public transportation and the routes between job and potential homes. By walking in the area one can see whether there is a good deal of new construction or rehabilitation going on. If there is work going on, assume the neighborhood is being renovated and may be a good place to live. These neighborhood conversions go on for three or four years. When complete,

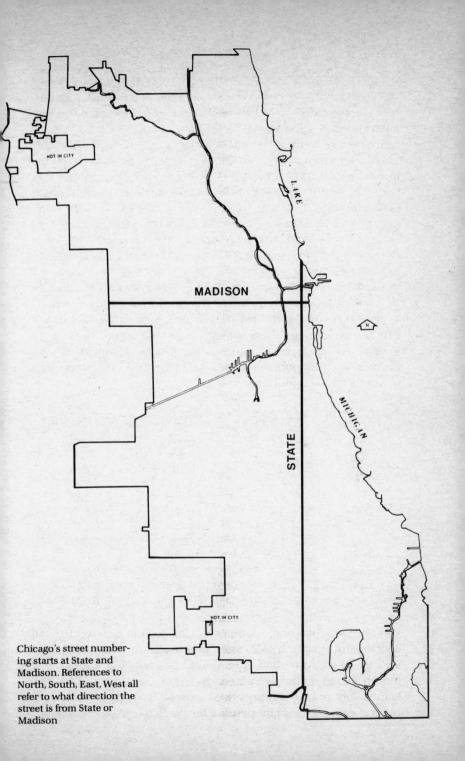

MADISON

LAKE

STATE

MICHIGAN

N

NOT IN CITY

NOT IN CITY

Chicago's street numbering starts at State and Madison. References to North, South, East, West all refer to what direction the street is from State or Madison

the block is usually clean but with high rents, tight parking, and a high burglary rate. On the other hand, the not-so-nice blocks may have similar problems plus much litter, street gangs, noisy tenants, and decrepit walls, plumbing, and wiring.

Apartment hunting requires patience, stamina, comfortable shoes, organization, and time. Start at least two months before the move. May 1 and October 1 are the big "move days" in Chicago. Last-minute hunts in April or September will be a disaster. It might be interesting to note who "the competition" is when on the hunt. My research indicates there are about 668,000 apartment dwellers in the city, about 55% of the population. We can probably assume that at least 75% of all moving that takes place in the city is out of or into an apartment.

The Census Bureau reported that in 1976 17.1% of the American population moved. My research, based on the utility company statistical reports, indicates that in 1976 better than 20% of the Chicago population changed residences. We cannot statistically account for all moves because some people do not have telephones or pay for utilities. The following list shows the percentage of moves for each month.

MONTH	% MOVING	NO. OF PEOPLE	NO. OF APARTMENTS
Jan	1.2	15,345	6,016
Feb	1.3	16,624	6,517
Mar	1.5	19,181	7,520
Apr	1.5	19,181	7,520
May	1.8	23,016	9,023
Jun	1.4	17,903	7,018
Jul	1.3	16,624	6,517
Aug	1.4	17,903	7,018
Sep	1.8	23,016	9,023
Oct	2.1	26,854	10,527
Nov	1.6	20,460	8,021
Dec	1.5	19,181	7,520

We can see that each year some 235,288 people move and 92,240 apartments change hands. More practically one can see that an average of at least 6,000 apartments are changing hands each month. Based on the estimated low vacancy rates of 1 to 7% that leaves only a few hundred more spaces than people wanting them. Assuming that competition for the better places is going to be very rough, you must be well organized and well prepared to be a successful bidder in this seller's market.

One will be completely overwhelmed by the vast number of available apartment listings if some "prehunt" decisions are not made. First: *What part or parts of the city are acceptable?* In addition to asking friends and reading some of the excellent guides to the city, a long, leisurely casing of the area will be in order. After all, the area is going to be home for one, two, three years or more.

Next: *How much room is needed? How many bedrooms? A study or office? Living room, dining room, full kitchen? One or two bathrooms? Storage? Parking space? How much should the rent be?*

Write all of your specifications down. Later, in all the confusion, they will be needed.

Be fairly sure of your needs and desired location. Work out family or roommate differences before the hunt starts. After screening ten to thirty places in a couple of weeks, only a calm head, good organization, and the patience of Job will sustain you.

The hunt actually starts with a late Saturday night trip to the newsstand. Get a Sunday *Chicago Tribune*. The *"Trib"* is the basic bible of the apartment hunter. The other weekend papers usually have some repeats of the *Tribune* ads, but the *Trib* usually has all the ads. Additional general reading could be the Chicago *Reader* (for North Side and Hyde Park apartments, free and published on Thursdays), and the Thursday, Friday, or Saturday editions of the *Tribune*. For sport, pick up the *Sun Times*. There are also a number of local newspapers in Chicago. In the suburbs, locals are the only real source, besides the *Tribune*. In the city, the locals are sometimes helpful. The Chicago Redbook (Yellow Pages) "B-guide" has a complete list of local papers. Check the papers for the part of town desired. Some of the more complete locals are:

NORTH SIDE: *Albany-North Park News, Austin-North News*, the Leader papers, *North Town News*, the Lerner Home Newspapers.

LOOP AREA: *Near North News.*

WEST SIDE: Post Newspapers, Press newspapers, Peacock Northwest newspapers, *West Side Times.*

SOUTH SIDE: *Chicago Defender, Chicago Courier,* the Economist newspapers, the *Hyde Park Herald,* the Southwest Messenger newspapers.

Many of these companies publish a number of editions, each keyed to a specific small part of town. Call them and ask which paper carries the ads for your part of town. Also find out where the paper can be obtained. Many are free from merchants in the local area.

The Trib and Sun Times publish many specialized editions. Obtain those newspapers *in* the part of town you will be searching. If in doubt, call the circulation departments and ask them in which editions are the ads you require and where that particular edition can be purchased. Generally, papers sold north of the Chicago River will contain city ads for the north part of Chicago and those sold south of the river will have south side ads.

Circle with a felt-tip pen (it won't tear the paper) the ads that look promising. Keep in mind the triple goals of **location, size,** and **cost.** Go through the whole section. It goes quickly enough if the section is split between two people and each goes through half.

Trying to understand what some of these ads mean can be a pleasant side game. Everything is abbreviated or coded. Learn the language and save a lot of time later. Try this one: "Lrg 4rm (1bd) wf ac nr lk in new el bld, lndy, pkg." It says "a large four-room apartment (one bedroom) with wooden floors, air conditioning, near the lake" is for rent. The apartment is "in a new elevator building with laundry and parking facilities." What the ad may really be saying is that a smallish, one-bedroom apartment, (bedroom; living-dining room combined; narrow-no-space kitchen and bath) is for rent.

One should be a bit suspicious about parking, laundry, and near-the-lake references when coupled with "new elevator building." The description sounds like the typical come-on ad for a four-plus-one. Later, when checking out the places by phone, ask specifically if the building is a four-plus-one. Make your own decision from there. The following newspaper jargon definitions will help you interpret the ads:

fpl or *wbf:* fireplace or wood-burning fireplace. (When it doesn't say burning, don't expect the fireplace to work—leak water or gas, maybe, but not burn wood.)

wf or *hdwd fl:* wooden floors or hardwood floors (not tiled or carpeted, no cement or exposed decking, but maybe painted or not refinished).

lrg: large (hard to judge what *large* means).

spcs: spacious (big enough to swing your arms around in).

ampl or *ample:* plenty of parking, closet space, or what have you. (Old buildings seldom have enough closet space, and parking may either cost a fortune or be available on the street as you find it.)

blc: balcony (sometimes for real and sometimes a back porch or fire escape).

sm: small (microscopic).

mod, mod ap, or *mod kit:* modern, modern appliances, or modern kitchen (new kitchen sometimes, sometimes an electric refrigerator, running water, and a nonwood-burning stove).

pnty: pantry or walk-in storage area in kitchen (could mean there are no shelves, cupboards, or cabinets).

dbl plm: double plumbing (could mean many risers for hot and cold water so that water pressure is not affected by flushing toilets, or, it could mean hot and cold running water).

mstr bdrm: master bedroom (one large [?] bedroom, sometimes with a connecting bathroom).

mod bth: modern bathroom (newly decorated facility or merely one with a tank-type flush toilet and an old four-legger tub without a shower).

There are more abbreviations, but the idea is the same. If U CN RD THS, U CN RD N APT AD.

High-rise hunters, take heart. Although very few high-rise apartments are advertised, they are easy enough to find. Pick the area desired, and walk or drive around until a building strikes your fancy. There will be a rental agent on hand or a company name prominently posted on the exterior of the building. Contact the agent or company—they'll take care of the rest.

Some apartments are not advertised. These can be found by cruising in the desired area and looking for small white printed slips taped to the front window or door of the building. These are convenient 5x8 inch forms listing what is available in the building

FOR RENT
APARTMENT
IN THIS BUILDING

APT. NO.	DESCRIPTION	RENT
3A	2½ rm., 1 bdrm., bath, mod. kitch., no pets. North expos., heat incl. Ref. + sec. & dep. Sept. 1 lease. Ring apt. 1F or call 555-2368.	$225.00

and how much the rent will cost. It is best to walk when looking for these because they cannot be read from the street.

In most parts of Chicago, using the paper and checking the "For Rent" signs will work. Sometimes, when the pickings are slim, you may have to contact a real estate agency. These companies are also called management companies or services. They usually represent the owner, and they usually run the building for the owner. These management services will have from 100 to 500 units under their control. The large "downtown" companies have tens of thousands.

As an aside about real estate agents and apartment finding agencies, going to them may be a side track when hunting for a low-rise apartment. Most real estate or management agents advertise in the *Tribune*, but they will represent only a few properties. It is much better to go through the ads and find *all* the available apartments than to severely limit your choices.

Apartment finding agencies perform a service only if you do not have time to hunt yourself. If an agency asks for a fee before showing you an apartment forget them. Several agencies have been indicted for fraud and for cheating clients. Essentially, both the individual and the professional hunter have to have the same basic tools: a map (or knowledge of the city) and the real estate section of the newspapers. Checking out the area and seeing what is available (space, type, and rent) is really the only way to know when to grab a place or when to pass. The professional apartment finder can sell you some of his knowledge and some of his experience, but he doesn't have to live in the place (and leases are hard to break). He will also charge you $50 to $200 for his time.

After the streets have been walked, other sources attacked, and the interesting classified ads circled, very carefully cut out each small ad. A "Clipit" to cut things out of newspapers (a little gadget available at most stationery counters), or an Exacto knife are recommended. Take care not to destroy another ad when cutting. Tape each ad to a separate 3x5 inch file card. Write up each "nonnewspaper" lead on a 3x5 card. Use different colors for different types of apartments or different parts of the city or different dates of paper ads. The system should make sense and be useful to you. The important thing is to separate each ad.

When all ads are separated, organize them according to address or part of town. This organization is extremely important. The front of the Yellow Pages will help with street location coordinates

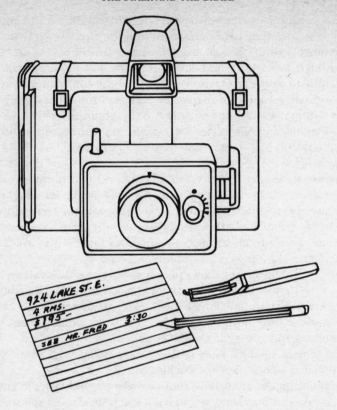

when an address is given. When no address is given, Illinois Bell Telephone offers a name and address service: the number is (312) 796-9600. The cost of the service is 4 units or 25 cents from Chicago phones. Give the operator the phone number and he or she will give you the name and address registered to that phone, if listed. It may be an agency, an owner at a different address, or the place itself, but it gives you more information.

Upon organizing the apartment cards by area or address, phone calls for appointments and details should be made. Do it an area at a time. Usually a phone call will elicit where the property is, how big it is, how much the rent is, and when the apartment is available. You'll want an apartment available about the same time you are ready to move, so dismiss all those available next week if it will be six weeks before it is needed. As some apartments strike your fancy, make an appointment to see them. Try to schedule the visits to one area only. Using the map or your knowledge of the area, give yourself enough time to get from one place to the next. Usually no more than two apartments in 90 minutes are advised when driving, and one every hour to hour-and-one-half when on foot or using public transportation. Sometimes one phone call will turn out to offer three or four possible places. Stay with the agent for all the places and plan other appointments accordingly.

Shopping the zone system way saves a lot of time and a lot of gasoline. It is still possible to log 50 miles in a day looking at eight apartments in two adjoining zones. As the phone calls are made and information taken, make notes on the file cards. Get the name of the company, owner, or agent. Make a schedule similar to an executive's day calendar and write down each appointment on the calendar, adding in enough travel time to make the appointment promptly. Mark the time and address on the calendar and the time on the card. Later, this cross reference will come in handy if you lose a card or need to reschedule.

Not all the phone numbers listed will answer; some will be answering services. With file cards and calendar, these later or "miscellaneous" appointments can be worked in easily. After appointments have been made, either for later in the same day, or for some time during the first part of the week, you are set to greet the happy agents. Take the file cards for the destined area, the appointment schedule for the day, a note book, and go.

If you have a small Polaroid Square Shooter, take it along, and bring extra film and flash cubes. If you have a tool kit, take it along too! The basic tools you might need are a regular screwdriver, a medium-sized vice grips or pliers, a $.98 neon glow tube circuit tester, a flashlight, and a portable radio (to check sound transmission). Inspect the apartment (if it looks like it could be the one) from top to bottom, from windows to toilet. Take pictures and use those tools to check into things.

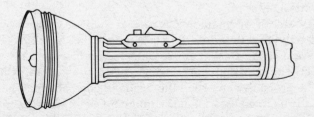

3

Checking Out an Apartment

Inspecting the Exterior

When you walk up to the building, LOOK AT IT. What condition is it in? If it is spring, summer, or fall, is the grass mowed? Is there any grass at all? Are the grounds clean, picked-up? How about the front of the building, including the entrance? Are the window frames painted? Are bricks or stone fronts in good repair? Is the stonework relatively clean? What is the condition of the front walk and steps? Is the entrance door structurally solid, painted or varnished? Look at the lock. Is it secure? Will it discourage salesmen,

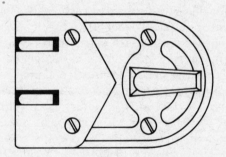

kids, drunks, and burglars? Is there an intercom/security system? Can you see combination screens and storm windows? If it is winter, are there signs of snow removal and ice salting? Walk around to the back. Is the area clean? Does the porch look OK? Does the alley seem safe?

The exterior of a building is one of the first things a typical landlord will fix. He wants the place to *look* nice. He thinks that if you see a nice exterior, you'll want to see more ... and he is correct. If he can't keep the exterior of his building clean, neat, and safe, he probably can't keep the inside in good shape either: beware the blighted exterior. If the intercom is not working and the front door is not locked at all times, you probably can't afford to

live in the building. One good hour's work by the local neighborhood thief will probably clean you out. No sense in living where
the thief can walk right in!

As you walk past the entrance check the condition of the lobby
area. Some are just large enough for mailboxes, others for a bit of
waiting for the bus in the rain. Are the walls, steps, doors (most
entrances have exterior and interior doors) in good repair? Are
there mailboxes? Are these in good shape? Are they lockable? Is
there a working light in the lobby? Is the floor clean and free of
debris?

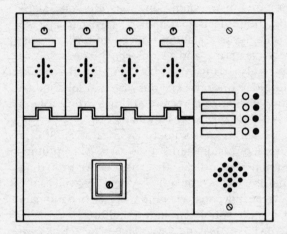

Sometimes only the inner door is secured and not the outer
door. It is better that the outer door be the locked door to protect
against mail thefts and weirdos. But it is imperative that one of the
doors be safely locked at all times. In smaller buildings there may
be no working intercom/security/buzzer system. It is really no
problem if every tenant has to go downstairs to open the door for
guests. Much better this inconvenience than letting anybody at
will roam through your building. But, if there is no doorbell or
intercom in the building, better try another place because the
building will be left wide open and you will probably be ripped off,
promise.

Generally, a building without a good front door, door closer, and
lock is not a good place to live. A landlord who will not take
reasonable precautions to protect his investment as well as his

tenants' security is probably not going to take care of most problems, should they arise. If the mailboxes aren't in good shape, it
means they have been broken into, and that means your mail isn't
safe. Best to skip the chance to pay this man your money for a new
experience you don't want or need.

Walk into the hallway/stairway. There may be an anteroom or
area, but usually not in small buildings. Check for three things:
cleanliness; condition of the walls and floors, woodwork and lighting; and, the smells. These are key indicators to the kind of building you may live in. A filthy building is just that—filthy! It shows
that either the tenants are slobs or your prospective landlord is, or
both. General conditions in the common areas are good signs
about how well the building is maintained. Torn carpets are
dangerous and worn carpets are about to become torn carpets.
Burned-out lights are dangerous and a landlord who doesn't care
about these items is also dangerous. Look for the fire extinguishers—there should be one on each floor. Also look for a smoke
detector at the stairwell. Smoke detectors and fire extinguishers
are required in all buildings of six flats and larger.

Building odors are good signals about many things. Strong
smells of sewers, urine, or disinfectants indicate that the plumbing isn't working. It may also indicate that there is overcrowding
which, by its very nature, will tax the utility systems as well as the
nerves of the tenants. Strong cooking odors will likewise indicate
overcrowding and/or poor ventilation in the building.

Gas odors show, obviously, leaking natural gas. These leaks are
of four types: bad stoves or space heaters; poorly or improperly
installed gas connections; leaking gas pipes in the walls of the
building. Occasionally they indicate faulty furnaces, water heaters, or gas dryers. Whatever the source, they are dangerous as well
as undesirable.

What can be deduced from the smells may well be ascribed to
the whole building—this place stinks! Older buildings deserve
special attention. They have older plumbing systems, older gas
systems. Many of these buildings were originally illuminated by
gaslight and heated with gas space heaters. In a modern building
where one would find electrical wiring conduits, an older building
has gas piping instead. The gas pipes will be found wherever there
is a ceiling light fixture and usually wherever a wall switch is
located. If the building has been well cared for, these gas pipes
have been disconnected. Unfortunately, most owners pass over

this nicety. The result: the whole building is a gas bomb. A gas leak in the old gaslight piping is hard to find, easy to smell, unpleasant to repair.

Plumbing is a similar problem in that the pipes are in the walls and hard to repair. The old pipe diameters are much smaller than modern building code standards require. Over the years the pipes (especially hot water pipes) accumulate scale and corrosion. Overcrowding in the building will force the system beyond its capacity. You may not have to ask anybody—the nose knows.

If the landlord isn't seeing to these conditions, it is because he doesn't want to spend the money and he doesn't live in the building anyway. Under such circumstances, if he won't live there, why should you? Who needs the aggravation?

As you are shown into the apartment, listen. What kinds of sounds do you hear? If it is fairly quiet, you are in luck. If not, think about what it will sound like on a summer's night if what you hear now is bad?

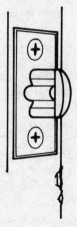

A door showing pry marks indicating an attempted break-in.

Another thing to check on the way into the apartment is the condition of the door, door frame, lock or locks. Look for pry marks. These will be gouges made with a little pry bar or screwdriver. They will be near the locks and latches. They appear as scars breaking the paint surface, deep scratches in the wood, or as dents when covered by paint. Check the door frame itself for cracks or splits near the latches. These both show the apartment was broken into, or at least an attempt was made. Find out about it. If the frame is cracked, the door isn't safe. Don't move in. Look at the locks. Are these flimsy? Do these locks evoke confidence or fear?

Up to now I have been talking about the general condition of the building based upon some quick observations. The conclusions to draw are basically about the landlord's attitude towards his job and what you might expect from him in the future. The real nitty-gritty comes next: THE CONDITION OF THE APARTMENT. The way the laws are now written, and in spite of some court cases to the contrary, when you take an apartment in the city of Chicago, "whats youse sees is whats youse gets!" Period. Good luck. Amen.

Inspecting the Interior

As far as the landlord is concerned, you will be renting the apartment as is. The landlord or agent can talk a good game. He will promise you almost anything to get your name on the application and collect his fee (i.e., his commission for showing the apartment). The law says, however, that if he promises to do things *IN THE FUTURE*, and then he doesn't do them, you are up that certain creek without a paddle, unless you can prove he never intended to do them.

Look the place over very well! Bring some basic hand tools along if you want to look "into" some things, so to speak.

Walls, Floors, and Doors

> What are the **walls** like? Holes, cracks, chips, scales?
> How about **sound** transmission?
> Are the walls thick or thin? Tap them and listen. Use your
>   portable radio.
> Are there water or rust stains in **ceilings** or walls?
> Are the **floors** smooth? Are there holes in the floors?
> If the floors are **wooden**, are they well-stripped? Sealed or
>   painted?
> If floors are **tile**, is the tile in good shape?
> If there is **carpeting**, is it clean and in good shape?
> What is **beneath** the carpeting? Rotten flooring, broken
>   linoleum or tile, concrete?
> Do floors and walls meet at the floor line, and are they
>   sealed so there are no **holes** or **cracks** between them
>   large enough to let **mice** run freely?

*Are the floors **level**? Do they ripple, sink, rise, or slant?*
*Are there **doors** for all doorways that require them?*
Do the doors open and close properly?
*Does the **door hardware** work?*
*Where **locks** are required, are they installed and working?*

Bathrooms

*Is the **sink** clean? Chips or mars? **Faucets** in good shape?*
*Does the **spigot** drip? Are there rust or wear marks in the bowl?*
*Does the sink drain? Does the **drain** leak?*
*Does the **toilet** flush and completely empty?*
*Is the **toilet seat** clean and in good shape?*
*Is the **toilet bowl** clean and not chipped or stained?*
Does the toilet shut off after flushing?
*How about the **bathtub**? Is it clean, unstained, and unchipped?*
*Does the **tub drain** work? Does it leak?*
*Are the **faucet fixtures** in good shape and do they work?*
*Is there a working **shower head**?*
*Is there a **shower curtain rod**?*
*Is the **hot water** hot enough?*
*What about the **water pressure**? Can you fill the bathtub or take a shower without a problem?*
*Is the **water** rust-free and clean?*
*Is there a **medicine cabinet**? Is it clean and in good shape?*
*Are there **mirrors**? Can they be used?*
*Are there **towel rods**?*
*Is the bathroom **vented to the outside** of the building through a window or vent fan?*
*What about **lighting** and **electrical outlets**? Are they usable and safe?*
*Are there holes or leaks where the **water pipes** come into the bathroom? Any stain marks?*
*Is there a **linen closet** or some other type of storage for towels?*

Kitchen

*What is the condition of the **kitchen sink**? Is it clean and* *cleanable? Is it marred, scratched, stained, rusted, or dented?*

*Are **faucets** and **controls** working? Any dripping?*

*Does the sink drain well? Does the **drain** seal?*

Does the drain leak under the sink?

*Is the **stove** clean? Does it work? Is it safe?*

*Is the **refrigerator** working? Does the door seal tightly? Is it clean?*

*Are there adequate **kitchen cabinets** and **counter tops**?*

*Is the **kitchen floor** in good shape and clean? Is the floor cleanable?*

*Can the kitchen be **ventilated** either through a window opening directly to the outside or through a vent fan?*

Pests

Do you see any signs of roaches or mice?

Smells

Does the apartment smell clean? Are there any gas, mold, or bathroom odors?

Windows

*Do the **windows** have **locks** and **handles**?*

*Do they have **counterbalance chains**?*

*Can they be easily opened and **closed**?*

*Are there **storm windows**? Are there full **window screens**?*

Heating System

*What kind of **heating system** is present?*

*If there are **space heaters**, do they appear to be new or in good shape?*

*Are the space heaters **vented** directly to the outside?*

*Are there **enough of them** to heat the entire apartment?*

*What is the approximate **gas draw** in cubic feet when they operate?*

*Is the apartment equipped with **steam heat radiators**?*

Are there radiators in each room?

*Do all have **air valves** and **handles**?*

*Are radiators rusted, dirty, or painted with anything but
   aluminum paint?*

*Can any evidence of **leaking water** be seen? Any rust stains
   or corrosion deposits?*

*Is there a **thermostat** in the apartment to control the heat?*

*If heat is supplied via a **hot water system**, are the radiators
   clean? Are they **along one wall of every room**? Is there
   evidence of leaking? Are there accessible **shut-off valves**
   on each side of each radiator? Is there a thermostat?*

*If heat is supplied by a **forced air system**, are there
   registers (vents) in every room? Is the furnace properly
   vented to the outside? Is there **sufficient air flow** into
   the furnace room to allow for efficient burning? Is there
   good air movement through the registers? Is there a
   cold air return? How **noisy** is the furnace when the fan is
   on?*

*If the apartment is heated by **steam from a separate
   boiler** in the apartment, is the boiler in good shape?
   Does it have a city of Chicago **inspection seal** on it?*

*Does the landlord supply **hot water** or do you?*

*Where is the **hot water heater** and how does it work (gas or
   electric)?*

Electrical Service

*How many **circuits** does the apartment have?*

*How are the circuits **divided**?*

*Are there **enough** for your needs?*

*How many **outlets** can you find in the average room?*

*Do all the outlets and circuits work? (Use the neon glow
   tube tester.)*

*Are the outlets the kind that will take a **grounded
   (three-prong) plug**?*

*Is there a **220-volt service** in the apartment for a big air
   conditioner?*

*How does the wiring appear? Are there modern switches?
   Have the plates been painted over twelve times?*

***When** was the apartment **rewired**?*

*Where is the **circuit breaker box** located?*

*Can you see evidence of **old gaslight fixtures**? (These will*

appear as "hook" affairs near the light switches and as
round covers in the middle of ceilings or on walls where
you might expect to hang a lamp.)
*Have these old gaslight pipes been **disconnected from the***
***gas mains** or are they still "hot"?*

This list obviously represents a long and detailed examination of the place you may live for the next one to three years. *Now* is the time to ask the questions and check things out. After you sign a lease, it will be too late. *Remember: the landlord is renting the apartment "as is." Even if he promises you things will be fixed or added or improved, he is not legally obligated to make good on his promises.* You can't break your lease just because he doesn't do what he promises.

Later, you will have the choices of asking him to make good on his promises, doing it yourself, living without, withholding rents, moving out, or taking him to civil court. In Part V where I cover tenants' rights and organizing, I will discuss these options and more.

4

What's All the Fuss?

The Inspection (Continued)

It is important at the inspection stage to understand what it is you are looking for, and why. The general construction of the apartment will not improve—it has to be in good shape prior to moving into the apartment.

Walls and Floors

Inspection of *walls and floors* will give good warnings about future problems. Uneven or poor flooring will cause no end of problems later. Problems can range from tripping and falling to catching shoes or cutting feet. Poor floors will also make it difficult to level a table, chair, or bed. Problem floors will be hard to clean. Floors with holes will house vermin such as silverfish, ants, roaches, centipedes, and other furry friends. These holes will also make a good home for the resident mice. Finally, poor floors represent an unsanitary condition allowing filth to filter into the apartment from the in-between parts of the building structure.

The holes or spaces at the floor/wall meeting point represent an access into your home for mice and sometimes rats. These rodents live under the floors and in the walls. Giving them free entry into the apartment is asking for trouble. For six months I was awakened two or three times a night when mice ran through the walls behind my bed. The scratching feet of mice within inches of my head was very unpleasant and frightening, a true 1984 experience. These mice would then exit at the base of the wall and run under and around the bed. Mice, alive and dead, could be found in the pantry, the dresser, the dirty clothes hamper, under desks and tables. I put down traps and littered the place with poison. The mice avoided the traps, ate the poison, and prospered. Unpleasant does not cover the experience. Finally I insisted that the landlord complete the floor trim he started but had not finished. The mice stopped running in the walls when the job was completed and the problem ceased. To be forewarned is to be forearmed.

Walls represent another problem. Bad walls will not hold paint, the paint will scale and peel. This looks bad, and flaked paint falling into food and onto tables and clothes is not healthful. The simple act of trying to hang a picture can end in disaster. A small nail can start a crack. Ultimately a piece of plaster from the size of an egg to the size of a basketball will fall out of the wall along with whatever was hung with the nail. Glue stickers react with the old plaster and the layers of paint and fall off, taking a hunk of wall with them. If you have children, it is highly dangerous to live with bad walls. Lead poisoning of the blood is a killer, and the lead is contained in those many coats of paint. The plaster itself is also poisonous if inhaled or ingested. I am speaking not of aesthetic considerations, but of sanitary necessity.

Stains in the ceiling or walls are indicators of another potentially more serious problem. The stains are transmitted through the walls by moisture. The source of the moisture will be water leaking from the roof, water pipes, heating pipes, sewers, or drains. The inevitable results are running or dripping water on furniture, clothes, or food. Then comes mildew, scaling paint, flaking and cracking plaster walls. If not corrected, a wall or ceiling in the affected area will collapse.

In one place I lived a leaking air conditioner drain allowed water to soak through the ceiling in my bedroom. I noticed a darker section of ceiling, but thought it was just a small patch job or repainted area. While I was asleep one night, thirty pounds of plaster fell on my bed. A ten-pound hunk just missed my head. Another large piece of plaster fell about five feet away on a very expensive rented motion picture camera and knocked the lense alignment out of kilter. The place, by the way, was a modern building, about five years old. It can happen.

Doors and Door Frames

The importance of solid *doors and frames* for the entrance and exit to the apartment is obvious. They are security features. Pry marks indicate the place has been burglarized. If it has happened before, it could happen again. The door frame must be solid, not cracked or splintered. There should be two locks, one a long bolt. You can't stop someone from breaking in, but you can make sure that it will not be easy.

Inner doors to rooms are helpful. Every room in an apartment has a doorway, but not necessarily a door. They all should. In the winter, doors are useful for controlling drafts and keeping the house warm. In the summer, doors are useful for sealing off rooms with air conditioners. It is nice to be able to isolate cooking smells and keep them in the kitchen. Doors also keep sounds in where they belong. They keep children and pets in or out, depending on the situation. Think about the doors when inspecting an apartment.

Bathrooms

The *bathroom* is the most consistently used area in the apartment. The fixtures should work well. Because of the nature of bathrooms, it is imperative that they be sanitary. Chipped fixtures are unhealthful, and the Chicago building codes require that chips be repaired or the fixture replaced by the landlord before an apartment is rented. That the toilet must work is obvious—it should not leak sewage onto the floor.

The bathtub should drain rapidly and should not let water seep out of the floor trap drain. There should be towelracks and a shower rod. (The curtain is your problem.) The piping for the sink

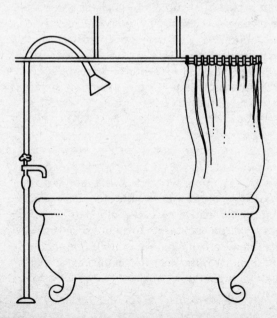

and toilet will come through the walls or floor. These openings should be tight and sealed with metal flanges, tile and grout, or plaster. If not, roaches, mice, and silverfish will find pest heaven and make a palace out of your little half-moon facility. Use your flashlight to check out the pipes.

Run the water in the tub and shower. How is the water pressure? Try to fill the tub with hot water. If it takes more than about three minutes to get to an acceptable level, there is a plumbing problem which will only get worse. Chances are you are filling the tub when nobody else in the building is using the hot water. Think what it would be like if the whole building were home: no water pressure. Check the shower. Does the shower head produce enough of a stream to really rinse off the soap? Will all the fixtures shut off? No dripping faucets and no perpetually filling toilet dripping, wheezing, or moaning at 3:00 A.M.? Check them out and make sure.

Look at the medicine cabinet and light fixtures. Are they safe? Exposed wiring in the bathroom or shorted wiring to metal medicine cabinets are common. The jolt you get in the morning should be from your toothpaste and not from the cabinet.

Finally, there is the problem of ventilation in a bathroom. City codes provide there must be a window to the outside or a working ventilation fan. Custom prefers that you should be able to air the bathroom—that warm, damp environment where all kinds of things necessitate ventilation. After a while an unvented bathroom will mildew and smell, and smell and odorize, and stink. Unpleasant and nonworking bathrooms are not required parts of apartment living. A place should be rejected if the bathroom suffers from problems.

The Kitchen

The *kitchen* is perhaps the second most important place in the apartment. Don't take an apartment with a poor kitchen. Everything should work. A bad refrigerator will spoil your food and cost you a lot of time and money. A bad stove can explode or prevent you from doing much cooking. Ovens seem to go out first—make sure your oven works. Pilot lights going out will fill the kitchen with gas fumes in about eight hours. A stove leaking gas is unacceptable. Either it must be repaired or replaced *before* a lease is signed or there is no bargain.

The sink must be free of chips and rust marks, clean and easily cleaned. There must be hot water and good water pressure at the faucet. The sink should hold water for doing dishes and not leak water from the taps, pipes, and drains. The kitchen sink is a general headquarters for roaches. Underneath and behind the sink must be dry and sealed. Pipes coming in must be sealed off. Remember the little vermin and the mice travel through the walls from apartment to apartment. Don't invite them into your house unless you want a pet and can't think of what else to get!

Kitchen ventilation is another important factor. Your kitchen must open directly to the outside through a large window. That is generally the building code requirement. If not directly vented, then it must be part of a large room where there are several large windows to the outside. Without this option, it must be ventilated directly to the outside via a vent fan. A combination of both a vent fan and a window are desirable. Without mechanical ventilation grease, food smells, garbage odors, and smoke will permeate the rest of the apartment in a short time. There is nothing worse than today's sweater and pants filled with the aroma of yesterday's hamburgers and burnt potatoes.

The floors also must be well-sealed and cleanable. There should be adequate shelves, cabinets and storage for kitchen utensils, foods, and supplies.

Windows

Windows are important for several reasons. In addition to lighting a room during the day, they also provide fresh air to the apartment.

Most high-rise buildings use windows mostly for light and have other provisions for air exchange through window conditioning units. If air exchange is *au natural*, then windows must open when they are needed, stay where they are positioned, and close when they are supposed to close. Most high-rise building windows are thermopane (double thickness). The main problem with the high-rise windows is the air leakage because of strong winds, and wind noise because of poor sealing. The inside of a high-rise on a moderately windy night can sound like the moaning call of the dead.

More concern should be shown for older buildings and low-rises with conventional windows. Typically, these windows are the double-hung sash type: the bottom half rises and the top half lowers. The windows ride in a frame called a sash frame. There is a set of chains that connect near the top of each window and disappear into the window frame. Connected on the other end of the chain is a counterbalance weight. These double-hung sash windows must have the chains and counterbalances connected because if the chains are missing, windows will open and shut only with much difficulty. The windows will have a tendency not to stay open (bottom) and not to stay closed (top). When opening a window, it is possible that it will fall on your hand if the counterbalance isn't holding the window in check. Windows can also slam shut and shatter.

Nonworking windows become major problems in the heat of summer and the cold of winter. Winter is particularly pesky. The windows not only have to work, but the whole window frame— that structure which holds the window to the rest of the building—has to be in good repair and snug fitting. A poor window can cause the loss of perhaps 30% of the heat in a room in the winter. A poor window can allow rain and snow to blow into the room and set up wind tunnel breezes. For this reason, it is highly advisable that all windows be equipped with storm windows.

In summer the main concern is for screens. Screens are required in all windows on the first three stories of every apartment building in Chicago from April 15 to October 15. The landlord *must* supply them and they must cover the window opening and be attached. No screen means mosquitoes, flies, bugs, and an occasional cat, squirrel or bird. Sanitation particularly against flies and mosquitoes carrying encephalitis, polio, malaria, typhus, and cholera are special reasons for screens. Combination storm windows and screens are the best solution and they should be provided by the landlord.

I have a reassuring word for you. You need not be self-conscious about being so curious about the conditions of a prospective living place. You are simply trying to insure your health, safety, and comfort. You know that if you don't look out for yourself, no one will. Least concerned of all will be your landlord. Check it out, and keep checking if you think you might take the apartment.

PART TWO

The Hunt,
the Kill, and
Other Rituals

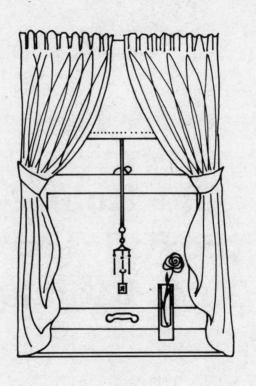

5

Before Applying
For a Lease

Deciding on an Apartment

Days and weeks of hunting have gone by. You are frazzled. You have seen three places you really like. You study the pictures you took of each place to remind you of what they looked like. You read the notes you have made. You call back the management company agent and "Yes, the apartment is still available." What is next? That depends on you and the apartment.

Shoot for a bit more research information about the management company and the building. Try to talk to current residents in the building. Look for a tenants' group or union. Introduce yourself, telling them you are considering renting an apartment. Ask them to tell you about the building and about the management. Ask about rent raises. You should be able to get an honest character reference for both the landlord and the building from some people in the building. If this source tells you that the management is OK, that the building is in decent shape, and that maintenance is good, you have been given a degree of confidence that things will work out well for you if you move in.

But what if you can't find anyone who will talk to you? What about a building that is empty when you are visiting? How do you check up on the management? It's not easy. One thing to do is to call the local neighborhood or community group (a list is provided in Appendix A). They may have information or can refer you to another group who might have information. You might try the neighbors around the new building, but seldom will they know anything more than if the building is quiet, dirty, or has a lot of noisy kids or that the cops are always there. This may or may not be helpful. You can also ask the management what other buildings they manage or own. Look at the other building(s) and ask residents in those places how things are. This will give a hint about the building you are considering. If you are still not satisfied and want to find out a little more, you can call the City Corporation Council (see Appendix B) and ask if the building is currently involved in any complaint, Compliance Board or court actions. You can also contact the office of the Compliance Board (Appendix B) and ask them the same question.

You may or may not get complete answers but if you are persistent, the phone calls are one way to get some information. Checking on the landlord is very hard. If any of the community or official sources yield some information, evaluate it carefully. Bad reports probably indicate trouble while no report means nothing at all—good or bad.

A final check of the neighborhood should be done to see how safe it is. Stop at the local police precinct house and ask the sergeant on the desk to let you talk to the community relations officer. About all you will be able to learn from this source is whether you are in a high crime area or if your building is something special. If things sound OK, it's almost time to make an application.

Before you contact your prospective landlord to make the plunge, ask yourself two questions: Am I compatible with this building/neighborhood/parking situation/etc.? Can I afford to pay the *net rent* (the rent on the lease) and the *gross rent* (extra payments for heating, gas, electricity, real estate taxes [a new landlord trick], parking, etc.)? The extra costs of utilities for heating, hot water, and electricity can easily add $35 to $50 per month to your rent. If the landlord has tacked on a real estate escalator clause, this might mean another $20 to $50 per month. If you are presented with a real estate clause in your prospective lease, reject it. It is a rip-off tactic. You could be obligated for thousands of dollars in taxes. You also have no control over the computation of the tax, nor can you protest the tax to the County Assessor, nor can you get income tax deductions for paying the tax. I cannot be too adamant: never sign a lease with a real estate tax payment clause. Parking can run from $10 to $55 per month. Can you afford the gross rent? If so, proceed to the next paragraph. If not, lose your turn, go back two chapters and inspect another apartment.

Applying for a Lease

Before applying for a lease, go back to the apartment and take a really thorough look, checking out all the factors detailed in the previous chapters on apartment conditions. If everything clicks, it is time to sign an *application* for a lease.

Up to now, the exercises have been preliminary. Gathering facts, taking notes, making careful observations of conditions, asking questions. You have invested no more than a little time, a little effort. What you haven't done, yet, is to make a commitment. You haven't put your money on the table or your signature on a piece of paper.

Landlords have it "good" these days because they are controlling a sellers' market. There are limited number of apartments available in the city and occupancy rates are close to 99% in full use. This means that almost all rentable apartments are occupied and the rest are probably not livable. Under such tight conditions and with money to be made, any real human consideration is sometimes tossed out the window for some rather underhanded and sharp business practices.

Practice 1: Promises, Promises

Do not believe what an agent promises you. Do not fool yourself. Once a lease is signed, the management is under no lease obligation to comply with agents' promises unless you get them in writing with conditional clauses. What I tell you is true. To protect yourself against this rip-off, wait until all the promises are kept BEFORE SIGNING THE LEASE. Also, be sure your application fee (deposit) is refundable if the promises are not kept prior to signing the lease. Usually promises have to do with decorating, replacing old kitchen or plumbing fixtures or appliances, repairing locks, intercom systems, installing storm windows and screens, preparing storage space. Sometimes promises have to do with major renovations. If an apartment isn't ready, forget it, now. Do not sign a lease, do not make an application. You may have to wait months until the place is livable. In the meantime, you will have to find another place to stay and a place to store your belongings. You will have to move twice. Remember the horror tales I told earlier about a landlord's "innocent" promises about fixing up things before you move in.

Practice 2: The Landlord's Hot Box Rush

The standard line is that "this is the nicest apartment we've got for rent right now, and it's a real bargain. I suggest you make an application today because three others are very interested." It's that old hot box. Better do it fast because it will slip away quickly. Well, it may be true or it may be jive. Don't allow yourself to be pressured into making an application until you have completed your own investigation. It could cost you a bundle.

Practice 3: Oh, That's No Problem

Want to make a bet? "How's the parking?" you ask. *"Oh, that's no problem,"* she says. "I may be transferred to another city next year, can I work things in the lease so I can move out early?" you inquire. *"Oh,"* he exclaims, *"that's no problem."* "My mother (sister, friend, son, grandmother) is planning an extended visit with us next summer, several months . . . is that OK?" *"No problem."* "I notice that the front door doesn't lock (or the mailbox is broken)" you say. The landlord replies, *"Oh, that's no problem."* And he or she is correct. It is no problem for them because they are not going to do anything about it. IT WILL BE A PROBLEM FOR YOU when the time comes to have your friend stay, move out early, try to find a parking spot, or protect your mail.

Practice 4: Yes, We Can Take Care of That

Variation of sharp Practice 3 as above. Read this to mean, "Yes, we can take care of YOU later."

Practice 5: Now, If You'll Just Fill Out the Rent Application . . .

In sales parlance, it is called *the close*—closing the deal, getting the signature on the dotted line, hitting home. The standard rent application form in Chicago is an out and out license to steal. Once you've signed that application, they have you. I will explain further in Chapter 6.

6

Getting Straight Answers from the Rental Agent: The Truth-in-Renting Act

Making an Application

Knowing what to look for in an apartment, and knowing why you are looking is just as important as where you wish to live, how big a place you need, and what you can afford to pay. The apartment is going to be the place you call home for a period of months or years. To be able to live comfortably, conveniently, and safely are prime concerns. It may take more time to check a place out and it may appear that you will ask "tough" questions of the agent or landlord, but you know WHY you have to ask the questions and you know that it is better to find out about the apartment before you move than to suffer through a list of horrors—both physical and emotional—after it is too late to really do anything.

In addition to the physical investigation you have just completed, there are some important questions the agent should be asked:

Are there any conditions in the building that require repairs (roof, new plumbing or wiring, replacement of the rear porch, new heating system)?

Is the landlord involved in any housing court or building code compliance hearings? What is the reason?

Are there roach, mice, or rat problems in the building? Is there a regularly scheduled extermination service provided?

Have there been any burglaries in the building? What are the details?

Has the building had any fires in the past several years? What happened?

Who is the owner of the building? Is the building up for

*sale? If so, will your lease be cancelled? Will your
apartment be lost?*

*Is the building cleaned regularly? How often? By whom?
Somebody living in the building or one of the
management maintenance people?*

*What repairs will management make and what repairs will
the tenant have to take care of?*

*How do you report maintenance problems? How long does
it take for repairs?*

Are there emergency, after hours phone numbers?

*Will the management company reimburse tenants for parts
and labor if tenants make their own repairs?*

*Is storage available? Where? How safe is the storage area
against theft, moisture, or dirt damage?*

*Is parking available in the area? How much will it cost?
Who should be contacted?*

*Does the management maintain fire and accident liability
insurance? What are the details?*

*Are there any special conditions for tenancy placed upon
residents in the building: replace hallway light bulbs,
shovel the snow, pay rent before the first of the month to
avoid a late penalty fee, no water beds, no pets, no
children, no dishwater, no washer/dryer, no extra locks
on the door, no overnight guests (yep)?*

If the rental agent or landlord does not want to fill out the
"Landlord's Application" (Appendix C) or answer a few honest
questions, can you trust him to maintain your building and be
straight with you later on? You must be strong on this point. The
time has come where prospective tenants have to stop being jived
by honey-mouthed bandits.

Remember after you sign the application, YOU HAVE LOST
YOUR APPLICATION FEE; AFTER YOU HAVE SIGNED A LEASE YOU
COMMIT YOURSELF TO PAY RENTS. It is in your best interest to be
sure you get what you are paying for!

Flip to Appendix C and look over the Landlord's Application
and Warranty of Habitability Statement. Make a photocopy and
use it!!!

Now how about your application form? This form is essentially
a credit reference form. The agent can find out a lot about you and
your finances when you fill out the application. "Fine," you say,

"that's business. There has to be some way for the landlord to learn about his prospective tenants." Well, OK, but what about that application fee that the landlord requests? What is that for? Earnest money? Maybe. "Well," you say, "that will be applied to my security deposit if the application is approved." But, why do you have to pay your money *before* the landlord approves the application? Management agents say this is because they have "expenses" involved in making the credit check.

In no other business besides real estate or used cars will retailers take your money *first*, and then decide whether you are approved. This is an old con game called the "pigeon drop" and you're the pigeon. The money is supposed to *"hold"* the apartment for you. If you back out, he keeps your money. He is protected against lost income during the time he has to find a new tenant.

Well, let's clear up a few myths about credit checks: to belong to the Cook County Credit Bureau costs $50.00 per year, and it costs less than $10.00 for each credit check inquiry. In every other business I can think of the cost of doing business (including sales and credit checks) is a part of the general operating expense of that business. What department store or credit card company charges you to apply for credit? None. They encourage people to apply and accept the cost as part of their normal business expenses.

The real reason you have to pay a rent application fee is because *the agent charges the owner a fee for every application completed*. The rental agent is a commission man. The more people he signs up, the more money he makes. Occasionally he will have to refund that application fee, but usually he can keep it. The fee is to be refunded if the applicant is "not acceptable." Well, it's pretty hard to fail the test to qualify to rent an apartment. If you can pay money, you are approved. Often, the agent will announce that he could not accept your application for your first apartment choice, but he has other apartments. He may put out his bait, sharpen his hook, and then switch. Happens all the time. You may or may not get the money back.

It is not unusual for a management company to take four or five applications for the same apartment and keep all of the application fees. Usually one or two applicants will decide against the place, one will take it, and one or two will be shuffled off to another place not as desirable or perhaps more expensive to rent.

What happens if you make an application, put your money

down, and find out that the landlord is "not acceptable." Well, that's tough. The rent application is usually a one-way street going in somebody else's direction. Usually the application will read that the owner or owner's agent has x number of days to contact you to announce the acceptance of the application. Why shouldn't the renter have the same grace privilege of refusal? Because the landlord wants your money and wants to tie you down. He doesn't want to give you the free choice of approval, nor the time to think about your decision. He wants to freeze you out of the market. It is grossly unfair.

Once you have signed an application, your apartment hunting ends, but the landlord will continue to show the apartment until a lease is actually signed. He will continue to take applications and application money. What he doesn't tell you is that there is a waiting list. He can start at the top and as an applicant is refused, he moves down the line. When an applicant is approved, he contacts the applicant. If the prospective tenant accepts the lease, the agent's job is over. If the applicant refuses the lease, then the agent pockets the money and makes the next phone call. Seldom does a decent apartment go unrented.

The rent application fee ought to be used to reserve your place on the list. If things don't work out, then you should get your money back. There is no justification for the huge sums confiscated by management companies through holding back application deposits. These fees are scam cons.

When you want to make an application, ask whether there is a waiting list. You have a right to know. After all, you are giving your money in good faith. If you wait ten days and find out the apartment has been rented to someone else, it is ground zero for you. Remember, while you are frozen, he is fluid. You deserve the same chance to look, and protect your time and money as the landlord has to sell. *Insist, when you make an application, that you be given the same number of days to refuse the management company as they require to judge your acceptability.* If they take ten days to approve you, then you should have ten more days to approve them!

When the agent asks you to fill out his application you ask him to fill out your application. It is Appendix C, Landlord's Application and Warranty of Habitability Statement. The actual "license to steal" appears at the bottom of the application. It states that if you (the applicant) shall fail to execute a lease for the apartment in the application you will lose your deposit which is called "liquidated damages." Don't be fooled by a clause giving you x number of days to sign the lease. That doesn't mean your money is coming back—it means you have a few days to decide whether to take the place or not (by signing the lease). It doesn't say you can change your mind without losing the money. Did you know that in Illinois a contract signed for a vacuum sweeper or encyclopedia can be cancelled within three days because the law assumes that high pressure tactics are sometimes used to close contract deals? You can get your money back for a $200 sweeper, but the same protection does not extend to the apartment renter and his $4000 lease!!

Why such a big deal over a little transaction? Well, because the transaction is not a little one. Typical rent application fees range from $50 to a full month's rent. If you see several places, and if you have to wait 10 days to get a reply about one place, you can lose all your research and hunting time if you do not hedge (by applying for more than one place). Remember, the agent is showing your place to many people and taking as many applications for that same apartment as he can. It's his roulette wheel with your money.

The agent is calculating that you will put money down in several places. He is hoping that you'll put money down with him and then not be able to sign the lease. BANG! There goes your month's rent. On the other hand, if he does not approve you, and you have not taken an application on another place, you'll have to start the process all over. You will have probably lost your chances with other spots you liked, and you may have lost the opportunity to move on time. You may have to delay moving, hold over your current lease, take temporary quarters, and so on. My strong advice is to insist that you be given an equal number of days after your application is approved to approve the landlord and the building. Don't forget to also determine if there is a waiting list and how long it is.

7

The Landlords' Leases

Analyzing Your Lease

Generally speaking, a *lease* is an agreement between you (the lessee) and the manager (the lessor) of a piece of property. When you *rent* property, you agree to pay a certain sum of money at specified times for the use of the property. You will have limited use of the property for the length of time specified in the lease. Ideally, as long as you abide by the limitations of the lease, and pay your rents on time, you should have no problems. Legally, you are exchanging a consideration of value (money) for the use of a valuable consideration (the apartment).

But, what has really happened is quite different. You have signed a legal contract, in the form of a *property lease*, which obligates you to pay the lessor (landlord) a specific monthly sum for the *opportunity* to use the apartment. In many cases you are obligated to pay the rent NO MATTER WHAT CONDITIONS MAY ARISE. Under certain limited conditions, you may break your lease and move without further obligation, but this is not usually possible. Landlords have the right, and on occasion will exercise the option, to sue you for breach of lease including early move out and rent withholding.

The principal concern when preparing to sign the lease for an apartment is understanding what it is you are signing. You are signing a document that obligates you to pay a monthly rent for an apartment, but doesn't necessarily obligate the lessor to provide you with more than the "opportunity" to occupy the apartment. Basically, even if the landlord shuts off your heat, your water, and your gas (all violations of city and state statutes), you are still obligated to pay some rent for as long as you stay in the apartment. Under such circumstances (and others that I cover elsewhere in the *Handbook*) you may be able to break your lease by moving out. However, the landlord is almost never responsible for your damages, losses and moving expenses. For problems less drastic you owe the full rent and cannot break the lease. In case of a fire, the landlord can still collect at least two months' rent from you if he can fix the place up before that two-month period expires. You may not be able to live in the apartment for the two months, but you still owe the rent. It is this type of clause and covenant that governs us when we sign a lease.

Appendix F is a detailed layman's analysis of several lease forms used in Chicago. Of the four forms currently in use, two are published for the Chicago Real Estate Board, the third is not attributed to any organization but is very heavily weighted toward the landlord and the fourth is a very balanced, neutral lease sponsored by the Chicago Council of Lawyers. These forms are copyrighted and we cannot reproduce them. I suppose this is just one more tactic of the real estate interests to avoid giving the tenant an even break.

If you are suddenly confronted with a lease you've never seen, full of small type and jargonese, you are quite defenseless against it. As a matter of fact, one of my legal advisors has spent quite some time researching the effects of three of these leases on the Chicago rental market and is currently gathering ammunition for a lawsuit to "free" the leases in the city. As it currently stands, practicality necessitates that you accept not only the type of lease offered to you, but also the wording and conditions of the lease. Because almost all landlords use the Real Estate Board or unsponsored leases, and because these leases are so lopsided in favor of the landlord, you have no real choice. Either accept "their" lease or live outside the city of Chicago. Because, so far, the real estate interests have generally rejected any true reformation of leases, and continue to publish repressive lease forms, only certain types of action at law will break the monopoly of lease tyranny. The Chicago Council of Lawyers' lease is a fair lease, but few landlords, so far, have seen fit to use it.

What should the "ideal" lease contain? This is what a lawyer for one Chicago community organization lists as necessary guarantees in any fair lease.

The right of any tenant to:

1. *live in habitable (code standard) conditions.*
2. *occupy the premises for the length of the lease.*
3. *pay rent only while occupying the premises and only while receiving the promised services of the lease, and withholding rents when necessary.*

4. *rely upon the word and good-faith performance of your landlord.*

5. *privacy, peace, and quiet.*

6. *due process under the law, including proper notices.*

7. *terminate your lease at any time for good cause.*

8. *renew your lease under similar conditions without excessive rent hikes.*

9. *self-help methods of fixing up and deducting such costs from the rent.*

10. *keep additions, fixtures, and other personal property temporarily installed for the term of lease.*

11. *protect his/her property from seizure or endangerment from illegal actions by the landlord.*

12. *legal redress, police protection, and full recovery of damages.*

So much for utopia. When the landlord's agent hands you their lease, to what should you pay particular attention? You do not have to read and sign the lease when it is given to you. Say "thank you very much, I wish to read it over. I'll call you tomorrow." Read it over and compare it to the detailed analysis in Appendix F.

Listed briefly here are the main dangers for each of three landlord leases. Appendix F contains a complete dissection so if you are considering legal action, go to the Appendix. If you are just curious, the following skeletal breakdown is sufficient.

Landlord Lease Number 12R

CLAUSE	SUBJECT	DANGER
1	Rent	*Rent is due the first of month. You can be evicted if you are one day late.*
2	Security deposit	*No fixed time for return of it. No repair receipt requirements.*
4	Condition of apartment	*Landlord makes no promise to improve, fix, repair, or maintain apartment, and you may have to make your own repairs. You accept apartment as is.*
5	Use of apartment	*Nobody can live in apartment*

		except persons named on front of lease.
6	Subletting	Hard to do and will cost you fees, expenses, and still obligates you to pay rents if the sublettee defaults.
7	Alterations	None without written permission. All improvements and additions belong to landlord.
8	Access	There is a fine if you refuse entry to your landlord. He can come and go anytime as he pleases.
10	Fire	You still have to pay rent for 120 days after a fire even if you are burnt out.
12	Surrender of apartment	When lease is over you must move out before last day or face a fine of 20% of monthly rent for each day of violation.
13 and 17	Waiver of rights; Confession of judgment	You waive your legal right to notice (legal due process), and appoint your landlord as your lawyer and grant him permission to plead you guilty for any lease violation he accuses you of committing. You also agree not to sue your landlord for any reason nor try to recover damages.
14	Fees	You promise to pay all your landlord's costs and lawyers bills if he sues you, regardless of outcome.

Landlord Lease Number 15

CLAUSE	SUBJECT	DANGER
1	Rent	You are subject to a late fee if you are more than five days late paying the rent.
2	Possession	If your apartment is not ready at move-in time you cannot sue the landlord for your damages.

4	Promises	Landlord promises must be in writing or they will not be honored as part of the lease.
5	Security deposit	Your landlord can "confiscate" your deposit at any time during the lease period without prior notice to you. You must then pay a new deposit.
6	Lessor to maintain	Your landlord can refuse to maintain the premises for "good cause." You cannot sue him for damages and you may not normally break the lease and move. You accept the apartment as is.
10	Alterations	No alterations, additions, etc., without prior written permission and any improvements become the property of the landlord.
11	Access	Landlord has almost unlimited access to your apartment (without your permission).
12	Subletting	Hard to do and costs you money.
13	Abandonment	If you are late on your rent payments, your landlord can enter your apartment and seize your property until you pay him.
17	Lessor's mortgage	If your building is sold or is in financial trouble your lease can be cancelled (say, so the owner can convert the building to a condominium).
20	Rules and regulations	The landlord can make more and new rules after you sign the lease and incorporate them into the lease.
21	Insurance	Residents agree to have proper fire, casualty, and liability insurance because landlord is held harmless and cannot be sued.
24	Tenant's waiver	Tenant must pay rent no matter what the landlord does to break the

conditions of the lease.

25	*Lessor's remedies*	*It is possible that your landlord can personally and directly evict you without benefit of a court order, and still collect rents until the lease expires.*

Landlord Lease Number L17

CLAUSE	SUBJECT	DANGER
2	Security Deposit	No fixed time for return. No repair receipt requirements if not paid back.
3	Condition of premises	Landlord makes no enforceable nonwritten promises and tenant accepts apartment as is and in good condition.
4	Limitation of liability	Landlord is not liable for any damages of any sort nor responsible for keeping the premises in repair.
5	Subletting	Hard to do and will cost you money.
7	Access	Landlord can enter your apartment just about whenever he wishes.
9	Holding over	It can cost you twice your monthly rent for up to a whole year.
13, 14, and 16	Forcible detainer; Confession of judgment	You waive your rights to due process and service of notices. You appoint your landlord to be your attorney and to confess your guilt in court (even though you may not even know you have been sued). You also promise to pay all your landlord's legal costs.
18	Fire	You must pay two months rent even if your place is rendered unusable due to disaster, even if you can't sleep there. Your landlord owes you nothing and you cannot sue him.

The worst of these clauses are unenforceable in court and you need not worry about them BUT you had best consult a lawyer if you get into lease trouble. There are a thousand twists and nuances.

There is another lease: Apartment Lease Agreement Number L19. It is the newest of the leases published by the George Coles Company, as are all the others. L19 is the latest Coles form and therefore the most up-to-date. The L19 is considered a "neutral" lease and one that more fairly represents both landlord and tenant. It is written in very clear language and does not contain the types of "sleeper" clauses the other three leases contain. A direct reading of the lease is all that is needed to understand it but I will cover briefly some of the more important points.

Chicago Council of Lawyers Lease Number L19

CLAUSE	SUBJECT	ANALYSIS
2	Rent	Landlord is required to provide a rent receipt if so requested.
4	Repairs	Landlord makes a list of repairs he will make by an agreed-upon date.
6	Parking	Landlord provides parking at no extra charge.
8	Option	The lease can be renewed with the renewal rent stated (now, before the first lease is signed).
11	Warranty	Landlord expressly states the premises are livable and in code compliance.
12	Decorating	An allowance for painting, etc., can be made part of lease.
13	Security deposit	The deposit has to be returned two weeks after the end of the lease. The landlord has to inspect the apartment one week before move-out and give a written estimate of deductions and later back it up with paid receipts. He also has to pay 5% interest per year on the deposit.

14	Entry	Landlord must make advance arrangements to enter your apartment and he must state the reason for the visit. He can only come during the day.
15	Tenant obligations	Common-sense requirements to take out the garbage, not tear the place up, and not make too much noise.
16	Lessor obligations	Common-sense requirements to keep building clean, make repairs, fix doors and windows, exterminate and generally keep things as good or better than they were at the start of the lease period.
17	Alterations	You must have written permission to make alterations, but the landlord has to tell you why you cannot if he denies permission.
19	Self-help	If, after a reasonable time, your landlord does not make necessary or promised repairs, or fails to supply you with heat, hot water, and so on (times and specifics are in the lease), then you can make the repairs, hire the repairpersons, pay the utilities, etc., out of your own pocket and deduct the costs from your rents until the total costs have been recovered.
20	Termination for good cause	If you get transferred or lose your job and living at the present apartment works a hardship on you, you can break the lease with ninety days notice.
22	Common areas	You have the right to use all the common areas of the building, including the grounds.
23	Renewal	Your landlord cannot refuse to renew your lease nor discriminate against you with unreasonably high

> *(or selectively high) rents. If the*
> *building is to be converted to a*
> *condominium, you must be given*
> *twelve months prior notice.*

If you are moving into a new situation you may not have much of a choice about accepting or rejecting the lease as is. If you are renewing a lease and you have a tenant's association in your building, you have a lot of power to make changes. I will explain how in Chapter 18.

Modifying an existing lease is not hard. All you need is to attach a set of "riders" to the existing lease form. You can strike clauses (as I suggest in Appendix F) or simply "correct" the faulty clause with a rider. In the case of completely rehabilitating the lease both strike-outs and riders are preferable.

Nobody should sign a lease without a *rider* (a supplementary agreement) stating that the landlord and/or his agent guarantees that the building and your apartment are habitable and that he will make sure that he will keep the place in good shape as it relates to heat, water pressure, hot water, structural soundness, repairs, cleanliness, and vermin. If a landlord won't guarantee habitability what kind of chance do you have when the heat fails, or the place is invaded by roaches? The Illinois Supreme Court believes (in *Spring* v. *Little*, see Chapter 15) that your landlord is obligated to insure and maintain habitability.

You should not sign a lease that allows the landlord to sue you for damages, but prevents you from doing the same thing. You should also not sign a lease which obligates you to pay rent no matter what happens to your apartment or no matter what your landlord fails to do to keep his building livable.

Attaching Riders to the Lease

There are four types of riders that you may need to attach to your lease.

Promises and Permissions

The first type of rider is a list of what your landlord has promised to do and is going to allow you to do. If he is going to fix things, these must be spelled out. The completion dates of the work must be included. If you are allowed to have pets (a sore subject in itself), this should be spelled out. Rules about guests (if this is a special problem) have got to be laid down. If you wish to put up shelving or paper the walls, get written permission and get in writing whether you will be fined or have to remove the paper, or whether the landlord wishes to buy any improvements you've made when you move out.

In older places some tenants are forced to rewire in order to accommodate air conditioning (or even a toaster). Arrangements as to who pays (always split the costs of these improvements) and who takes care of the work have to be in writing before the lease is signed.

The list is endless. You may want a specific agreement on decorating (up to one month's rent a year to pay for improvements installed by tenant). Landlord will usually only credit renter for money spent for materials or outside suppliers. You may need a separate parking agreement or a storage agreement. You might own a dishwasher or clothes washer/dryer. These need special approval. How about a TV or CB antenna on the roof? Special locks or a burglar alarm system? Appendix D contains a sample of this type of rider, but you will have to write your own to suit your needs.

Check-in/Check-out—Exceptions Rider

The second type of rider is really an adjunct to the first. It is an exceptions report. I have included such a report form as part of Appendix D. It can also be used as a conditions check-in/check-out form and as a "punch list." The idea is to go through your prospective apartment and check the appropriate boxes and make the necessary notations. You will be evaluating the walls, floors, and so on. You will check off things in good condition, make notes of exceptions to good condition, and end up with a ready list of work needed to be "punched out" (completed) in order to bring things up to specifications.

The list should be saved for move-out when you can once again go through the apartment. Conditions you noted as not acceptable when you moved in can be used now to prove you were not at fault if the landlord comes after your security deposit. You will also see what work you need to do to preserve your deposit if you caused some damage.

Both you and the landlord/agent should go through your place before you sign the lease *and* just after you have moved in (and found out about those little quirks you hadn't expected).

Universal Tenants' Rights Riders

The third type of rider is a universal tenants' rights rider. These are designed to correct inequities in the lease and insure that you have a fair deal with the management company and owner. You may wish to add more to the universal rights riders, but you should at least start with something like one of the two samples in Appendix E (a long and a short form). They are designed to protect you against being ripped off with no legal ground on which to stand. The long form rider (Appendix E) comprehensively protects against confiscated security deposits, retaliatory evictions, and payment of rents without a return of services. It frees you from pleading guilty to whatever your landlord accuses you of in court (confession of judgment).

Collective Bargaining Agreement

The fourth type of rider is a collective bargaining agreement between the tenants' union and the building management. This comes only after a building is organized and you are a member. If you are new to an unorganized building, this agreement is useless. (See Appendix K for the Collective Bargaining Agreement and Contract.)

Frankly, I don't believe in all the legalese mumbo jumbo of the lease or the riders. If we had a fair system of landlord/tenant relationships we could do very well with a shake of the hand. Unfortunately the system is heavily stacked against us. The laws are "their" laws and not our laws. We have to protect ourselves by using some of the same tools that "they" threaten us with, meaning that when they force a ballbuster lease down our throats we have no choice but to protect ourselves with a strongly worded set of riders.

These riders should prove beneficial if you ever get to court and they may make it easier for you to avoid court if you decide to move out and break your lease.

The law does not exist to help you and me. It exists to protect the landlords and bankers and to keep lawyers in the bucks. If we could avoid the whole formalized legal system, the happier we would all be, but a lease is a legal contract so we have to be legal in our response.

Please remember: "If it ain't in writing, it don't exist." "Promises are the hot gases that fill sewers." "When you sign an apartment lease, what you see is what you get." "The apartment you rent, you get (as is)." Protect yourselves. Take a look at the rent chart in Chapter 12, page 113. Look how much money you will spend a year with the landlord. Can you afford not to be careful?

I do not propose that renters attempt to write their own leases. The riders we have outlined are tricky enough to get signed. I doubt that tenant's rights lease L19 will have much of a chance, at least not without the pressure of a tenants' union.

In addition to the written leases discussed, there are also verbal leases. These are for terms of thirty days or even one week at a time. They give a tenant very little protection against being thrown out or having the rent raised at the whim of the landlord. These leases are also discussed in Appendix F.

PART THREE

In Transito, Post Hoc, Ad Nauseam, Et Cetera

8

Moving: Getting There Is Not Half the Fun*

Planning Your Move

Before you even start packing, there's lots to do. One month or so before you move, take a good look at what you really want to take with you. This is a great time to have a garage sale. Whether you're paying movers or doing the job yourself, you've no doubt accumulated several or many items that just are not worth their weight to bring along.

Tell the gas, electric, and telephone companies when you'll be disconnecting service at the same time you make utilities arrangements for your new location. If you have regular home delivery of items such as newspapers, milk or a diaper service, let these companies know what your schedule will be.

Change of address notices should be sent to the post office, magazines you subscribe to, credit card companies, insurance companies, the Social Security office, relatives, friends, and others with whom you correspond regularly.

Send out rugs, carpets, and clothes that need cleaning—these are better shipped in the cleaner's wrappings.

A few days before you leave, gather together jewelry and other valuables. These and your personal records should be carried with you even if you are using professional moving services.

If you live in an elevator building, find out whether building management requires you to schedule the time you're moving and make arrangements to use the elevator. Long waits for elevators at either end can add to your bill, particularly if you're using professional services.

The day before you leave, defrost the refrigerator and freezer. If

*The first part of this chapter originally appeared in slightly altered form as an article written by the staff of the *Uptowner*, a magazine published by Uptown Federal Savings and Loan Association, 4545 North Broadway, Chicago, Illinois 60640, and is reproduced here with permission.

you own your appliances and will be taking them with you, they may have to be professionally disconnected (and possibly, serviced) before shipping. Check on this in advance. Many movers will offer this service at an additional charge, otherwise an appliance specialist must be called in.

Should you move yourself or use professionals? Moving yourself is tempting, especially if you're moving locally, can talk some friends into helping, and have the price of a rented truck. But, before you make that decision take a good look at what you have, where you're going, and what the problems might be.

Self-moves are most practical at the local level, at least in part due to the pricing structure of most professional movers. On local jobs, they will charge by the hour, but on longer moves (over 50 miles) rates will usually be based on weight. On the weight system, it's possible that when you add up the costs of mileage, gas, and one-way fees on your rented truck, the cost of doing it yourself on a long move can approximate a professional mover's charges, with none of the fringe benefits.

Even if you decide on professionals for a local move, you still may want to do part of the moving job yourself, particularly the packing, and have the movers come in only for the really heavy furniture and other large items. Moving companies offer a wide variety of services, everything from packing to maid service to baby sitters, and it's up to you to decide which of these services you'll need to take advantage of. The moving company is not responsible for boxes you pack yourself unless the carton itself is damaged in some way, or a Declared Value Protection Plan is in effect.

Doing it yourself—the right way. Obviously, the basic reason you move yourself is to save money, so it's a good idea to save in all aspects of your move, starting with the cartons you pack your belongings in. Grocery store cartons are free but do not have tops and generally offer inadequate protection. The right cartons for moving purposes can be purchased at a carton manufacturer for a fraction of what a mover would charge you.

As for a truck rental—shop around. Not all rates are the same, and if you are willing to pay for a somewhat larger truck, you'll likely make fewer or only one trip instead of several. Recognize that you'll need a deposit or a major credit card to pick up the truck, so be sure you've made the proper arrangements in advance. Reservations are usually necessary. It will do you no good to

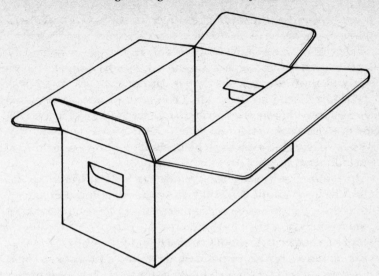

have five friends waiting to help if it turns out you can't get a truck.

When you're loading the truck, the important thing is to create a base, putting appliances and other heavy items on the bottom so that lighter items can be stacked on top. If possible, you should try to rent a truck with slats on the inside walls. This will allow you to lash your cargo down, pile boxes as high as you like and prevent anything from tumbling down. Many rent-a-truck firms also have pads that will protect your furniture as it is piled. (These can also be used to pad stair railings—a common cause of damaged furniture during moves).

If you or your landlord do not have a dolly, it would be a good idea to rent one—a two-wheeler if you're carrying heavy appliances and a four-wheeler if the distances to be covered between house and truck are great.

Good Packing Makes the Move

It's worth it . . . and not too difficult . . . to pack your belongings carefully and correctly.

China and *glassware* should be placed in dishpack containers or barrels with tops. There should be several inches of cushioning material at the bottom (linens will work fine), and each piece should be wrapped with at least two thicknesses of paper. Newspapers offer adequate protection, but frequently rub off on china. White paper, or the plain, uninked newsprint available from most movers, is more desirable. The first wrapped pieces should be placed toward the outside of the container with additional pieces being filled in towards the center. Dishes, platters, and bowls should be placed on their side. Each layer of dishes should be alternated with a layer of cushioning material. The most fragile items—glassware, stemware and other highly breakable pieces—should go in last. Just before sealing, add an extra layer of cushioning at the top.

Silverware can be packed in a regular silver chest, trunk or cedar chest or in a carton with bedding. If a chest is not used, major silver pieces should be wrapped separately in nontarnish tissue paper.

Books and *records* should be packed in the not-too-large cartons designed for this purpose. Both records and books should not be packed more than about 30 pounds to a box—no matter who's doing the lifting. Their weight adds up quickly, so remember to check.

Lampshades should be wrapped in clean white tissue or mover's newsprint—regular newspaper will generally rub off. Because shades are light and easily crushed, they should not be forced inside one another.

Large *mirrors* and *pictures* usually require no packing, just extra care for local move situations. Wrap them in a blanket.

Many *televisions* and *stereos* require special servicing prior to being shipped. An appliance service man can do this or your mover for an extra charge. Stereo turntables should be screwed down and the tonearm secured with tape.

Refrigerators and *freezers*, as mentioned, may need servicing before being shipped, although many late models do not. The inside of these units should be completely dry. Glass trays and containers should be wrapped and packed as other breakables. Each shelf should be wrapped in paper with the paper hanging over the edge to prevent scratching the door. In some cases, the power unit must be tied down.

Kitchen appliances such as toasters, blenders, mixers and grills should be treated as large breakables. They should be placed in the bottom of containers, carefully wrapped.

Washers and *dryers* require servicing before they can be moved long distances. The agitator on the washing machine must be secured and the dryer bolted together—your mover or a machine service man can do the job.

Rugs not already wrapped and rolled from the cleaners should be rolled (never folded) and tied tightly in the middle and at both ends. Throw rugs may be tied together into one roll or placed inside of a larger rug. Rugs without backing, such as cotton throws, may be folded and placed in boxes or other containers.

Kitchenware should be wrapped in a double thickness of paper and placed in a strong container, again, with heavier items on the bottom.

Table lamps require as much care as china or crystal. Barrels, large dishpacks or wooden boxes should be used, although small lamps can be wrapped and placed in containers with clothing or bedding.

Clothing can be taken directly from closets and placed in specially constructed wardrobe boxes supplied by all movers. These help avoid the possibility of rewashing and ironing upon arrival and aid in extremely simple clothes transfer on both ends. Professional movers generally prefer to move dressers intact with the drawers in them and the clothes in the drawers. If you are moving yourself, this may prove too heavy for you, in which case drawers may be removed, covered with paper and carried in separate trips.

Linens and *bedding* such as blankets, pillows, sheets and towels can be used to fill dresser drawers, trunks and cedar chests or placed in cartons. As mentioned, these items make great cushioning when packing other items.

Medicine and *toilet articles* should be secured carefully around their closures and if there is any question about potential leakage, closures should be taped. Containers should be placed in boxes with all spaces filled in with tissue. The box should be marked "fragile" and "this end up."

Items that cannot be carried by professional movers include perishable food, inflammable substances or anything likely to cause spills or fires (gasoline, paint cleaner, aerosol cans, etc.) and articles for which a value cannot be established, such as original manuscripts and research documents. Again, you're best to carry valuable papers, money, jewelry, coin or stamp collections with you—don't leave them in a dresser drawer to be moved.

If you are packing your own goods, but actual transporting is to be done by professional movers, your costs can be kept to a minimum by stacking all of your boxes near the front door or in one easily accessible place. Remember, on a local move you'll be paying by the hour so the less work the movers themselves have to do, the better.

How to Choose a Moving Company

First, ask friends or relatives for any firms with whom they may have had a recent, satisfactory experience. Of course, you can simply "let your fingers do the walking," but in any event, be sure to get an estimate from several moving firms. The Interstate Commerce Commission, which regulates all interstate carriers, does not rank, rate, or recommend movers, but does require each to supply you with a performance record which can be examined and compared to others. This record includes such information as how many shipments the mover shipped, how many were received late, what damage claims were, and other pertinent information.

What Should Your Move Cost You?

All interstate long-distance moving rates are regulated by the ICC and are identical. When a mover examines your household goods in order to estimate your moving expense, he will look at what you own and compare it to a chart that gives an approximate cubic foot measurement for each item. For example, an arm chair might take 10 cubic feet, a gas range 30 cubic feet. Using the rule of thumb of seven pounds per cubic foot, he will give you an approximation of the total weight of your belongings to be moved. Rates are based on weight, but change over longer distances and with heavier loads. If the mover underestimates your weight, you may still have to pay for the average. Movers report this is one of the most misunderstood elements in the moving process.

Because most movers will only accept cash, checks, or money orders, it may be necessary for you to arrange to have the check or cash payment ready in advance. But since actual shipping weight is determined by weighing the truck when empty and after your goods have been loaded, your mover may try to "cover himself" by adding on an extra 10% to his estimated weight, and thus the cost. If the actual weight is still lighter, you will be billed for the additional amount.

To give you a rough idea on how moving weights and rates run, a small house might have 8000 pounds worth of movables including appliances, a small apartment 4000 pounds.

On a local move, cost may vary widely. Independent operators can run as low as $40 an hour for 3 men and a truck. A high rate from a major firm could be as much as $65. On local moves, mileage may or may not be a cost factor, and packing, if required, will usually be figured on an hourly rate. In estimating a local move, the mover will have a chart, using cubic feet, that approximates the time it will take to load and unload from various areas of the house.

Most movers belong to a *tariff organization*, such as the Illinois Movers Tariff Bureau, Inc., which sets a rate ceiling and standards for its members.

Potential Problems

What problems can arise when you move? The Interstate Commerce Commission (ICC) identifies four major sources of misunderstandings between movers and clients. The first is confusion about pickup and delivery dates. The second, confusion on costs. The third and fourth areas—mover liability and claims settlement—are always the largest areas of controversy.

Unless you have made arrangements with your moving company to pay an additional charge for protection, movers are not liable for the full value of damaged goods. On a local move a liability of 30¢ per pound is, in most cases, included in the cost of your move. (That means that if a ten-pound article is damaged, you will receive $3.00.) You must, however, say that you want this minimum coverage to receive it. Otherwise, you will receive and be billed for additional coverage under the *Declared Value Protection Plan* of your mover. This coverage changes the total liability of the shipment to at least $1.25 per pound for the total shipment weight. Each item, however, is insured for full value or actual damage. You have the option of stating that you will limit the liability to $1.25 per pound or you may enter a lump sum value you consider adequate to cover your shipment. It cannot, however, be less than $1.25 per pound.

Local insurance coverage might run about 35¢ per $100 valuation. If you plan on using your own insurance company in addition to the carrier's coverage, you may need a special floater on your homeowner's or renter's insurance. Check with your insurance agent.

Moving company drivers, incidentally, are generally empowered to settle minor claims on the spot—usually situations that involve $100 or less. Once you sign a release, however, you cannot reintroduce a claim.

If you do have a claim for damage or missing goods, you will obviously need proof of it. One of the best ways of doing this is through the ICC regulated inventory that the mover must take. At the time the shipper picks up your goods, he will write down every item being moved with a notation as to its condition. You should check this list to see that it is accurate. When the shipment is delivered that inventory listing is again checked. If you notice any damage or items missing from the inventory, the shipping papers should be so noted. This is considered to be the most valid proof of your claim, and it's wisest to enter your claim at this time. You have, however, up to nine months to realize damage or missing articles from the move and to enter claims.

Moving day is here—what to do? For starters, you or someone you trust should be present during packing, loading, and unpacking—and be sure to read and sign that inventory and keep a copy of it. You should also check to see that your Declared Valuation Protection Plan is entered on the bill of lading in the proper amount.

Next, make sure children are supervised and out of the way—they may find excellent opportunities to play with the articles they usually can't reach.

There is much you can do to help the movers (and yourself) just by being a "good supervisor." Be sure to point out and tag items that are especially breakable and articles you don't want packed or moved. It's also a good idea to put the items you'll need immediately in a separate, marked container and identify it to the movers. All cartons (and for that matter, everything being moved) should be labeled or tagged as to which room in your new home they are to be delivered.

In general, help avoid delays in any way you can. Without actually joining in the loading process (leave that to the professionals), you can speed things up by leaving furniture in place but clearing the tops of all tables, dressers, and so on.

Before the mover leaves with your belongings, be certain he

knows how to reach you in case of an emergency during any phase of the move.

If you arrive at your new home ahead of your mover, use the opportunity to clean up the house and decide in advance where you want the furniture placed. The carrier will reassemble whatever articles they disassembled at the old location, but not the items you packed yourself. Movers will usually install and attach appliances at an extra cost.

Once you've moved in, immediately start tracer action on any items that are missing. If possible, notify the mover before he leaves and ask for claim forms and instructions.

Helpful Hints About Moving

Where can you get boxes? They can be rented from movers, lucked-into at the grocery store, or purchased at the box factory. These are the "official" sizes for moving boxes:

Books and records	$17'' \times 12\,\%'' \times 12\,\%''$
Lamp shade	$18'' \times 18'' \times 16''$
Linen	$23'' \times 23'' \times 20''$
Dishpak	$18'' \times 18'' \times 28''$

The Iroquois Paper Company sells boxes. They are located at 2220 West 56th Street (just west of the tracks). Their number if 436-7000.

You must call ahead to place your box order and make arrangements to pay by cash or check.

You can also buy their stock box sizes which will do the trick very nicely:

*Books, tapes, small fragiles, and medium sized very
   heavies: Stock box #W2, $12'' \times 12'' \times 12''$, 25 for $12.00.*
*Records, most kitchen items other than dishes and pans;
   most everything else that will fit. Get lots of them: Stock
   #W96, $18\,\frac{1}{2}'' \times 12\,\frac{1}{2}'' \times 14''$, 20 for $13.00.*
*Linens, pillows, pots, pans, and other big items that are not
   too heavy: Stock #W39, $18'' \times 18'' \times 18''$, 10 for $9.10.*
*Dishes, glasses, and other fragiles that need lots of
   cushioning: Stock #W12, $20'' \times 20'' \times 20''$, 10 for $11.00.*

As far as the fancy tissue and chipboard the movers have, I have found that newspaper works as well and is much cheaper. Start your newspaper collection about a month before packing and you will have no problems.

Stock boxes come flat so they must be "built" and sealed on the bottom and top. I recommend Horder's, Utility, or any other stationer's store to buy several 3-inch × 600-feet rolls of reinforced kraft paper tape. You'll use 6 or more feet per box. I don't recommend the PVC plastic tape, although this is what the movers use. It is expensive and very hard to handle. Working with PVC tape is like a vaudeville routine with fly paper. Use a scissors to precut your paper tape and a fat sponge sitting on a plate of water to moisten the tape. You can build thirty boxes in an hour.

When you do your packing, pack those boxes tight and full. The contents are best protected when they are (1) wrapped in several layers of newspaper, (2) neatly placed in the boxes, (3) packed tight and full in the boxes. This protects them from being damaged because a full box cannot, under ordinary circumstances, be crushed when stacked. Do not pack a box heavier than 30−35 pounds. Remember: you will have to carry it!

Also get some self-stick labels. Avery S4848 3″ × 3″ labels to identify what is in the box and/or into what room the box is supposed to go; and some Avery 2020RG 1¼″ diameter dayglow red "dots" to number each box. Make a brief inventory list keyed to the box number. This way if you should need something or lose something, you'll know what to look for without reading every label or tearing through every box.

If you want to rent a truck, reserve your vehicle well in advance. Remember, between 6,000 and 10,000 apartments change hands every month. If you want to hire a mover, book him early. Some will ask for an advance payment of up to $100 at the time they estimate the job. They will want the balance of the money at the time the move is completed. A couple of six-packs of beer will not be unwelcomed, and a cash tip of $5 to $10 to each mover is not unheard of, either (for difficult moves, up the ante).

If possible, move out a few days before the end of your lease. In this way you'll have an opportunity to patch any holes or remove any goodies that you have left. You might want to sweep up (this assumes that you are a good tenant, and you actually believe your landlord is going to refund the security deposit). But, if you do fix things up, your landlord won't stand a chance in small claims court if he sues you for damages. Sinkloid is a patching product which dries quickly and can be sanded or painted immediately. Use it on the holes you've made and smile.

If you have a chance, take pictures of the place after you vacate. This is for evidence in case you have a troublesome landlord who will not refund a deposit or sues you for damages.

I also suggest that you be able to move in early to your new place. You can set-up special things like your plants, refrigerator, special lighting, carpeting, shelving, or a burglar alarm before everything else comes in. It is also sometimes easier to move the fragiles before the movers.

Don't forget, one of the first things you should do when you move in is to take Polaroids of the new place and save them. You may need them when you move out to (once again) protect yourself from the new landlord.

Moving is unpleasant and disruptive. It is a time of physical and emotional stress. Prepare yourself. If you live with somebody (roommate, spouse, parent, etc.) try to understand the tension that exists. Premove jitters probably started when you first worried about finding a new place. Postmove jitters won't stop until everything is found, put away, or replaced (if broken). It takes pets about a week to settle down. Children require several weeks to several months. Some marriages never recover.

I have no sage advice about the trauma of the whole thing. Just try to take it easy and hope you haven't moved into a hornet's nest of building problems or nasty landlordism. Cross your fingers, try some yoga meditation, a joint, or a shot of whisky. A vacation about three weeks after the move is also a good calmer.

Two final words or shall I say phrases: *Unready apartments* and *holding over.* An unready apartment is just that, not ready to receive you and yours. If you attached the universal rider (Appendix E) to your lease you will have some protection because your landlord is obligated to pay for your movers, your temporary lodging, your time off from work, and any other damages of that sort. If you did not attach the rider, you could be in trouble if you arrive and the place isn't ready. My suggestions here are to keep in *constant* contact with your new landlord and the "old" tenant, and make a physical inspection prior to moving in.

If you have a problem, tell the new landlord and ask him what he plans to do. You may have to write him a letter, based on the rider, saying he has ten days to be ready after the start of your lease, and that you will hold him responsible for all your costs and damages while you wait until the place is ready. If the place isn't ready after ten days you have the option to break your lease. At any rate he is obligated to pay all your expenses until you can move into any new place. If you have to pay a higher rent for a comparable (or less than comparable) apartment, he will have to compensate you until the end of the lease period if there is a rent differential.

Your landlord letter will be a nasty letter, but if you don't do something like this you will be out of luck and in trouble. What do you do with your belongings? Who pays for the movers to come again? Where will you sleep? What about your mail and how about a phone number? If your landlord does pull an unready apartment on you, size up the situation, talk to him and if you think you are about to be dumped upon, send him the letter, and call your lawyer.

Holding over is when you stay in your apartment after the lease expires. The Illinois State law allows the landlord to collect double monthly rent prorated on a daily basis as "damages." Your lease may also have another hold-over clause allowing even higher damages. If you have to hold over, make arrangements very, very far in advance with your landlord. If he has rerented your apartment there will be somebody else trying to move in on their scheduled move day. This could cause the equivalent of a chain collision on the Dan Ryan with everybody smashing into everybody else's tail and nobody going anywhere—very bloody.

If you know you'll want to stay on for a few more months, ask your landlord to extend your current lease for that time period. Agree to adjust your rent (upward I am afraid) for the period, or accept a month to month lease (remember no protection against cancellation or arbitrary rent hikes). In either case you're protected against hold-over damages and hold-over evictions.

My advice is never to consider an apartment that is not complete and just the way you want it. Never get in a situation where you have to plead for a hold-over at the last possible minute.

9

Helpful Hints for the Harried Apartmentier: Roaches, Mice, Repairs, Utility Bills, and More

Roaches and Mice

So you've moved into your new quarters. There's you, your roomie, your pet fish, three plants, a half dozen mice, and a squad of roaches. Mice and roaches? Roaches and mice? You mean they aren't yours? You didn't bring them from the last place? They weren't meant as a secret gift from an admirer? Well, then you've got a problem!

Roaches are the subject of songs, books, jokes, and long conversations. Franz Kafka has died and gone to heaven. He is no longer a beetle and these are not his cousins. Kill them dead, as the ad goes. Oh yes, you can get rid of the roaches, but to do so requires dedication.

First, the roach needs water. Water can be found in the bathroom and kitchen. Water can be found as moist condensation on the outside of the cold water pipes running in the walls. Find where all the pipes—hot, cold, sewer, gas, and conduit—come into the apartment. Seal the wall around them with grout of Sinkloid spackling mix.

Inspect all the sinks, tubs, drains, and so forth for leaking water. Tighten up loose connections and have the landlord repair anything else, including dripping faucets.

Control of roaches will now be in three steps: Clean out and empty all your kitchen cabinets, bathroom shelves, and any other dark hiding places you have seen roaches. Roaches eat soap powder, glue, paper, and other nonfood stuffs, as well as people food. Roaches are found where people live because people bring these delicacies with them. Empty your shelves, wash them, and dry them. Be sure you leave no trace of soap or paper lint. Do not, I

The lady roach with egg sac.

The royal consort: Poppa Roach.

repeat, do not put liners on your shelves until after the roaches are purged.

Everything replaced in storage should be wrapped in plastic. Nothing should be accessible to the beasties for about three months.

I do not believe in sprays. I have used them. They work for a while, especially if you actually hit the roach with the sauce, but sprays smell so bad and they have to be used so often that they are worse than the problem. On to step two.

If you have no small children and no pets, either boric acid powder from the drug store, or roach powder poison from the hardware store is effective. The powder should be sprinkled along all the baseboards in the entire apartment. If you have cornices or crowns over your doorways, sprinkle there also. Don't forget to sprinkle around the toilet. In addition, place, by the score, those little anti-roach cans that have poisoned peanut butter or stick-em stuff, in every cupboard, closet shelf, cabinet, and drawer.

For a three-month-long period dry every dish, keep the sinks absolutely free of water except when you are using them.

If you have children or pets, or prefer not to use powder, you should spray with Raid, Black Flag or something similar along all the baseboards, door frames, and under and around the sinks, drains, and toilet bowl. Do note, however, that the sprays are toxic—dangerous to breathe, ingest, or touch.

Next, you must have the whole building exterminated. If your building cooperates by controlling water and the tiny debris, and puts out the poisons, you will lick the problem in about three months.

As an alternative, try to get the landlord to do a series of exterminations which hit the corners and baseboards, pipe openings, and other water-collecting spots. Have this done in every apartment every week for a month, every two weeks for the next month, and every month from then on, and you will also beat the problem.

To stamp out roaches you need the cooperation of everybody, including the landlord. You can do it. But, as I said, it is very difficult.

How about those mice? Best way to get rid of mice is to have a cat or dog in the apartment. Mice seem to avoid places with animals.

If you don't have a pet contact your landlord. Ask him to supply you with mouse traps (yech!) and packets of strycnine poison. Supposedly the mice get very thirsty from the poison and go towards water to die. If you have done a good job of roach-proofing your place so there is no available water, there won't be any mouse Valhalla there either. When they die, they stink to high heaven.

Your landlord should also seal the floors and close up the baseboards between the floors and walls, if there are openings. Also seal between the door frames and trim and the walls and floor. Any place suspected of harboring the mice should be stuffed with triple- or four-ought steel wool and then covered. Your whole building should be similarly treated.

If the pest problem gets really out of hand, call the city health inspector and the city building inspector. Collect as many "examples" of roaches and mice as you can to prove your case. Do not let your landlord pull some sort of token attempt—keep on him. Of course, such a problem is a good start for a tenants' union.

Repairs

Well, there are a thousand other problems that can go wrong in your castle. Generally speaking, when something "breaks," if you can fix it with a few simple tools and no expense for parts, fix it. Don't mess with anything you cannot afford to replace if you break it. Don't venture into deep waters without knowing the currents. For instance, if you want to replace a washer in a faucet, do you know where and how to shut off the water supply? If a light fixture starts crackling away, do you know how to kill the breaker and inspect the wiring?   Stick to the simple stuff. First, you could goof, and if there was an accident as a result of what you did, you would be liable. Secondly, if you do goof, you might have to buy a new garbage disposal, stove, etc. Lastly, it is the landlord's responsibility, in most cases, to make repairs and maintain the premises. If you start out doing his work for him, he may never respond to your call for help. It is bad training. Besides, what happens if you spend a bundle and then he says he didn't want you to do it, and won't reimburse you?

When you have a problem you cannot correct, call your landlord. Make an appointment for the repair to be made at a certain time or by a certain date. If nothing is done, send your landlord a letter detailing what needs to be done and that nothing has resulted from your first phone call and appointment. If you do not hear from him, and if when you do talk to him you are unsatisfied, send him a short letter telling him that if the repair is not made by such and such a date you will have the work done and deduct from your rents the cost. Indicate the price.

The complete process is detailed in Chapter 15 in the section dealing with *Spring* v. *Little*, a tenants' rights law case. If you think my approach is high-handed, then you'll sit around forever waiting to get the lock replaced on the door, to get the hot water in the shower, to get the front room lights to work without blowing a fuse, or to get the refrigerator door to seal properly. Do you get my point?

If the landlord isn't going to act right away, he probably isn't going to act at all. Did you know that 0% of most small building budgets are spent for maintenance. (See Chapter 14.) For $3000 or $4000 a year, you deserve some service!

I suppose the next most helpful hint is how not to destroy the walls and ceilings when you try to put up shelving, ceiling hooks for plants, or swag lamps. I suggest buying a happy house book for the weekend handyman or handylady. Get an inexpensive electric drill and a set of bits, including a masonry bit. The masonry bit will drill the holes through the plaster.

Never, no, never pound anything into plaster. Use mollie bolts, anchors (ask your hardware man or read that fancy household book), or toggle bolts. Spackle-up your mistakes immediately.

And if you are really planning a project, find a friend or neighbor with the tools and the experience. Bribe him or her with dinner or something, or trade off a bit of your expertise for theirs. Besides, it is always easier to let somebody else do it anyway.

Utility Bills

Now, how about your utility bills.

If you pay for your own cooking gas, it costs the minimum billing of about $2.25 per month. You do not use that much gas, that's just the way the gas company charges. If your bill is any higher than that, somebody else may be tapping your gas pipes. Call the gas company to check it out and ask your landlord to correct the problem.

If you also pay the gas bill for your own hot water heater, the charge runs to about $2.50 per month per person. You might also want to know that if you use your oven every day for 45 minutes and cook with all your burners full blast for half a hour you would burn about $.03 of gas each day. So for one person, your monthly gas bill would rise to $3.46 (or $6.92 for a two-month billing period). Add another $2.50 for each additional shower taker and you can estimate your bill. Again, be sure you are not paying for somebody else's gas service.

If you have a gas furnace, your costs are supposed to equal the number of square feet of your apartment multiplied by $.40. That is what your heating bill should be for the year. If your apartment does not have storm windows and is not weather-stripped and caulked (i.e., needs insulation) your bill could be double the formula. At any rate the gas company says you need an 80,000 to 110,000 BTU (British thermal unit) furnace to heat a five to seven room nonhigh-rise apartment. They say your furnace will run an average of 2000 hours during the heating season (unless the weather was like the winter of '77 when it ran 3000 hours). I have worked out a formula that takes BTUs divided by 100,000, multiplied by the heating season, multiplied by the cost of a therm (1 therm = 100,000 BTUs). Complicated, well yes, but it tells you what to expect. To figure your heating bill, multiply your furnace's BTU capacity by $.005. So, on an average winter, with an 80,000 BTU-capacity furnace, your heating bill would be $400.00. Divide that by the five months when the furnace runs and figure for two people paying for cooking gas, hot water, and an 80,000 BTU furnace the monthly bill is about $86.92 for each winter month. If you had good insulation, your bill could be as low as $57 per month.

Space heater usage is calculated on the BTUs divided by 100,000 times $.25 for each hour it runs. Space heaters probably cost twice what a furnace does simply because they are typically inefficient.

By the way, if you were to run your stove and oven to keep warm, if the carbon monoxide didn't get you, the bill might. Running the stove as a heater would cost about $.05 an hour, $1.20 a day or $37.50 extra a month.

Who cares? you ask. Well, I previously mentioned these costs in relationship to what a heating bill would do to your yearly gross rents. I include this discussion here because of the great chances of being robbed on gas. So far, every old building I have been in has been mispiped, and somebody gets stuck for a huge bill.

The same is true for electricity, except it is much harder to compute average uses. For one person, in a small apartment without a lot of fancy gadgets, one might expect to use about 250 kilowatt hours per month. The bill would be about $12.00 per month or about $24.00 per two-month billing period. A frost-free refrigerator would add about $2.00 a month.

Basically a kilowatt hour of electricity (1000 watts of electricity used for one hour) costs a little less than $.05 when you add in the taxes and other adjustments. (See Table 1 for a complete range of equipment and electricity costs.) If you can figure out what your daily usage is, you can compute your bill estimate.

TABLE 1. **Typical Appliance Operating Costs**. These cost estimates are based on averages. Actual cost of operation varies with frequency of use, condition of the appliance and from user to user.

Food Preservation

Freezer—15 cu. ft.	340	14.1¢ per day	$4.08
Freezer—Frost Free 15 cu. ft.	440	19.7¢ per day	6.01
Refrigerator			
12 cu. ft.	240	8.6¢ per day	2.48
Frost Free 12 cu. ft.	320	14.2¢ per day	4.15
Refrigerator/Freezer			
14 cu. ft.	325	12.9¢ per day	3.88
Frost Free 14 cu. ft.	615	20.6¢ per day	6.24
side by side	800	27.3¢ per day	8.19

Food Preparation

Blender	390	1.60¢ per hour	$0.05
Broiler	1,400	5.90¢ per hour	0.34
Carving Knife	90	0.10¢ per use	0.03
Coffee Maker	890	0.75¢ for 8 cups	0.36

Deep Fryer	1,450	5.94¢ per hour	0.28
Dishwasher	1,200	$1.24 per month	1.24
Egg Cooker	520	2.13¢ per hour	0.05
Frying Pan	1,200	4.91¢ per hour	0.63
Hot Plate	1,250	5.16¢ per hour	0.31
Mixer	130	0.53¢ per hour	0.04
Microwave Oven	1,450	5.94¢ per hour	0.65
Range with Oven	12,200	6.5¢ per meal	4.01
Self-Cleaning Oven		11¢ per cleaning	—
Roaster	1,300	5.32¢ per hour	0.68
Sandwich Grill	1,160	4.75¢ per hour	0.11
Slow Cooker	200	5.5¢ per use	0.48
Toaster	1,150	0.80¢ for 6 slices	0.13
Waffle Iron	1,120	1.40¢ for 4 waffles	0.07

Waste Removal

Trash Compactor	40	1.64¢ per hour	$0.11
Waste Disposer	450	1.84¢ per hour	0.17

Home Entertainment

Radio	70	0.35¢ per hour	$0.29
Radio/Record Player	100	0.45¢ per hour	0.37
Television			
Black & White			
Tube Type	160	0.66¢ per hour	1.19
Solid State	55	0.23¢ per hour	0.41
Color			
Tube Type	300	1.30¢ per hour	2.25
Solid State	200	0.80¢ per hour	1.50

Laundry

Clothes Dryer	4,800	12¢ per load	$3.39
Iron (hand)	1,000	4.10¢ per hour	0.49
Ironer	1,300	5.30¢ per hour	—
Washing Machine			
(non-automatic)	290	0.40¢ per load	0.26
Washing Machine (automatic)	510	0.67¢ per load	0.35
Water Heater (See Note "A")			
Avg. Per Family	4,500	25¢ per day	7.65
Avg. Per Family with Washer	5,500	37¢ per day	11.31

Light Bulbs

40 Watt Bulb	40	0.16¢ per hour
60 Watt Bulb	60	0.25¢ per hour
75 Watt Bulb	75	0.31¢ per hour
100 Watt Bulb	100	0.41¢ per hour

150 Watt Bulb	150	0.61¢ per hour
200 Watt Bulb	200	0.82¢ per hour
300 Watt Bulb	300	1.23¢ per hour

Comfort Conditioning

Air Cleaner	50	0.21¢ per hour
Air Conditioner		
Portable (5,000		
BTUH w/EER of 8)	625	2.56¢ per hour
Window Unit (9,000		
BTUH w/EER of 8)	1,125	4.61¢ per hour
Central Unit (30,000		
BTUH w/EER of 8)	3,750	15.36¢ per hour
Blanket	180	2.75¢ a night
Dehumidifier	260	1.10¢ per hour
Fans		
Attic	370	1.51¢ per hour
Fan Coil Unit (See Note "B")	125	$1.16 per month
Furnace (See Note "B")	300	$2.72 per month
Portable	170	0.69¢ per hour
Window	200	0.82¢ per hour
Heater—portable	1,000	4.10¢ per hour
Heating Pad	65	0.27¢ per hour
Humidifier	180	0.74¢ per hour
Oil Burner (See Note "B")	270	$2.46 per month

Houseware and Outdoor

Clock	2	$0.70 per year
Floor Polisher	300	1.23¢ per hour
Lawnmower	1,600	6.55¢ per hour
Motor—1 HP	1,000	4.10¢ per hour
Sewing Machine	75	0.31¢ per hour
Snow Blower	1,500	6.14¢ per hour
Sump Pump—⅓ HP	330	1.35¢ per hour
Vacuum Cleaner	630	2.58¢ per hour

NOTES:

Based on 1976 rates.

One kilowatthour (kwh) is the use of 1000 watts of electricity for one hour.

* — Costs calculated using an estimated average Rate 1 charge of 4.096¢ per kwh, (based on rates effective September 2, 1975) including an average fuel adjustment of .496¢ per kwh, but no state or municipal taxes.

A— Based on water heating rate of 1.996¢ per kwh including an average fuel adjustment of .496¢ per kwh, but no state or municipal taxes.

B— Average cost over the six-month heating season.

Health and Beauty

Germicidal Lamp	20	0.08¢ per hour
Hair Dryer	380	1.55¢ per hour
Heat Lamp (infrared)	250	1.02¢ per hour
Shaver	14	0.06¢ per hour
Sun Lamp	280	1.15¢ per hour
Tooth Brush	7	0.03¢ per hour
Vibrator	40	0.16¢ per hour

Again you say so what? Well, in the last two places I lived I either powered all of somebody else's apartment or lit the hall lights for the building and powered the landlord's color TV. I have inspected AC terminal boxes in other buildings and found that many people are paying for the landlord's electrical service. Who is paying for the hall light outside your apartment—find out!!!

If your bill is higher than you think it should be, call the electric company (Commonwealth Edison) and ask them to inspect your meter. They cannot do anything if the tap is on the building side, but usually the man will help you determine if you are wrongfully hooked up. Edison, if you request it, is supposed to notify your landlord to make corrections. But sometimes Edison won't cooperate and you have to do things yourself. At any rate Edison will still hold you responsible for the bill, even if your electricity is being "stolen."

On your own, if you suspect you are being ripped off for the power, how do you find out for sure and stop it? First, turn off everything in your house and unplug the refrigerator. Nothing is on but a clock. No radios, no fish tanks. Go to your meter (usually in the basement or outside) and somehow identify, by either a reference to your apartment number or your account number as printed on the bill, which box is yours. Watch the disk in the center of your meter. It shouldn't move at all, or just barely. Wait and watch for twenty minutes. If there is an "illegal" appliance like a refrigerator it will take time for the refrigerator to cycle, but when it comes on, the disk will spin fairly fast.

If you observe that your disk has not stopped, even though you've shut off everything you own, then you have uninvited friends. Your next step is to turn off all the breakers to your apartment and wait. I suggest doing this at night. You'll be turning off somebody's lights and they will come down to the breaker box to

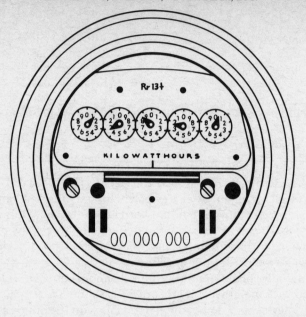

see what happened. If nobody comes, you may have shut off the building's lighting system or some pumps, or the washer/dryer. If you can locate what you killed, make a note of it. If someone comes downstairs, tell them you're sorry for the inconvenience, turn their power back on and call the landlord and the Illinois Commerce Commission to figure out who owes you how much money for the use of your electrical service.

Write a letter to your landlord and ask him to correct the problem as soon as possible. If he does not promptly respond, write him again giving him a specific date after which you will no longer supply electricity to who or what and that you will make the necessary arrangements to disconnect the improper wires from your service. Send copies to Commonwealth Edison and the Illinois Commerce Commission.

Also make the arrangements to be paid for your lost power. Three small light bulbs in a hallway burning 24 hours a day cost about $25.00 a year. Somebody else's refrigerator can cost you an extra $52.00 to $90.00 a year. Inspect the outlets under suspicion and calculate what the power draw is in kilowatt hours. Figure out how much things cost by the day and multiply that by the days you have been paying the bill at that address. Either that tenant or the landlord owes you the bread.

10

Introduction to Thermodynamics and Fluid Mechanics: The Heavy Stuff— Water Heaters, Furnaces, and the Gas Bill

The longer we live in a place the more we learn about its idiosyncrasies. Lots of times we find out more than we care to and are placed in a situation where we have to learn more than we want to learn.

The initial apartment inspection made before a place is rented cannot possibly reveal all the secrets. Well, what happens now. You are in, the lease is encased in granite and nothing seems to be working. It is time for a noncredit short course in building engineering. Welcome to "Introduction to Thermodynamics and Fluid Mechanics" or "where has all the heat-hot water-utilities bill money gone?"

Hot Water

Hot water is a problem in some buildings. If the landlord is providing hot water, he must supply water that is at least 120°F hot day and night. If the water heater is in your apartment (and/or you are paying for the privilege), you can set your own temperature, but the heater must be capable of providing the necessary minimum temperature. The heater should be a gas heater because it costs a fortune to heat water via electricity. If the heater is solely for your apartment, it should have a 35 gallon/30,000 BTU capacity. The cost of operating your own 35 gallon water heater at about 120° runs about $.08 a day or $2.50 per month per person.

Most central building water heaters are in the basement and

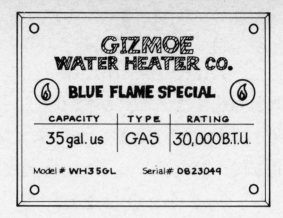

you should inspect it. In a building, a capacity of 15 to 20 gallons per apartment is a minimum for assured hot water with normal usage. It should heat with a capacity of 150,000 BTUs. If there are washers, add 5 gallons per washer to the capacity needs, and heat recovery should be 185,000 BTUs. If the building houses large families, add more capacity.

Heating Systems

A lack of heat in the winter can be a serious problem. It is therefore very important to check out the heating system at the first sign of trouble. The landlord is required to heat your apartment to 68° during the day from 8:30 A.M. to 10:30 P.M. After 10:30 P.M. and before 6:00 A.M., the temperature may legally fall to a chilling 55°. These are the minimums—he must do at least this well. If you pay for your own heating, you can set the temperature as you wish, but your heating apparatus has to be capable of heating to the minimum. Heat is required by the city to be available (if needed) from September 15 to June 15.

Most of the very old apartment buildings were originally heated by gas or coal-burning fireplaces. There would be one of these gas burners in the living area and perhaps in the dining room. Other rooms would be equipped with smaller gas, oil, coal, or even wood-burning Franklin type stoves. In many older apartments one can see pie-plate type covers over the chimney access ports. When the heating was upgraded, these gas stoves and fireplaces were pulled out. The replacement heating systems, typically, were either steam-heated radiator systems or space heaters. Recently, when buildings have been converted or rehabilitated, the trend has been towards individual apartment steam or forced air systems.

Space heaters are not desirable. They are the cause of many fatal fires and carbon monoxide or smoke poisoning. Small children are in constant jeopardy of being set afire or burned from the hot exposed surfaces.

A space heater, basically, is a metal box about the size of a two-drawer file cabinet. Natural gas is burned on a grate similar in function to, but much larger than, an oven burner. The gas heats up the metal box and the combination of the exposed flame and the very hot, metal box surfaces radiate heat to the room. Space heaters are usually set in a room near an outside wall. The hot burning gases are supposed to be vented directly to the outside.

Space heaters are very inefficient. It will cost from $35 to $55 for each heater each winter month. Bills of $75 to $100 per cold winter month are common.

Avoid space heaters. They take up valuable floor area, they are dirty, and they do not provide much heat to other rooms in the apartment. Space heaters can also explode. The presence of space heaters indicates that the owner or landlord has not been too interested in keeping the building in good, safe livable condition.

A much finer and efficient heating system is the *steam-heated radiator system*. Usually this consists of a low-pressure boiler sending hot steam up pipes to classical steam radiators. The cast iron radiators transmit the heat in the steam directly to the air via heat radiation. The steam in the radiator, as it cools, condenses to water and falls back down the same pipe that the steam comes through.

The integral parts of the steam system are a burner (either gas or fuel oil (coal is usually not burned because of pollution regulations), a boiler, a set of pipes, and the radiators. The burner heats the water when activated by a thermostat. The positioning of the thermostat is an important point and bone of contention. In smaller buildings, there is usually only one set of thermostats for the whole building. (There will be a day thermostat set at 68 degrees and a night thermostat set at 55 degrees. A timer is connected to the thermostat and selects which heat control unit will activate the burner during the day or night hours.) The thermostat is usually installed in a part of the building that always gets warm fast and stays warm. Sometimes they are in an apartment (and locked to prevent "unauthorized" adjustment) or high in a hall-way. Typically, the results can be perfectly legal temperatures in one part of the building and freezing conditions elsewhere.

Steam systems are not without problems if the landlord has allowed the system to fall into disrepair. The most troublesome problem is scale and corrosion accumulation in the steam risers and radiators. This restricts the amount of steam to the radiators, and subsequently, the amount of heat available in a room.

When clogged pipes and radiators exist, the radiators will not heat properly and will fill with condensed steam water. Some-times removing the air valve on the radiator when the steam is down will release the internal pressure and let the water go back down the pipe. The air valve will have to be washed or shaken to remove the sediment that tends to clog it, or will have to be re-placed. A lot of problems can be avoided in a steam system if the proper style of air valve is installed on the radiator.

The purpose of an air valve is to allow air which is in the radiator to escape when the steam rises in the pipes. The valve is designed to remain open when little or no internal pressure is in the radiator. As the steam rises, it slowly pushes air out. That familiar hissing sound is the result. When the steam actually hits the radiator and snakes its way through to the air valve, it has a pres-sure of .5 to 3.5 pounds per square inch. This is enough to close the

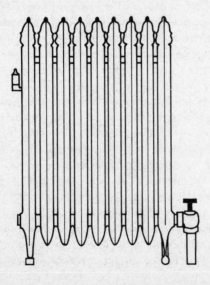

air valve and let the steam circulate in the radiator and not your apartment.

When the boiler shuts off the steam cools back into water. The air valve opens up because the pressure has been relieved. As it opens, it breaks a vacuum caused by the condensing steam. With the vacuum eliminated, the water can flow back down the pipes to the boiler.

Air valves can cost from $2.50 to $9.00 apiece, but the cheapies are not designed to work well with low-pressure systems. They are made not to release immediately after the steam pressure drops. This means that water cannot drain back to the boiler. Two problems develop. One is that the radiators clog up with water and will not allow steam to pass. When steam pressure pushes from below, some of the water may be forced out the air valve or the steam valve handle. Thus, rusty water and stains on the rug and furniture.

The other problem that attacks the system is that when condensed water does not return to the boiler, an automatic control pours more water into the boiler from a city water pipe. If the boiler has gone dry, it will explode. If not, now there is twice the water in the system. (This process of overfilling takes several hours to several days.) Finally everything—radiators, pipes, boiler—are full of water. When the boiler comes up, it converts some water into steam but the steam has nowhere to go—there is no heat in the building. If the boiler is not emptied and each radiator "bled" by removing the air valve, the party is over.

The more expensive air valves are designed specifically to work with low-pressure steam systems. Find out what type of boiler your building has. Either the janitor, landlord, or the building department should be able to tell you. Get a low-pressure steam air valve with an adjustable breather. By setting the air valve nob, you can control how much heat will come into each radiator and will also ensure that the water will drain back, benefitting you and the entire building.

The cheap air valves last for only several months. The expensive valves go for years. Insist on the good valves when these must be replaced.

This type of clogging, filling, and heat failure are chronic conditions. It is not always possible to detect the problem during nonheating periods, but there are some indicators. Rust stains flowing down from the air valve port indicate that water has filled up to that level throughout the entire radiator. The steam pressure from the boiler has pushed the water out of the radiator through the air valve or through the threaded port that the valve screws into. The water will leak steadily on the floor and spray out several feet from the valve. The water usually contains rust, scale, and a corrosion inhibitor and will stain or ruin rugs, furniture, and clothing. Occasionally, the valve will burst and allow a spray of dirty hot water and live steam to hit the wall on the other side of a room. Look for water stains on the floors around the radiators to confirm whether the iron sections are leaking also. Check the flooring for rotting or severe sagging. Check the radiator steam control valve handle to verify that it works and can shut off the steam. *Radiators should be tilted so that they drain back toward the steam pipes*, allowing the condensed steam water to return to the boiler.

An old, improperly operating steam radiator system will also give you another headache. When the heat is on, and when there is only one thermostat for the building (or section of the building), you have no good way of controlling how much heat you receive. This is because the only control usually present is the steam valve handle at the base of each radiator. *A radiator will not function if that valve handle is partially closed. It must be either wide open or shut all the way.* An in-between setting will allow steam to enter, but because of corrosion and scale, it will not allow water to return. Thus, the radiator will quickly fill with water, cease all operation, and leak. One cannot successfully control heat using the steam valve handle—forget it. Get an adjustable air valve instead. Messing with the steam valve is asking for problems.

Steam radiators also present some danger to small children because the radiators can become very hot; however, serious burns are rare.

Hot water systems operate in a similar manner to steam systems with thermostats, burners, boilers, and pipes. The radiators usually run along the outside walls of an apartment and are usually present in all rooms. Hot water is pumped through the pipes and radiators. The radiators have a valve to control water inflow and also to control water outflow. Ideally, each radiator is connected in parallel to the supply and return pipes. This allows individual setting of each radiator. If the water flows in series through one radiator to the next, several difficulties will arise. The first is that the water will cool off before it gets to the last room. The second is that you cannot restrict the flow of water through any of the radiators without slowing down the water flow in all of them, causing the whole system to cool down. Series-connected hot water radiant heating is not a good bet for a Chicago winter. The same cautions about leaks and corrosions apply to hot water systems as they do to steam systems.

Forced air heating systems are part of many rehabilitated apartments. These are usually found as individual apartment units. A forced air system consists of a thermostat in the apartment, a gas-fired furnace, an air blower in the furnace, and a series of air ducts and registers or vents to distribute the heated air. The furnace is usually located in what used to be a closet. It must be vented to the outside via a closed stack.

In many ways the forced air system is most convenient for apartment living because it can be controlled directly by the tenant. Forced air can heat a room rapidly and also circulate air throughout the apartment. The forced air furnace usually can be expanded to a year-round central air cooling/air heating system.

Drawbacks include the fact that the tenant must almost always pay for forced air heating and cooling in addition to rent in a low-rise building. If filters are not cleaned regularly the furnace loses efficiency and the house becomes very dusty. The blower and the moving air can create a sound that is carried throughout the apartment. If duct work and blower are properly sound-damped, the noise is minimal; if not, the system creates quite a racket and may be very undesirable.

The hot air registers should be located in each room of the apartment. The registers should be positioned near outside walls and ought to be at floor level. This combination of locations permits even room heating and the most efficient use of the system.

Occasionally hot water furnaces or steam boilers are placed in individual apartments. Be sure to inspect for general appearance to get a feeling about the age and safety of the equipment.

Heating Requirements

Because there is a trend towards tenants paying their own heating costs, in addition to rents, it is important to consider just how much it can cost to heat an apartment. The formulas get very complicated, but basically it is a question of apartment size and how much "heat loss" takes place during the winter. *Heat loss* is the amount of heat energy that escapes through the floors, walls, windows, and ceilings to the outside. The gas company experts in Chicago have come up with a few simple ways to approximate costs for an average-to-hard winter in the city. These statistics apply to low-rise brick apartment buildings in the city (not to high-rises or homes, they require a different set of calculations).

Based on a winter where the combination of wind and temperature gives an average wind chill factor of $-10°$, an average five-to-seven room apartment will require the same number of therms (100,000 BTUs of gas) that there are square feet of floor space in the apartment to be heated, *provided that the apartment has storm windows, sealed window frames, and insulation*. If not, *double* the amount used and money spent.

Gas bill charges are for the number of therms used. If an apartment has a 12×12 foot living room, a 9×12 bedroom, an 8×10 bedroom, a 9×9 kitchen, a 9×12 dining room, a 6×8 bathroom and a 4×4 hallway, there would be approximately 641 square feet plus a few closets and other miscellaneous corners. The number of therms used during the year would be about 650 or so. The cost of one therm was about $.25 in 1977, so, the cost of running a gas fired heating unit for a water, steam or air system would be about $160 for the year or $32 per month extra during the five winter months. If your apartment is about 1000 square feet (a three- or four-bedroom place of medium size), your gas heating bill could add at least $250 per year to the rent or $50 extra a month during the winter. For a cold winter like 1977 add 50% more to the heating bill.

There is another side to the tenant-supplied heat question: is the heating system adequate for the job? There is a simplified way of determining what is required. The gas experts say that a heating furnace in Chicago operates about 2000 hours each year. They also say that one therm of gas is equal, when burned, to 100,000 units of heat (or BTUs, British thermal units—the amount of heat energy required to heat one pound of water $1°$ Fahrenheit). Using the seven-room apartment as an example, we know that 1000 therms are needed during the year for heating. If we multiply 1000 therms times 100,000 BTUs, we get the number of BTUs consumed: 100 million. Divide 100 million BTUs by the 2000 hours the furnace is burning during the average year to find out how many BTUs are needed each hour the furnace operates: 50,000. In an apartment without storm windows double the BTU rating—100,000 BTUs would be required.

All furnaces have a specification plate which gives the furnace capacity in BTUs per hour. If the furnace rating varies much from the computation, you will find it will not supply adequate heat, or it will cost too much to operate.

For your information, windows without storm windows can cost $175 to $200 combined per year in lost heat costs. Windows covered by storm windows lose about half of the heat of the single-pane, exposed windows and can save you as much as 50% a year on your heating bill. Insist that your landlord supply and install storm windows. Every apartment, regardless of who pays the heat, should have storm windows. It should be a mandatory code requirement. With so much emphasis on energy conservation maybe something will be done.

Remember:

> *Hot water at 120° Fahrenheit is required 24 hours a day.*
> *Heat is required to be available from September 15 until June 15 each heating season. The temperature minimums are: 6:00 A.M., 60° Fahrenheit; 7:30 A.M., 65°; 8:30 A.M. to 10:30 P.M., 68°; through the night a minimum of 55°.*
> *The capacities of individual heating systems should be as follows: first-floor apartments: 100,000 BTU/hr capacity; middle-floor apartments: 80,000 BTU/hr; top-floor apartments: 110,000 BTU/hr capacity. The system will be more efficient and save much money if storm windows are installed.*
> *A simple way to figure the cost of heating an apartment for the year: multiply the number of square feet of the floor area of the apartment by $.40.*

Be prepared for a pop quiz next winter and go on to your next class: "Pipes and Lights" (bring your own tools).

11

Pipes and Lights

Pipes

Plumbing, which we have talked about in relation to the kitchen and bathroom, needs to be explored. Basically, clean water (hot and cold) should be delivered to the taps in the apartment at a useable pressure, and the used water should drain away rapidly and completely. Older apartments suffer from "underplumbing." If the original riser and branch pipes are still being used, there could be serious problems because these old pipes are clogged with scale. *Scale* is a combination of rust, corrosion, and hardwater deposits—Chicago's very own version of arterial sclerosis. We'll call it hardening of the water pipes. This condition generates two problems: (1) the interior diameter restrictions of the piping reduces water flow and water pressure; (2) accumulated crud breaks off from the piping and clogs the valves and taps, further reducing flow and pressure and staining the water a rust red.

To determine whether there might be a problem, snoop a little bit. Lift off the toilet bowl tank cover and flush the toilet. As the water leaves the tank, observe the tank bottom for rust stains, dirt, sand, silt, and caked calcium deposits. If there is even a small accumulation of such crud, there is a plumbing problem.

If you wish to be bolder, use a vice-grips or adjustable crescent wrench and remove the bubbler spigot from the kitchen sink faucet. It should come off with a little effort. There are one or two screen strainers in the bubbler. If there is "sand" present, there is a problem. The more junk, the worse and more frequent the prob-

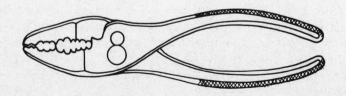

lem will become. In one building I lived in, all water stopped flowing after 5:00 P.M. on a daily basis. After numerous complaints, the landlord sent a plumber around. In twenty minutes he cleaned the strainers in all the faucets and the tubs and showers. VOILA! . . . water returned. But the building had had water pressure problems for months and the problem returned.

Some water problems can be corrected only when pipes are replaced. A stopgap measure that sometimes works is for a plumber to open up the existing pipes where they rise vertically into the apartments. The pipes have to be pounded. This usually will loosen some crud. The best tool is a landlord's head, the next best is an iron hammer. Either is hard enough for the job.

The water service itself to older buildings can be a problem. The supply pipes are usually inadequate. The minimum pipe size for smaller buildings is a 1″ inside diameter service for a three-flat, a 2″ supply pipe for a six-flat, 2.5″ to 3″ incoming service for an eight- to ten-flat. The way to determine the water supply pipe diameter is to look at the incoming side of the water meter. If there is a big pipe, (2″ or larger) you are OK. If not, here come the Saturday night bathtub drizzles.

Old buildings usually were "plumbed" using a main riser and several branches. These branches serve each sink, tub, or toilet. If there are too many branchings, or if the riser pipes are restricted or too thin, the old problem of the hot and cold heebee jeebies will plague you. When a toilet is flushed elsewhere in the building or apartment, a jolt of hot water screams out of the shower. All the cold water is diverted to that toilet. When someone runs their shower or the hot water in the kitchen, the reverse takes place. When clothes washers are used in the building, the problem can be acute.

Finally, just general advice about working fixtures, fast draining drains, and completely flushing and normal, rapid refilling of toilets. Make sure things are as you want them to be. Don't shrug off a slow-draining bathtub. In five minutes, while taking a shower, you can fill the tub up to your ankles. Under such conditions, you can fall and crack your skull. If the toilet doesn't empty properly, you can either make a part-time hobby of flushing every time you walk by the bathroom; reveal secrets about yourself you won't even tell your doctor; or start the first coliform typhus breeding farm on your block: think about it. Make your landlord fix these problems.

Lights

There is no question that most older Chicago apartments are underwired. The need for and the uses of electricity have expanded many times since these buildings were put up. As mentioned earlier, most buildings were originally lighted with gas. When they were converted to electric lighting, only a few wall outlets were provided. There simply wasn't much need. Well, today there is. Not only do we need many outlets for clocks, lamps, TVs, hi-fis, kitchen appliances, hair dryers, Christmas trees, air-conditioners, we need a much greater capacity of power.

Generally speaking, an apartment should have at least one duplex convenience outlet on each wall of each room, and more on long walls. The kitchen should have outlets placed so that small appliances can be plugged where needed. The outlets should be of the grounded variety, the kind that have the extra round hole just above and in between the regular flat slots. Most new electrical devices have the three-pronged plugs. The bathroom should be equipped with a convenience outlet for a radio, shaver, or dryer, but one far enough away and shielded from the tub, shower, sink and toilet.

Having enough outlets is only part of the battle. Ample "supply" is necessary. It is great to be able to find outlets for the TV, the refrigerator, and a reading light, but what happens if you blow a fuse right in the middle of the 6 o'clock news? In one place I lived, you couldn't turn on both the room light and a clothes iron at the same time—there went the fuse. Ever try to iron in the dark?

Most older apartments have only two circuits to cover all requirements. The circuits are rated at 15 amps. In this country most electrical consumption rates are expressed as watts. Basically, 120 watts are equal to 1 amp (at normal house service of 120 volts AC). To determine your needs, just add up the wattage of appliances, lights, and so on, that you might have on at one time. And determine in what parts of the house they are usually used. Then you can figure how many circuits are necessary and where. (See the electrical usage chart in Chapter 9.)

There are very good reasons for this exercise. Overloaded circuits result in problems: room lights flicker and never get up to full brightness; television sets operate poorly, the size of the picture changes constantly, color TV sets present erratic results; the refrigerator runs constantly, will not cool sufficiently and will not keep foods frozen; wiring overheats giving rise either to fire, wires breaking in the walls, or additional loss of power due to the overheating. And there are the constant circuit breaker or fuse failures, an inconvenience to say the least. Clocks run slow, and FM radios require constant retuning because of power drift.

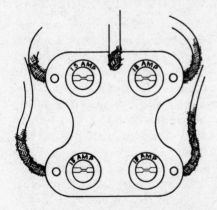

The underwiring of an apartment prohibits the use of air conditioning. This problem makes necessary the careful planning of what to turn on when. For instance, when the toaster is used, it has to be when the refrigerator is off. Ironing and TV don't mix. All the room lights at one end of the house have to be killed when the hi-fi is on at night. You can't use the hair blow dryer or styling comb when both the kitchen and bathroom lights are on, or when the refrigerator is running. And so it goes. Does this sound familiar, or more importantly, do you want to continue to live like this?

Generally, five to seven circuits are needed in an apartment. The kitchen must have two: one for the refrigerator and the lights, and a second separate 20-amp service for kitchen appliances. There should be a suitable number of outlets.

The division of circuits in the rest of the apartment is less precise. Normally, there should be at least one ceiling light circuit for the entire place, better yet is to divide the ceiling lights onto two circuits, front and back.

The convenience outlets should be divided into two circuits, one for the front part of the apartment, one for the back. This is the minimum to insure relatively trouble-free electrical service. It may be possible under such a division to run an air conditioner. It is almost certain that normal activities will not have to be curtailed because of insufficient electrical service.

Because of the way old buildings are wired, this five-or six-circuit division may be the only way of upgrading the electrical service. Sometimes it is possible to have separate circuits to each room, or two rooms. This is a most desirable scheme because it balances the load and gives you a lot of freedom in arrangements.

Often the fuse or circuit breaker box will be located near the electric meter in the basement. Breakers are more desirable than fuses because the circuit breaker is an overload protection switch that can be reset with the flick of your finger. The fuses burn out and have to be replaced, and a damp floor and a slipped finger could give you a little jolt, so be careful. It is also possible to substitute higher rated fuses for circuits but this may overheat wires. Best to play safe and be sure your landlord is playing safe with a safe breaker system. An inspection of the breaker box will give you the opportunity to count how many circuits your apartment has. And while you're at it determine, by asking your landlord the question, whether your meter is feeding electricity to any other part of the building, like outside hallway lights, back porch lights, washers or dryers, furnaces. You might be surprised to learn what is connected to your meter through that breaker box, and what goes through your meter you have to pay for! Beware.

About those old gas-lighting pipes I mentioned earlier, ask if they have been disconnected from the gas main. In some cases the electrical wiring will be pulled through the old pipes, so you can be sure the gas is disconnected. In other cases, the wiring is pulled around the pipes and there may still be gas in the pipes. This is not

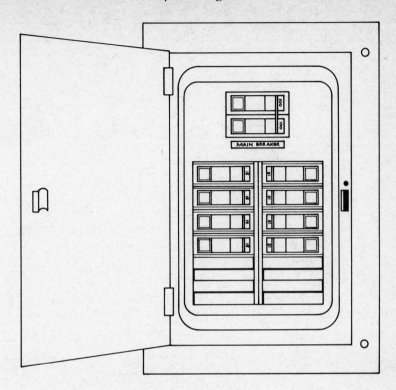

a good condition. The gas line will be capped with a brass screw-type cap. The method of sealing off the pipe and screw threads, more often than not, is to stuff a plug of regular hand soap into the hole and coat the threads with the soap. After a period of years, the soap dries and the gas leaks out. The unpleasant smell of gas odorizer seeps into the apartment and is particularly evident during humid or damp conditions. Far more dangerous is having the leak occur in a ceiling fixture or a wall switch. A spark from a loose wire can set off an explosion. Be sure the gas is dead. Ask your landlord or call People's Gas.

PART FOUR

The Real Estate Conspiracy

XYZ MANAGEMENT CO.   Receipt # **4567**

RENT RECEIPT

From _____

Received $_____

For Apartment _____

_____

Date _____   _____

                                        XYZ MANAGEMENT CO.

12

Some Observations About the Realities of Tenant Life, Landlords, and the Merry-Go-Round of Big Money

While the heart of this book attempts to construct a step-by-step, practical guide to apartment hunting and living, I think it is important to understand the business of real estate.

The tradition of landlords and tenants is an old and dishonorable one. The original English concept (the basis of American law) was that the landlord would rent or lease land to a tenant for a period of time for a certain consideration of money or goods or both. The landlord's only responsibility was to allow the tenant use of the land and to collect rents from the tenant. The tenant's only duty was to pay the rent. The landlord made no promises as to what condition buildings were in or whether the land could raise a crop. These were the tenant's problems. Any repairs or improvements were up to the renter. The concept was based on a rural and agricultural life growing out of the Middle Ages.

Today, many landlords still have their heads in the Middle Ages and their hands in our pockets. Tenant law is just beginning to realistically reflect the problems of urban life in the twentieth century. Too many landlords believe their only responsibility is to give you the key and collect your money. This attitude pervades in almost all landlord-tenant transactions.

Just what is it, this apartment renting thing? In the big city it is a biological function of the city dweller. Construction of residential single-unit structures (houses) is down, way down. Construction of apartment complexes is zero. A number of the new high-rises are in financial trouble, and the older high-rises are converting to condominiums. The low-rise buildings are in two classes: the buildings going down, and those moving up. Those going down aren't worth what you have to pay to live in them, and those moving up are prohibitively expensive. Inflation? Yes, and *greed*.

Apartment buildings are a great tax dodge and quick money makers. Lots of people with too much bread look for a nonfattening way to convert their financial calories into cake, and still look thin. The intrigue is complicated. The results of the investment game are quite depressing. Money, looking for a way to preserve itself and prosper, buys into the housing market. This happens thousands of times in a few years. As the number of available apartment buildings drops, the prices of available buildings shoot up. The higher the prices, the more buildings are put up for sale. Classic economics, you say. Up to that point, maybe. But enter the United States tax structure, and God knows what else. The price of apartment buildings should stabilize but it doesn't, it keeps going up. Do what you will, it climbs. Make money short, add more buildings to the list, reduce the number of buyers (not likely): the price keeps going up. So does the cost of borrowing. One result is that the rents charged are going to reflect the profits skimmed off the building by the previous owner at the time of the sale or transfer of the building. And when an owner sells one place, it is in his best interests, taxwise, to reinvest the money. Generally, he gets the best tax advantages by buying another building, waiting a few years for the price to double, then selling out. By the way, the cost of improvements are tax-deductible also. Worked smartly, and the people in real estate know the ropes, one can buy a building, do some work on the place, take a loss while the building is empty, deduct the cost of improvements from income, deduct the cost of paying interest to the bank, sell the building for twice what one paid for it, and still pay taxes in a lower tax bracket than most poor renters. This is a travesty.

We, who pay both taxes and rent, are the real "bankers" for the real estate investors. There is no equity in such a situation. At the same time, the cost of buying a single-family home is out of reach of most young couples (who traditionally have been the best market for such housing). The required down payment for a house in the city is 20% to 30%. The cost of a single-family dwelling (in decent shape, in a decent neighborhood) is from $40,000 to well over $100,000. So, while most of us are unable to save the necessary $8,000 to $15,000 down payment, we still require a place to live.

The only alternative is an apartment. Apartment-renting is a good proposition for the real estate interests who keep the rents high enough that we can't save for our down payment, restrict the number of new starts by keeping the costs of new housing and construction loans high, and keep the purchase costs of all housing on an upward spiral. This is the unhappy truth, and a very sad tale.

As apartment dwellers, we pay a very high monetary price for the place we live. In the accompanying table, find your monthly rent and the yearly total. Can we afford NOT to demand something in fair exchange? I think we must demand equity and fairness.

Landlords, owners, and management companies play a horrible game of gouge—high rents, sharp business practices, and a barbed lease with all the subtlety of a grappling hook. Once ensnarled on its spikes, you lose no matter what. Landlords' laws and leases are instruments of legal oppression. This is not a statement of political rhetoric, but a fact that any person who has suffered through the travesty of a bad landlord can attest to.

TABLE 1. **How Much Rent Do You Pay Every Year?** Find your monthly rent in the first column, and find the yearly rent your landlord collects from you in the second column. Read it, weep, and then ask yourself if you are getting what you are paying for. If you think not, it is time for action.

Month	Year	Month	Year	Month	Year
$100	$1200	$300	$3600	$500	$6000
110	1320	310	3720	510	6120
120	1400	320	3840	520	6240
130	1560	330	3960	530	6360
140	1680	340	4080	540	6480
150	1800	350	4200	550	6600
160	1920	360	4320	560	6720
170	2040	370	4440	570	6840
180	2160	380	4560	580	6960
190	2280	390	4680	590	7080
200	2400	400	4800	600	7200
210	2520	410	4920	610	7320
220	2640	420	5040	620	7440
230	2760	430	5160	630	7560
240	2880	440	5280	640	7680
250	3000	450	5400	650	7800
260	3120	460	5520	660	7980
270	3240	470	5640	670	8040
280	3360	480	5760	680	8160
$290	$3280	$490	$5880	$690	$8280

There is a conspiracy between real estate people, lawyers, the courts, law makers, assorted politicians, bankers, insurance companies, and other focuses of vested money and power. The conspiracy is quite simple: keep the money flowing and keep the system "working." As we are about to see, the system is not our system, but their system.

In the social organization of Western *Homo sapiens*, in the grand classes of species, the most lowly is the apartment dweller. We don't assign ourselves this position—it is visited upon us, gratis. Thus assigned the tail end of things, we must quickly learn to become suspicious and wary. As a thing of prey, we must guard against our arch enemy: the landlord. Do not scoff at what I say—the sad tales are nasty and manifold.

1. A young couple spent several weeks finding the "right" apartment in New Town. They had suffered through two years of roaches and clogged toilets and were ready for a good place. They found it. A management firm promised delivery of the new apartment in three weeks. At the end of five weeks, the place wasn't "quite" ready, but the couple had to move. The lease, a Chicago Real Estate Board 12R, had an additional clause written in giving either party the right to cancel with 90 days' notice. The couple was tempted to use it and thought they were very clever in having this clause included.

The people decided to stay, and they spent one month painting six rooms, installing wiring in two rooms, cleaning up old woodwork and plumbing, redoing the floors, putting up shower rods, shades, curtains, and shelving. The place looked great and they were pleased. So was the management company. When the rents were paid after the first month, the management company gave the couple 90 days to move out. The rents were raised 50%, the place re-rented and the young couple was out on the street.

2. Three roommates, two cats, and a small jungle found a home in a three-flat on the North side. It was winter, the place was just passable, but everything worked. At least that is what the management company told them, and that is what the roommates wanted to believe. Shortly after they moved in, the heating system failed and some of the plumbing froze. The landlord was very sorry and said he would try to take care of it "right away." That's all he did: make mouth music. The roomies stopped paying rent, the

landlord was enraged. Two of the roommates caught lingering colds, both cats became ill from the cold, and many of the plants in the jungle died.

The landlord refused medical bills, veterinary bills, and plant replacements. He also did not fix the heat or repair the plumbing, but he did sue the tenants for the rent. The tenants moved out. When the court date came up, the tenants were in court to ask that the landlord pay them for their losses. The landlord failed to show up so the tenants were out of an apartment, work, and money. The landlord lost one month's rent and then sold the building at quite a profit.

3. A young couple found a super apartment. They made an application. The agent said that usually he took a $50.00 rent application fee which was applicable to the first month's rent, but, he said, because of the desirability of this particular place he would require a full month's rent as a deposit. The couple paid up. After 10 days, the couple, not hearing again from the agent, decided the rent was too high and they wanted their $385.00 returned. They called the agent. The agent said it was too late, their credit check had just gone through; they had passed. He would have to keep all the money because they failed to exercise their option to take the apartment. The lease had two months before it even started and there was a waiting list with other paid-up applications, but the couple was still out the bread.

These are real horror stories for the people who had to live them, and these stories are just the crust of the messy pie: no heat in zero weather; 50% rent raises; mice running through the walls and over beds at night; roaches, rats and small children fighting over the same piece of food; windtunnel speed drafts from broken windows in the winter; broken toilets that make a visit to a war camp latrine seem like a gift; stoves that explode when lit; refrigerators that stay an even 60 degrees no matter what; light switches and wall sockets that arc more light in sparks than the light bulbs they are supposed to control; raw sewage backing-up through kitchen sink drains and bathtubs; the world-famous four-hour bathtub—that's a bathtub that takes four hours to drain after a shower; door handles that fall off; windows that fall out; radiators that explode; space heaters that spill carbon monoxide into rooms they are supposed to heat; ceilings that collapse when leaking pipes soak the plaster; kitchen faucets that won't stop and kitchen drains that won't start; door locks that won't lock or locks that won't open; sash windows that can't be opened or can't be closed; landlords with a deaf ear to the problems and a good ear that lets them know when you are home as rent time comes around.

Suffice it to say: most landlords (owners, managers, agents) are sharpies who are out to collect rents and keep costs down—period. There is no sense walking blindly into their lairs.

A last comment about the situations I have been describing: this is what is going on in the "higher class" parts of town. The poorer sections of Chicago are even worse and those tenants are even more cruelly victimized.

13

The City From The Eye Of The Computer: Statistical Chicago

An Overview of Chicago Apartments

Let's look at statistical Chicago as it relates to apartment living.

There are approximately 3,100,000 people living in the city.

The city is ethnically 46% white, 40% black, 11% North, Central and South American Latin, and 3% Asian and American Indian. The white population is decreasing (it was 50% in 1970) and the black and Latin populations are increasing (they were 33% and 7%, respectively in 1970).

Since 1970 the city has lost a net of 250,000 persons (−8%), some to the suburbs and some to the south and southwest of the country. The rate of lost population is climbing to more than 1.2% each year.

In 1970 there were a total of 1,210,000 dwelling units of all sorts. Apartments comprised 742,940 of them. In 1977 the number of total dwelling units shrank to 1,027,500, a loss of 15%. The number of apartments available for rent in 1977 shrank to 668,400, a loss of better than 10% since 1970. When you add in the lost single-family dwellings, the number of total dwellings lost in seven years was a staggering −110,800, and this is the figure after all the new construction has been factored into the calculations.

We are an apartment-living city. Fifty-five percent of our population lives in rental units while 42% lives in owner-occupied homes. In 1977 we had 190,000 unlivable housing units and 159,000 units that needed work to bring them up to the Chicago building code standards. It could be argued "statistically" that only 60% of Chicago's housing was in good shape in 1977.

The city building department also generates its own set of statistics. They sound impressive but I wonder what the results really are.

The department received 110,000 complaints during the latest yearly reporting period. The department made 70,000 housing inspections, 200,000 electrical inspections, and 61,500 work-in-progress inspections. They ordered 28,500 building owners to report to the city's administrative Compliance Board to follow-up on violations of the code. Of these compliance citations 9,200 cases went into housing court and have not been heard of since, but 2650 buildings were demolished as a result of city diligence.

No landlords were charged with criminal negligence to property and 20 porno shops and more than 100 massage parlors were raided by the inspectors and closed because of dangerous building conditions. Thirty people burned to death in substandard housing, and several thousand persons were treated for conditions relating to exposure to cold due to lack of heating in their apartments.

The landlords are not usually due in court until eight months after the violation and then often only for another continuance.

The percentage of city inspectors driving expensive cars is not available.

There are over 400 city inspectors. Nearly 200 of them are assigned to building inspections.

It is very hard to determine the vacancy rate for apartments. The real estate experts claim less than 1% vacancies, the city thinks the number is 7.5%, and the Census Bureau's guess, based on "idle" electric meters, is 5.1% vacant apartments (available for renting). According to the city, in 1977 there were 85,000 vacant apartments of which 64,600 were for rent.

In 1970 the median amount of monthly rent was between $100 and $200 for about 65% of the apartments in Chicago. Now it is well over $250 but there is no current census information on this point. In 1970 57.5% of renters paid less than 25% of their incomes for rent while 38.2% paid more than 25% of their incomes in rent.

Of existing apartments in the city 8% are single-room units, 25% are one-bedroom units, 36% are two-bedroom units, and 25% are three-bedroom units. And, glory be, 97% of all apartments in the city now have a toilet.

We live close to the ground with 42.2% of our population living in 2- to 3- and 4-flats, and probably another 25% living in six-flats and low-rise buildings.

We are also an old city as far as age of apartments is concerned. Sixty-seven percent of our housing was constructed before 1940 and 70% of our population lives in this pre-war housing.

There has been little new construction of apartments in the city. There are several new high-rises with rents starting at $400.00 for a closet, but there basically has been no new residential construction started in the city since 1974. "The year the bottom fell out," as the in-crowd likes to say.

By June of 1975, there were 12,000 condominium apartments in the city, and the number is estimated to have doubled. Most of these condos were apartments converted for sale, however, not newly built units.

The leaders in the world of real estate, finance, and construction announce that little apartment construction has taken place in eighteen months because of the cost of financing, nor will construction pick up until the cost of borrowing drops or profits open up. They are also proud of the condo conversions they are parenting. These, of course, cost them much less, and costs whoever buys them much more. A recent report from a real estate research group puts the baseline cost of buying a home or condo at $40,000 for the Chicago area. Most condos in the city are now selling for over $60,000 and their prices are rising at almost 1% a month in some cases.

Banks and other lending institutions have also put a stop to lending mortgage money to small-time buyers who are looking for a six-flat. One downtown savings and loan said the risk was too high and there were no profits in small housing units. They also flatly claimed that the prices for small buildings were ridiculously high. A three- or six-flat that was selling for $40,000 three years ago is going for $80,000, and a totally rehabilitated six-flat commands $225,000.

The city tears down about 2500 buildings a year. The *Chicago Tribune* claims there are about 1600 abandoned apartment buildings standing right now, somehow saved from the bulldozer. The cost of renovating a six-flat runs between $5000 and $20,000 per unit plus another $10,000 to $60,000 for the building. Taxes run about 10% for small buildings and the mortgage payments can be as high as 50% in some cases. What this adds up to is that it costs too much money to buy, fix up, and maintain small apartment buildings. The banks don't seem to want to help, and taxing structures discourage improvements. The city has no policy except to tear down buildings when they ultimately and miserably fail the codes and die.

In the so-called changing neighborhoods, there is also the problem of getting any money at all to make repairs, let alone purchase buildings. The term is called *redlining* and the practice is for banks to refuse all loans in certain redlined "undesirable" neighborhoods or areas.

So the bottom line is that we have a high apartment population; more apartments are being taken out of the market by conversions, blight, or demolitions than are being built to replace them; no real effort is being made to solve a shrinking vacancy rate; and the very expensive and hard-to-get-at money market discourages repairs and purchases and encourages blight.

Among other things, slumlord milking has cost Cook County about $50 million in unpaid property taxes. Little is done to collect the money even though there is an occasional attempt.

Playing at the Numbers Game: The Financial Picture

The predictions are as follows (quoting the experts): rents will have to jump automatically 25% now and then to keep up with inflation of 6% to 10% a year in order to make the market profitable enough to encourage new construction. The market will have to sustain a net profit of 7% to 12% on total investment for people to want-in on the game. Rents for apartments in the city will have to climb to something like $350 for a studio, $500 for a two-bedroom with tenant paying for all utilities. This is what the bankers and real estate interests want to have happen in the next two years.

The banker/real estate dream is to squeeze that last dollar from the good ol' middle- and working-class tenant, toss out all the poor and ethnically "impure," and build the third century of their own empire on the prairies of Illinois.

The city is actually collaborating in all this by failing to set up working mechanisms for neighborhood stability, housing construction, code enforcement and rehabilitation, and tenants' rights. Instead of allowing the owners of slum properties to milk and bleed a building to death, the city should join forces with tenants and at least try to reverse the process of blight. As it is now, the building department does nothing to help a building back on its feet. It watches and waits. When neglect catches up with the place, the city tears it down, and in effect, raises our rents.

The whole concept and operation of Chicago 21, a plan to rebuild the South Loop, is a perfect example of how to destroy old neighborhoods, unstabilize areas, and direct resources to the most profitable places for the banks and not to the most needed plans for the people.

If middle-class tenants, and even middle-class landlords, cannot stem the tide of shrinking housing and no new construction, in ten years only the rich will be able to afford a decent apartment in the city. The word is out. One of the city's larger real estate management firms has raised the limits as to how much a person can spend of his income to qualify to rent. The amount allowable has climbed from one-quarter to one-third of one's gross income. After take outs for taxes and Social Security, that amount is almost 50% of take home pay!!!

Now more than ever, it is important for tenants to recognize what will happen to them if they do not fight back. Tenant organization is needed: at the building level to make sure it is maintained; at the block level to protect the neighborhood; and at the city level to bring pressure to bear on political officials and the courts.

Read on.

14

A Peek Through the Looking Glass: Management Costs and Operations

Operating Costs

Into the misty murky areas of apartment management we go to find out what we get for what we pay, and how much others are making from our hard-earned rent money. In summary, and without a doubt, the bankers walk away with the biggest plums, cherries go to the landlord, grapes to the real estate taxes, and olive pits to the maintenance man.

Not very much is published about operations. The Institute of Real Estate Management publishes an "Income and Expense Analysis" every year. The Institute analyses major types of apartment buildings and the general breakdown of what they take in and what they spend. The report shows national trends and also hints at the local situation. The problem is that they do not receive enough data from any city to really paint a sharp picture. The research only covers larger buildings and only those that are making money.

For the smaller buildings from three-flats to twelve-flats, there is no officially available operating information. I was able to study financial statements of twenty-five randomly selected buildings in Lakeview and seventeen summary statements of buildings in Uptown. This information comes from *The Best Seller's Book*, a computer compilation of the North Side Real Estate Board Cooperative Listings Service, and is published weekly by International Graphics Corporation. Between the two publications mentioned and a lot of interviews with bankers and real estate and management types, I have constructed a profile of costs and profits for buildings in the city of Chicago. These are for the 1978-1979 period.

If you can believe what any landlord says, these figures are as valid and accurate as any available, and very revealing.

There are two separate and distinct real estate markets in Chicago just as there are big buildings and little buildings. Big money buys large high-rises and large low-rises. These buildings cost millions. Three- and four-story flats, up to twenty-four apartments, cost from $50,000 to $250,000. The high-ticket buildings turn over occasionally while the lower-priced buildings are constantly being bought and sold. The statistical observations will also reflect differences by building size. There are different tax rates, different loan rates, and different ways of stating operating costs.

Let us first look at the larger buildings. Basically we can only evaluate the yearly operations of these buildings because we have no information on what the initial price of the structure was or how much the loan payments are. Taking into consideration the upward moving rents and the costs of heating, this is the expenditures and profit picture.

On an average, the profits from operations of a high-rise building are about 31% of its total income before mortgage payments. About 25% of total income is spent on operations including staff, supplies, water and plant utilities, insurance, and so on. Management fees amount to about 6% and real estate taxes come to almost 20%. Over the years repair, maintenance, and painting costs have climbed to about 8% of the total income of a building. Heating has jumped from 5% of total income to about 12%. So, in rough numbers, you pay about 70% for your apartment needs and about 30% to the investors and their banks.

Broken down, the figures predict that you will be paying $1092 per room each year, either now or in the near future. If you live in a high-rise one-bedroom (four-room) apartment, you pay nearly $4368 per year (that's $364 a month) for rent with $1200 going for regular building expenses, $328 for maintenance and painting, $437 for heating, $262 for management service fees, and $525 for Cook County real estate taxes. If your building is air conditioned, part of the regular building expenses include the air conditioning.

In low-rise large buildings the costs of heating are higher and so are maintenance expenses. I suspect that much of the maintenance has to do with decorating (painting), but at least it is an ongoing process. You pay more for a high-rise apartment, but you seem to get your money's worth.

TABLE 1. **Profitable Larger Building Apartment Statistics.** * Expenses in dollars per room, 1978 estimates.

	Elevator High-rise				Low-rise Between 12-24 units**				Low-rise over 25 units			
	National		Chicago		National		Chicago		National		Chicago	
	$	%	$	%	$	%	$	%	$	%	$	%
Rental income	920		1092		575		672		747		734	
Operating expenses	253	27.5	266	24.4	118	20.5	130	19.4	157	21	176	24
Maintenance–Repair	69	7.5	87	8	63	11	64	9.5	52	7	59	8
Heating	92	10	131	12	69	12	121	18	90	12	103	14
Management fees	55	6	62	5.7	40	7	44	66	46	6.1	50	6.8
Taxes (real estate)	110	12	207	19	92	16	128	19	92	12.32	122	16.6
Total costs	572	63	753	69	382	67	487	72.5	437	58.4	510	69
Net profits before mortgage and taxes	341	37	339	31	193	33	185	27.5	310	41.6	224	31
Turnover rates	30%		24%		31%		24%		43%		24%	

*Based on Institute of Real Estate Management Statistics and estimated out to current trends.

**Does not reflect classic 12-24 unit low rises found in most of city. Reports only Gold Coast and suburban type buildings.

As far as profitability of the large buildings are concerned, there is no good way of knowing. It is assumed (and this may be very wrong about a particular building) that the mortgage payments will be 20% to 25% or less of the gross rent receipts. If that is true, the average building analyzed here would leave about 6% to 11% profits per year. The real estate experts say they need to see a return of 7% to 12% profits per year, the accompanying chart also shows the operating costs and profits for high-class, low-rise buildings between twelve and twenty-four units, and low-rise buildings with twenty-five units or more.

The detail in the tables on three- and four-story apartments are much more complete and revealing about the small-building real estate business in Chicago. This is because of the access to the "for sale" slips posted in the North Side Cooperative Listings book.

In the Lincoln Park—Lakeview area (Old Town, New Town, De-Paul, etc.), the average real estate taxes paid are about 8% of the total income of a building. The average allowance for mainte-nance, repairs, and painting is 0%. Heating accounts for about 12% of the income where heat is provided as part of the rent; the water, sewerage, and building electricity (hall lights) run about 4%; and, another 2% of the income is spent on other miscellaneous ex-penses including lawyers to collect back rents and court costs. Insurance on the building accounts for the last 4% of the income expenses.

Heat is the largest expense in the building and taxes are next. After the insurance the rest is "profits." Well . . . today the average cost of the mortgage on a small building (after down payment) is 47% of yearly income. Profits average 25% of income but the amount of money is small in most cases. Finally, if you compare the net profits to the overall investment (the cost of the building), the return on investment is about 5%—not even enough to keep up with inflation. My real estate knowledgable friends challenge some of the figures for Lakeview. They say that the numbers for heating and insurance are too low. The numbers are those re-ported by owners who have made a financial statement as part of offering the building for sale. If these numbers are known to be wrong, then the owners and real estate folks are perpetrating a fraud. If the cost factors are indeed higher than reported, the purchase of these properties would spell automatic financial ruin for the small-time investor, and at any rate would mean that no matter who acquired the property, the building would have to be

TABLE 2. Total Financial Experience for 25 Low-rise 5–29-Unit Buildings in Lakeview (Current).

No. of Units	Selling Price	Taxes		Miscellaneous		Heat		Utilities	
1. 6	$ 48,000	$ 900	11%	$ 0	0%	$ 700	8%	$ 200	2%
2. 5	49,000	500	10%	0	0%	0	0%	100	2%
3. 6	52,500	600	6%	0	0%	600	7%	400	4%
4. 5	60,000	940	10%	0	0%	0	0%	250	3%
5. 6	62,000	750	7%	0	0%	0	0%	420	4%
6. 5	62,000	200	2%	0	0%	0	0%	300	3%
7. 5	64,000	770	8%	0	0%	1200	13%	200	2%
8. 7	69,900	710	7%	0	0%	0	0%	100	1%
9. 18	72,000	2900	10%	2100	7%	2400	9%	2000	7%
10. 8	75,000	700	8%	0	0%	0	0%	400	4%
11. 29	75,000	2000	8%	900	3%	2000	8%	1100	4%
12. 6	80,000	2200	15%	100	0%	1600	11%	300	2%
13. 6	82,500	600	4%	0	0%	0	0%	300	2%
14. 13	95,000	1900	9%	9400	46%	3700	18%	1400	7%
15. 5	96,000	800	7%	0	0%	1300	11%	700	6%
16. 13	119,000	1200	5%	600	3%	5000	22%	2800	12%
17. 7	130,000	1700	8%	0	0%	2000	10%	400	2%
18. 6	130,000	1000	6%	0	0%	0	0%	0	0%
19. 19	145,000	4700	15%	1600	5%	4100	13%	800	2%
20. 5	148,500	600	5%	600	5%	0	0%	400	3%
21. 13	149,500	2800	11%	500	2%	2400	9%	500	2%
22. 6	150,000	2200	15%	0	0%	2000	13%	500	3%
23. 19	150,000	3900	9%	400	1%	7200	17%	2200	5%
24. 10	160,000	1600	7%	1700	7%	2600	11%	600	2%
25. 7	$165,000	$1500	6%	$ 200	4%	$1500	6%	$ 700	3%
Total % of all entries			8%		2%*		12%**		4%†

	Repairs		Insurance		Total Expenses		Rents/Year (Income)	Monthly Rents
1.	$ 0	0%	$ 140	2%	1,940	23%	8,300	115/690
2.	0	0%	350	7%	950	19%	5,000	83/417
3.	300	3%	400	4%	2,300	26%	9,000	125/750
4.	0	0%	350	4%	1,540	17%	9,100	150/750
5.	0	0%	500	5%	1,670	15%	10,800	150/900
6.	250	3%	350	4%	1,100	12%	9,300	155/775
7.	0	0%	500	5%	2,670	29%	9,360	156/780
8.	0	0%	600	6%	1,410	14%	9,948	119/830
9.	2500	9%	1400	5%	15,300	54%	28,200	130/2350
10.	0	0%	400	4%	1,500	16%	9,420	96/770
11.	1000	4%	1400	5%	8,400	32%	26,140	75/2183
12.	0	0%	500	3%	4,700	31%	15,120	210/1260
13.	220	2%	500	4%	1,620	12%	13,680	190/1140
14.	700	3%	1000	5%	18,100	89%	20,340	130/1695
15.	0	0%	400	3%	3,200	27%	11,700	195/975
16.	0	0%	500	2%	10,100	44%	22,900	147/1908
17.	0	0%	800	4%	4,900	24%	20,700	246/1725
18.	0	0%	1200	7%	2,200	13%	17,100	238/1425
19.	0	0%	1400	4%	12,600	39%	32,580	143/2715
20.	0	0%	800	6%	2,400	18%	13,260	221/1105
21.	0	0%	600	2%	6,800	27%	25,464	163/2122
22.	0	0%	600	4%	5,300	35%	15,300	212/1275
23.	0	0%	1500	4%	15,200	36%	42,060	185/3505
24.	0	0%	1200	5%	7,700	31%	24,600	205/2050
25.	$ 0	0%	$ 600	2%	$ 5,500	20%	$26,868	320/2239
		1%*		4%		28%		

*Of all buildings reporting.

	Mortgage		Yearly Profits (after all expenditures including mortgage)	% Mortgage to Income	% Profits (to Total Expenditures including mortgage)	Return on Investment
	Mo. Payment	Yearly Total				
1.	294	3,528	2,832	43%	34%	6%
2.	300	3,600	450	72%	9%	0%
3.	321	3,852	2,848	43%	31%	5%
4.	368	4,416	3,144	49%	35%	5%
5.	380	4,560	4,570	42%	42%	7%
6.	380	4,560	3,640	49%	39%	6%
7.	392	4,704	1,986	50%	21%	3%
8.	429	5,148	3,390	51%	35%	5%
9.	441	5,292	7,608	19%	27%	11%
10.	460	5,520	2,220	60%	24%	3%
11.	460	5,520	12,270	21%	47%	16%
12.	490	5,880	4,540	39%	30%	6%
13.	502	6,024	6,036	44%	44%	7%
14.	582	6,984	-4,744	34%	-23%	-5%
15.	588	7,056	1,444	60%	12%	2%
16.	729	8,748	4,052	38%	18%	3%
17.	796	9,552	6,248	46%	30%	5%
18.	796	9,552	5,348	56%	31%	4%
19.	888	10,656	9,324	33%	28%	6%
20.	906	10,872	-12	82%	0	0%
21.	916	10,992	7,672	43%	30%	5%
22.	919	11,028	-1,028	72%	-7%	0%
23.	919	11,028	15,832	26%	38%	11%
24.	980	11,760	5,140	49%	21%	3%
25.	1010	12,120	9,248	45%	35%	6%
				47%	25%	5%

pulled down soon because between mortgage and insurance payments, there would be no money for heat, repairs, or taxes, let alone improvements.

Buildings held by the same owner for at least six years are spending considerably less on the mortgage payments than the buildings shown in Table 2. Their expenditures for taxes, heating, and repairs are assumed to be the same as the newly purchased high-loan buildings. If maintenance and other work are not being done to keep the building in good shape, there is something wrong. Somebody is milking the building. It is time for tenant action or your apartment will go down the tubes like the rest.

In the Uptown area the calculations show a higher rate of return on investment, about 8%. The total expenses are higher (about 45%) but the profits are about the same after mortgage payments. Knowing the area as one of blighted houses and rip-off landlords, and comparing the Lakeview figures, the only conclusion is that housing in Uptown is much cheaper to buy, and that expenses run about the same in both areas. This means essentially that Lakeview, in many of its neighborhoods, is an Uptown about ready to happen. Money is being spent on insurance, heat when required, and sometimes on taxes. No money is going into many of the buildings being put on the market and (I assume) other buildings not yet on the market. In spite of the rehabilitation programs in existence, these are not really touching the salvation problem. In five years, Lakeview may be in real trouble.

The Real Estate Speculators

If you study the numbers some things become crystal clear. There is no way to survive, as a landlord, when your return on investment is 5%. You can't do it. Inflation is much ahead of you. At 8% you may stay even. Profits of 25% a year on income are possible only if no improvements or repairs are made. If the cost of heating the place is passed on to the tenant, so much the better. But, in the long run, the landlord has to lose.

Nobody should go into the landlord/owner business unless they can afford to take losses and make improvements for at least 5 years (until rent increases outdistance the mortgage payments— the old game of hedging on inflation and hoping inflation wins).

What is going on is a giant market in land and tax speculation.

People are buying up anything they can get their hands on. They want to hold a property for two or three years and sell it. The money, as we can see, is not made in owning the property, because it is worth only 5% of its cost. The advantage is to sell out and realize a 50% to 100% instant lottery cash prize. This is where the game is. Buy it cheap, run it cheap, and sell it high.

And how do the landlords survive while waiting for their windfall profits to manifest? They try to take paper or book losses. Buying buildings is a great way for the rich to receive huge tax deductions. The trick is for the owners actually not to spend or lose money, just make things appear that way. In the first five or six years of a loan most of the money paid to the bank is for interest on the loan, but interest is deductible from federal income tax.

Buildings are usually purchased by the rich. Typically several men will get together and form a limited partnership. The partnership "shares" in the tax deductions by allowing each man to deduct his percentage of the business "losses" from his personal income. So while the building generates only a few thousand dollars profit on an initial down payment of $30,000 to $50,000, and while the return on investment is losing to inflation, these men make money through tax dodges. The only requirement for them to stay ahead of the game is not to spend any money on the building. If things get bad, they will cease payments for real estate taxes and utilities because they might actually get hurt if they were to lose "real" money. The building must be run at a true zero profit basis. The cost of the loan keeps the rents high, and fear of losing money stops any improvements or repairs.

While waiting to sell out such owners are taking our rents with no intention of maintaining the property, and then forcing us, through our higher income taxes, to subsidize their high style of living by allowing them all the tax breaks. This is double jeopardy and when the building you are living in is sold, be prepared for a huge rent increase.

The really smart money is out of the game now. They came in when a building could be picked up for $40,000 (three years ago), they sold out last year for $60,000 or this year for $90,000. The new owner that bought the building is paying a much higher mortgage and is finding rehabilitation costs are twice what they were three years ago. In short, the real estate market has been diddled with.

The dust is going to settle soon. We see the banks and savings

TABLE 3. Summary of Profits, Mortgages, and Regular Expenses for 17 Typical Low-rise Apartment Buildings (in Uptown).

	Price	Return on Investment	Mortgage	Percentage of yearly income	Income	Expenses	Percentage of yearly income	Profits	Percentage after all payments	Units
1.	$ 41,000	5%	3,014	26%	$11,760	$ 6,711	57%	$ 2,035	17%	6
2.	45,000	6	3,308	25	13,140	7,287	55	2,545	19	11
3.	49,000	9	2,602	29	12,240	4,299	35	4,339	35	7
4.	49,800	21	3,668	18	21,460	7,749	35	10,558	48	12
5.	49,900	7	3,668	28	12,960	5,904	46	3,388	26	6
6.	53,500	11	3,932	22	17,516	7,802	46	5,782	33	9
7.	58,400	4	4,329	36	12,120	5,978	45	2,313	19	6
8.	65,000	8	4,778	30	15,960	5,770	36	5,412	34	8
9.	68,000	9	4,998	26	18,972	8,155	43	5,819	31	12
10.	70,000	6	5,145	24	2,060	12,028	57	3,887	18	12
11.	75,000	6	5,513	37	14,820	4,822	34	4,485	30	6
12.	80,000	6	5,880	41	14,222	3,774	26	4,568	32	7
13.	84,500	3	6,210	33	18,900	10,397	55	2,292	12	7
14.	105,000	13	7,718	18	43,840	22,120	50	14,002	32	18
15.	109,000	4	8,012	30	26,500	14,452	55	4,036	15	13
16.	120,000	8	8,820	23	38,160	20,115	53	9,165	24	21
17.	$135,000	7%	9,923	33%	$29,940	$10,045	36%	$ 9,372	31%	13
Average of all buildings		8%		28%			45%		27%	

and loans wiping the grease off their lips after a fat meal, but disaster is predicted for everyone involved in this scandal, including the tenants.

The figures I have here shout out: there is no way a landlord can pay to keep his building up and also pay the ridiculous mortgages. The apartment-renting business is not one for great cash profits, only for long-term capital gains. Soon neglected buildings will not be sold. They will drug the market. The bottom will fall out. Nobody is going to buy an apartment building that cannot be resold. Few landlords (the ones in this speculation market right now) can afford to improve or repair their holdings, even for resale. The buildings go down, and so will the market. The banks will not be so smug when their default rates threaten bankruptcy.

Well, as an old friend once said, "what is to be done?" The solution is not just to pass laws and legislate speculation out of business—that may be a waste of time. The aldermen and legislators are among the speculators. Tough enforcement of the current building codes may help a bit, but the codes are there mainly to extract payoffs, so what changes? Cheap government insurance and rent subsidies? Sure, but look at the grand larceny by the banks in Chicago on Federal Housing Administration (FHA) loans. The banks made loans to the most unqualified of buyers (folks who couldn't possibly pay the mortgage), foreclosed immediately, and collected the entire mortgage amount from the government (HUD). The resulting scandal, replete with token indictments and charges, simply points out that government assistance and other programs assist only the rich and not those who need real help.

As tenants, I suggest we study the statistics, learn a bit about apartment management, pressure the slumlords out of business through court and rent actions, and take buildings in receivership. We should also support a new equitable landlord-tenant act.

By the use of our own labor, and a cooperative city building department, we can save our buildings, our homes, and our neighborhoods.

There should be no tolerance for the excuse that it costs too much money to fix up the old places. The old places should have been maintained all along. A landlord buying a dilapidated building (probably with no money nor intent to repair the place) should post a performance bond to guarantee that he will repair and maintain the properties acquired.

Instead of the housing court and the building department playing a sham game of inspections and continuance after continuance, the buildings should be immediately seized by the court, condemned, and then assigned receivership to the tenants or the not-for-profit community organizations in the immediate area.

There is money to be made in the real estate game by the lenders, the sellers, and the building inspectors. The rest of us, including anybody foolish enough to try and buy a building these days, is going to lose. If there is one thing to protect us, as renters, it would be a moritorium on the sale of buildings that are not in grade A condition. The banks could enforce such a condition, and at the same time issue rehabilitation loans from the surplus mortgage funds. The city could prohibit the sale of buildings without a clean inspection certificate and refuse to allow occupancy of any building sold without a clean certificate.

Such a plan would actually save money and it would ensure a safe, good place to live. It would protect and preserve the neighborhoods, and it would not, in the long run, drive the price of housing out of sight. It will take twenty years to correct the inequities that currently exist.

If you talk with the experts, as I have, you hear interesting stories. One is about how rents have only raised 135% whereas the cost of living has gone up 180% since the 1967 base period. These so-called statistics justify the rent raises we see of 35% to 40%. The experts claim that the cost of heating has climbed 100%. As we can see from the cost statistics, heat is only 12% of the total income so this increase should raise our rents only by 6% at the most and this should cover the last three years. Rise in maintenance costs is justified to 2% only if painting, maintenance, replacement, and repairs actually are taking place. Otherwise, there is no justification. Don't be bled to death by a rent increase! Start a tenants' union and fight.

Planning To Be a Landlord?

Would you like to become a landlord? Here are some facts to consider. To buy a 3- or 4-story small building you normally need 30% for a down payment. Your monthly payments will average about 10.5% per year of the original loan over 20 years.

The real estate salesmen say you shouldn't pay over 25% of your yearly income in mortgage payments. They also say that your total costs (including real estate taxes) should amount to less than 50% of your income from rents. This leaves 17% a year (if you believe their ideal setup) for all management, operating, repair, utility, and heating costs. It also leaves a 50% profit. The chart figures on page 124 show that it cannot work that way.

By the way, a management firm will charge $250 a month to collect the rents and keep the books on a small apartment building. They usually have neither employees nor resources to make any repairs. This fee comes out of your 17%.

The market is for existing buildings only, little new apartment construction is going on in the city. The city demolishes 2500 apartment buildings each year. Because of this, the prices of apartment buildings have doubled in four years.

The fastest and most profitable new real estate business in the city is demolition and wrecking. Old slumlords are getting out of the business of renting and into the business of wrecking. Many times they see "old friends" one or two owners down the pike and ready for the bulldozer.

How do you protect your building from the wrecker's ball? Regular cleaning and maintenance, of course, but you must do more. The Institute of Real Estate Management recommends that apartment buildings be well insulated, weather stripped, caulked, screened, and storm windowed. The apartment managment experts recommend that an apartment be painted every three years and between tenants. The washer and dryer (high-class living) should be replaced every seven years; the water heater replaced every nine years; the refrigerator, garbage disposal, and the dishwasher replaced every eleven years (we should be so lucky); and the stove every thirteen years.

Well, what do you do if you don't have a lot of money for a down payment and have no intention of keeping up a building? What if you are a milker and a bleeder? How can you, in short, become your very own slumlord?

Here is how some real slum landlord management companies and owners get their buildings. They use several techniques. One is called "leverage." When the railroad barons did the same thing it was called pyramiding.

The landlord will use the equity in one property as the collateral on a mortgage for another property. This reduces his down payment and secures his loan. There is usually a bit of slippery maneuvering involved, but after a while the landlord can own a dozen buildings. Through leverage the loan on each building is secured by another building. There may be 10 banks involved, fraud, and some dummy corporations. Well, what happens if he loses one of these leveraged buildings through a mortgage default. His whole deck of cards must tumble. Each loan rests on the foundation of equity in another mortgaged building. Call in one or two of the mortgages, and the landlord can't come up with the cash or additional buildings to secure his loans. Zap. He's finished. More about the power of rent withholding in Chapter 18.

Another way to become a landlord with only a little money is to buy a building on contract. It takes very little down and a mortgage is not necessary. But you will get caught in the middle of a nasty game. Slumlords sell properties to other slumlords on contract. Contract selling allows the "responsibility" and "profits" to go to the contractee. The contractor (the real owner) continues to get tax breaks and the real ownership of the building, while hiding behind the flunky contract buyer. Usually contract buyers last only a few months before they default on their agreements. This is because the buildings are in such bad shape and the tenants are so rebellious that the buyer can neither get the rents nor come up with enough cash to pay for repairs. He is making payments to the contract seller who now is raking in the cash with no obligation to manage or maintain.

When it comes to court cases (housing court) the owner is held safe because he has "sold" the building. So ultimately, the poor slob that contracted for the place is left holding the bag, and the real owner resells the building and starts the process all over.

It does little good to organize against the contract buyer. In such cases it is important to try and seize the building through receivership, thus depriving the hidden slum owner of any more chances to rape tenants.

PART FIVE

Is There Really a Santa Claus?

15

Tenants' Rights and Obligations in Chicago: Or, What the Landlord Won't Tell You

It has become clear to me since I finished my research on tenants' rights that I had been huckstered into believing that if you know what your rights are, you will prevail against all travesties. This is what I was taught in civics class. This is what the late mayor of this city would have you believe. It simply is not true.

In Chicago, no matter what rights you have or think you ought to have, there is no organism or mechanism that will act on your behalf. Ergo, we have no rights.

Our lives are controlled by big money and big real estate. Example. There is a Rent Complaint Bureau (see Appendix B for their number) that is the grand idea of a group of real estate typhoons. The Bureau has no enforcement power—*NONE!* The Commissioner of Human Services (in charge of the Bureau) has publicly admitted that he is understaffed and underfunded. He said that although the purpose of the Bureau is to investigate complaints, he will not send his people to tenant association meetings to hear the complaints or witness the problems. He announced that the Bureau would act as a conciliator between tenants and their landlords but refuses to set up, request, or attend such meetings. While he thought that 40% rent raises were an abomination, he said the Bureau was officially prohibited from trying to gain rollbacks. When he was told of retaliatory evictions, he said it was terrible, but the Bureau was not authorized to become involved with any legal matters.

The Rent Complaint Bureau is a joke. The same has to be said for most of the work of the city building department inspectors.

There are supposed to be 400 men protecting the lives and welfares of the 1.7 million occupants of apartments in this city. While they do respond to urgent requests for heat in the winter, they can't seem to get slumlords to clean up. I have watched inspectors drive around the city in big cars. I have seen inspectors go through an entire building, drunk as skunks, and give a clean bill of health to a place that even rats wouldn't live in.

I have seen the shenanigans in housing court. The owner says he's complied, the inspector, who knows there isn't compliance, agrees. Bang! End of problem. Case dismissed. Once it's tossed out of court it will take another year before the same situation will come before the same judge with the same inspector (and the same result?).

Come into eviction court and complain about the bad conditions. The judge there doesn't care about your rights. He cares about the landlord's rights. Pay up and/or move out. YOU HAVE THE RIGHT TO WITHHOLD RENT, but try to enforce that right in the city of Chicago!

The city and "the system" are geared to maintain the status quo. The reason we must ferret out our rights is so that thousands of us will start to pressure the city and the courts for protection and action. We must be prepared to take action which deals directly with our problems. We must learn how to capture our rights and enforce them by ourselves whether the city or the courts is ready to cooperate or is even involved. A properly operating tenants' group can protect its legal rights with its own mechanisms of power and enforcement.

This chapter, Chapter 16 and Chapter 17, discuss how to try and operate under the current system of process and procedure within the laws and the courts. Chapter 18 outlines how to organize and operate a tenants' organization. It is through effective tenants' rights associations that we will see the light at the end of a dark hallway. Instead of calling for more laws and more enforcement and more bureaucracies, the unified efforts of residents in a building will quickly and effectively get results. It's hard work, and dangerous (you could be sued or evicted), but rewarding.

Remember: there are more of us than there are of them. Also remember that the money they use to buy off inspectors, judges, lawyers, and legislators comes out of our pockets every month at rent time. We have the real power!!

Tenants' Rights

You do have rights. These rights are very difficult to learn about and even more difficult to capture, but they do exist. The rights are embodied in the Chicago building code ordinances, the revised statutes of the State of Illinois, and in some case law handed down by various courts in the State.

The problem—and it is the crux of our problem as renters—is that the courts in Cook County practically refuse to enforce our rights and protect us from the landlords. We are being cheated every day. We are being taken advantage of in the grossest of ways.

Generally speaking, we are supposed to be guaranteed a safe, healthful, sanitary, secure, and peaceful place to live. We are supposed to have repairs made for us when needed, and we are not supposed to be disturbed by the landlord. For our part, as tenants, we are not supposed to disturb other tenants or damage the apartment or building. We are responsible for keeping our living place clean and throwing out the garbage.

The city of Chicago, through the building codes, specifies a number of obligations the landlord has to his tenants. Violation of the codes is supposed to result in rapid actions causing the landlord to correct the problem or face stiff fines. I will discuss later how the procedure is intended to operate and how it really works. Right now, let's examine some of the major rights granted under the code.

A landlord must supply heat to all apartments (if that is part of the lease). Heat is required from September 15 through June 1 of each winter/spring season. The minimum daytime temperature is 68°; the minimum nighttime temperature is 55°. Specifically, these are the temperatures required by the code: 6:30 A.M., 60°; 7:30 A.M., 65°; 8:30 A.M. until 10:30 P.M., 68°; late-night hours, no less than 55°. While all temperatures—daytime and nighttime temperatures— are probably too cold (especially for small children and the elderly), at least we have some protection. There is no excuse for not providing the heat, except a heating system failure. In extreme cases of heat failure, the city will act with relative speed to correct the problem. Otherwise . . . well, otherwise is what the next three chapters are all about.

If the landlord supplies your apartment with the heating equipment (even if you pay for the gas), *he* is still obligated to ensure that you get adequate heat. So, if the furnace or space heater fails, it's the landlord's responsibility to get it fixed. If the apparatus is insufficient to heat your apartment, the landlord must supply enough heating equipment to meet the code.

The landlord is required by the city to keep his building roach- and rodent-free. You, as a tenant, are not supposed to raise roaches or rats as a hobby (the ordinance states that the tenant must exterminate his own apartment if the problem is ONLY in that one apartment). In order to keep the place vermin-free, the landlord is obligated to regularly exterminate all apartments (and the rest of the building). He is supposed to fill all holes in the walls and floors that would allow mice or rats to roam and he must seal his building to keep rodents from entering the basement.

Landlords like to claim that PEOPLE bring the roaches through bad habits or in dirty boxes. This may be true in some cases, but roaches are a prehistoric bug that have survived about every calamity known on earth. Roaches are very smart (for bugs). They are attracted to where people are. They eat soap powders, the glue from paper labels, sugar, flour, powered soups and milk, crumbs, bread, and most other dried foodstuffs. When you move out they leave also—not necessarily with you, but to another apartment. Keeping an apartment clean is helpful, but keeping the whole building properly exterminated is the only answer. If a landlord accuses you, personally, of bringing in the roaches, he is a willing liar. Roaches were here before we were born, and will be here when we are dust. The landlord simply does not care to do anything. The law, however, states that he must.

The landlord is required to supply hot water 24 hours a day at a temperature minimum of 120°. Needless to say, he must also supply cold water, and both must be at a sufficient pressure to be useful. When the water pressure falls too low, common sense is all that is needed to determine the problem. If you are supplying your own hot water, your water heater must be capable of heating to 120°, if not, the landlord must repair or replace the heater. IT'S THE LAW.

Plumbing and electrical facilities must work, and must be adequate and safe. If the drains don't work or leak, if the toilet won't flush, or the faucets drip, drip, drip, the landlord must repair them. If sparks fly out of the electrical outlets, or the lights constantly dim or flash, the landlord must make proper repairs.

The building code requires enough circuits and outlets to serve the normal needs of today's apartment dweller. If you must string extension cords around like cobras, your landlord can be made to rewire the apartment. You also must have direct access to the circuit breakers or fuses. If he locks them up, he is in violation.

In the city of Chicago, all taxicabs must be freshly washed and all apartment building yards must be manicured, clean, and litter-free. The common areas of the building must be clean, swept, and policed. Garbage is not allowed in the building hallways or stair-wells. There must be no trash in the basement. The landlord must supply garbage cans or refuse receptacles (in the rear of the build-ing) for the tenants' trash. Although each tenant is supposed to take out his own garbage, the landlord MUST collect the garbage from the halls and stairs if the tenants won't take it out. (A tenant may be evicted for leaving refuse in the halls, but the landlord must clean it up). The garbage must be collected from the building once a week, and more often if it becomes a nuisance.

The physical plant (of the building) must also be maintained in a safe manner. Windows and window frames must be in good shape. The windows must open and close. Window locks must be strong and must work. The doors must work and the outside doors must have suitable, strong, safe locks. The brick work, ce-ment work, sidewalks, roofs, gutters, siding, and fire escapes must be in good shape. No falling mortar, no leaking roofs, no dripping gutters. No major cracks or flaws. The inside parts of the building have to be in good condition. The steps have to be solid and not broken. There have to be handrails firmly attached to the wall. The common areas of the building must be lighted to see well and walk safely. They must be lit night and day. Outside common areas including front and rear doors, side passages, gangways, and courtyards must be lighted from dusk to dawn. The outside com-mon areas also must be well-drained (from rain and melting ice), shoveled, and salted during the winter.

If the building is larger than a three-flat, chances are fire extin-guishers are required. If the TOTAL floor area of the entire building above the basement is greater than 3000 square feet, a fire extin-guisher is required on each floor and no more than 75 feet from a front or rear entrance to each apartment. The fire extinguisher should be an "ABC" dry powder type. These extinguishers are the only type safe to use on grease, paper, and electrical fires. All apartments must have two fire exits, (usually a front and back escape means).

All apartment buildings with six or more units or four stories or higher must have smoke detectors, unless they are modern high-rises. There should be at least one in every apartment near the bedrooms, one at the top of the front and back stairways, and at least one on floors normally occupied even if there are no bedrooms (multilevel apartments). If the building is less than eighty feet tall, you need smoke detectors. The landlord must supply, install, and maintain them.

The landlord is required to provide screens for all windows each summer season, from April 15 until November 15. The screens should be permanently installed for the summer. The little collapsible types are not sufficient. The tenant may have to actually put them in the windows (if there are no problems with fitting or installation), but the landlord must supply the screens.

All the major appliances in your apartment and in the building must be maintained and repaired by the landlord (if he supplies them). If your stove or refrigerator goes on the blink, call the landlord. The same is true for heating and cooling systems, water heaters, and the intercom/security system. The trash containers have to be maintained, the fire extinguishers charged, and the electrical and plumbing fixtures repaired.

Even if you are responsible for repairs for a major appliance such as the furnace, stove, or refrigerator and can't pay for it, if it is his equipment, the city code requires the landlord to fix it. If you have no heat for whatever reason, it's the landlord's responsibility to make the repairs. Perhaps a sticky legal question, but still, the landlord must maintain the heat, even if you won't or can't. (By the way, it is a good idea not to sign a lease where you pay for repairs—you can get stuck for a fortune.)

The landlord's obligations are mostly common sense and for the benefit of the tenants as well as the protection of the landlord and his building. That landlords overwhelmingly fight against these seemingly reasonable requirements is a sad commentary about how one group or class of people insist on treating another group or class of people. It is this type of mistreatment and discrimination that tenants must fight against.

Tenants' Obligations

Tenants' obligations are also mostly common sense principles. Keep your apartment clean. Sweep, vacuum, mop, dust. Throw out the garbage. Don't misuse the plumbing. Cook only in the kitchen. Don't store dangerous or flammable chemicals (paints, etc.) in a way that they could catch fire (seal them up and keep them away from heat, flame, and children). Don't be slobs around the building. Keep the noise down at night.

Respect the fact that somebody else owns the building: don't break things up or smash windows. Keep bikes, kids' toys, and storage out of the hallways (so other people don't trip over them and so these things don't contribute to fire). Use your head. Being a good tenant is easy. When and if it comes to a showdown between yourself and the landlord, you'll want and need your hands to be "clean" so he can't nail you for something and cloud up the real issues.

Technical Problems

There are a few more technical problems which ought to be discussed. One of these is overcrowding. Too many people for not enough space. The building code states that a family unit must contain at least 450 square feet for a family of four (250 square feet for an apartment for two people). An additional 75 square feet is required for each additional member of a family. A bedroom has to have at least 70 square feet of space for one person and an additional 50 square feet (35 square feet for children) for each additional person. You, as a tenant, should not tolerate overcrowding in your building (and you should not contribute to the problem). Basically speaking, there should be one room in an apartment per person. This is not luxury living. It is sanitary and emotionally safe living. Overcrowding contributes to a higher incidence of disease, filth, vermin, rodents, fire, stench, and noise. It makes for uncontrollable children, drunken fights, garbage, and property destruction. Any landlord who knowingly allows overcrowding is a criminal. Any tenant who encourages overcrowding endangers himself, his family, and the rest of the building.

Other technical problems are ventilation and natural lighting. Every room where people normally live must have windows that open (and close) or proper and adequate mechanical ventilation. A window must allow enough light during the day that electric lights are normally not needed. The formula: window area must be approximately 10% of the floor area of the room. Windows must open to 5% of the floor area of the room for natural ventilation. These are health requirements. Apartments are not supposed to be prisons, but homes. Kitchens must have good ventilation to the outside through windows or vent fans. The same is true for bathrooms. If a kitchen or bathroom does not have a window (which can be opened as needed) and does not have a vent fan, then serious and unsanitary conditions exist and must be corrected.

The city publishes a booklet titled "Landlord and Tenant: Responsibilities and Obligations." Copies may be obtained from the Public Information Office of the Department of Buildings, 121 North LaSalle Street, (312) 744-3426. It is available in English and Spanish, and covers the same ground we have just discussed here.

Indicative of the attitudes of real estate interests is a brochure available through the Chicago Real Estate Board to landlords. The little publication is called "A Tenant's Responsibilities and Obligations: From the Housing Section of the Chicago Building Code." The Board reprinted *only the tenants' obligations*. They did not reprint the landlord's responsibilities nor did they reprint the section on how to make a complaint. For the Board it appears important only that the tenants keep in line, and not get uppity.

The code is much more complicated and far reaching than the few points I have detailed above. In Appendix G, I list, in summary fashion, the main points of the building code ordinances as they cover our rights as occupants, and the obligations of the landlord.

Legislative Backups

There is some legislation concerning tenants' rights and tenants' relationships with landlords. I have excerpted the most significant points of the law and placed them in Appendix H. Generally speaking, your apartment is your castle. The law says that you must pay your rent on time or the landlord can have you evicted after giving you five days notice to pay up or get out. You can also be charged double rent if you stay on after your lease expires (a good reason to move on time!).

Your landlord is allowed to enter your apartment, with your permission, most of the normal hours of the working day, but he cannot come around to harass or badger you. If he does, call the cops and your lawyer.

Normally you can neither be evicted nor can your landlord confiscate your property without a court order. The property which you have purchased and installed in your apartment (hanging lamp fixtures, wall systems, that nifty pulsing showerhead) all belong to you and you can take them with you when you move out as long as you do not destroy the apartment in the process of removal.

A landlord cannot deny you an apartment because you have young children.

If the landlord is supposed to pay for utilities and doesn't, you can pay the utility companies directly and deduct the bills from your rent.

It is illegal for the landlord to evict you or refuse to renew your lease because you made a legitimate complaint to the city inspectors, but it is very hard to prove why a lease wasn't renewed, even if you know it was retaliation. Good luck!

If you live in a building in Chicago with more than twenty-five units, the landlord has to pay you 5% interest in cash or as a rent reduction once a year on your security deposit. Also your security deposit must be returned within 30 days after you move out. The landlord owes you double if he doesn't pay up.

Check out Appendix H for a fuller view of the state laws and also their citations.

Spring v. *Little* Decision

There is a small, but potentially powerful collection of case law that contains the seeds of equity for the renter. The problem with the courts in Cook County is that too many judges are also landlords or the former lawyers of landlords. It is nearly impossible to use these court cases as a basis for a successful defense of your tenant rights. Courts in other states have handed down more case law and it has been applied more and more broadly and effectively, but here, in Illinois, there is little satisfaction. We can see the table laden with goodies, we can smell its savor, we even have the money to pay for the feast, but we are told it is a private affair and we are, therefore, excluded.

There is a sleeping giant waiting to be awakened and come to our collective rescue. The giant is the progeny of the Illinois State Supreme Court. Its name is *Jack Spring, Inc.* versus *Emma Little, et al* (280 N.E. 2nd 208), *Spring* v. *Little* for short. This is a landmark law case where the Illinois Supreme Court granted us very specific rights as tenants, and instructed the lower courts to respect our rights. Unfortunately, most tenants cannot obtain these rights because most judges, specifically Chicago judges, refuse to hear *Spring* v. *Little* arguments in renters' courts.

What happened was quite simple. Two tenants, living in different parts of town, with different landlords (and with no particular knowledge of each other), stopped paying their rents as a protest to conditions in the places they were residing. They were taken to Forcible Detainer Court (Renters' Court) and evicted. They hired lawyers and these lawyers appealed. After much legal wrangling the cases were combined and finally reached the Illinois Supreme Court. The decision was in the tenants' favor. In a nutshell, the Court stated that there is an implied warranty (or implied covenant) of habitability made by the landlord whenever he rents an apartment. The unwritten or unspoken promise the landlord makes is that the apartment (and building) is in livable or occupiable condition, that it is in acceptable repair and substantially complies with the building codes of the city. Further, the landlord promises to maintain the premises in a like condition for the term of the lease.

The Court further held that in eviction cases where unpaid rent was the reason for the eviction, a tenant could use the broken warranty as his defense for not paying rent; that is, the miserable conditions of the place caused by landlord inaction.

On the face of the matter, it would seem that if you live in an apartment with building code violations, you could withhold your rent until the repairs were made. You might even sue your landlord for damages (repairs, medical bills, moving expenses, loss of time due to apartment problems, loss of work, sickness, "mental suffering and pain," injuries, etc.). If your landlord tried to evict you for nonpayment of the rents, you could use the poor conditions as your defense for not paying.

Well, it just isn't working out that way. The courts in Cook County refuse to allow such defenses to be heard. This is an outrage. The judge starts with one question in any rent case: How much money is due? The judge asks the landlord, not the tenant. If the tenant cannot produce the rent receipts or cancelled checks, the case is closed and the tenant is out. The tenant is not allowed to produce repair receipts or pictures of the place or even protest that conditions are desperate. Is there money due and owing? Yes: then move out and/or pay up. Next case.

If you have money, hire a lawyer BEFORE you have your court date. If you don't hire a lawyer, hire a truck or trailer and move out before Mr. Sheriff arrives.

Why must we, renters-tenants-occupants, be given such short

shrift in our own courts? Because they are not the courts of the people, they are the courts of the landlords, the real estate interests, the bankers, and the lawyers.

Judges are lawyers first, politicians second, judges third, and landlords most of the time. They are in collusion with a system designed to squeeze money out of the poor tenant and not seek anything beyond a legal, fictionalized justice.

The *Spring* v. *Little* opinion is a gem of information. If you are considering seeking action based on *Spring* v. *Little*, consult a lawyer who will help prepare the groundwork and properly advise you on the merits and pitfalls of *Spring* v. *Little*. The *Little* case is not for everyone seeking redress.

It is interesting to note that the Chicago Real Estate Board (CREB), filing as a friend of the court in this case, stated their belief (and the belief of their membership) that under Illinois law "no implied covenant to repair is imposed on a landlord, a covenant to pay rent is independent of a covenant to repair, and a breach of a covenant to repair" has nothing to do with the fact that the tenant owes rent. In other words, the CREB argued simply: pay up and shut up. Nice folks, these real estate people. The CREB lawyers argued further that there is also no implied warranty of habitability. As we have stated over and over: you are renting an apartment as is, what you see is what you get. The CREB believes, apparently, that what you don't see is also what you get. To that I say *phooey!*

Tenant Versus Landlord

Spring v. *Little* implies a procedure to follow when trying to gain redress from landlords.

1. *Put repairs and maintenance clauses in the lease.*
2. *Make lease provisions for rent setoffs (reductions) caused by bad conditions.*
3. *Make lease provisions for repair payments or other costs that the tenant must undertake in order to keep the dwelling habitable and within the building codes. Make these deductible from the rent.*
4. *Make provisions for lease termination and damages because of landlord inaction and code violations.*

If these clauses are not in your lease, or you cannot get them put into your lease, you are still in luck. The Supreme Court has concluded that (1) you have the right to these implied warranties, and (2) you can do things yourself to enforce them.

If repairs are required:

1. *Send your landlord a letter stating specifically what the problem is and where it is located.*
2. *Ask that the problem be corrected by a specific date. State what damage, inconvenience, danger, or potential danger you are exposed to because of the uncorrected conditions.*
3. *State that you will make the repairs if he does not (if you can afford to do so). State the approximate cost of the repairs.*
4. *State how you wish the credit to be handled: rent reduction or rebate, rent credit, cash refund.*
5. *Or, you may inform your landlord that you will withhold part or all of the rent until such time that repairs are made.*
6. *Before you send a letter, consult a lawyer if you intend to withhold rents or seek rent credits.*
7. *Send the letter to your landlord via certified mail, with a regular mail copy to the same address. Keep a copy for yourself.*
8. *Be prepared for a lot of smoke and steam.*

The *Spring* v. *Little* case has strong "authority" from a section of the Illinois Public Aid Code (Sec. 11 – 23, chapter 23, Illinois Revised Statutes, 1969). This act allows that welfare recipients can, through the Welfare Department, withhold their rents when the building in which they live is substandard as defined by the building code. It allows rent withholding for up to ninety days. If after that time the landlord has still not made repairs, the tenant must pay the landlord the rent minus a 20% penalty which the tenant may keep. A similar procedure is employed for each 30-day period thereafter, as long as the conditions continue.

Opponents of *Spring* v. *Little* complain that the legislature should act to clean up the tenant laws. I agree. But it is clear that the legislature had to take action in 1969 to protect part of the renting public, and in 1972 (the year of *Spring* v. *Little*) the Illinois Supreme Court (without explicitly stating) extended the protection of the law to all of the renting public.

The options and opportunities are present. Complain, seek rent reductions and rent rebates for work performed, withhold the rents, receive penalty payments.

The Cook County Courts' usual response when such withholding cases come for hearing is that the tenant really wouldn't want to continue to live in such conditions and therefore the lease is terminated, the back rents are forgiven, and the tenant is ordered out. This is a paternalistic and vicious cycle of events. The result: housing is allowed to blight further, and the poor tenant is sent on to the next snake pit.

This cycle must be broken. The courts must recognize their responsibility to protect not just individual tenants, but the entire community from blight and destruction which has shaded Chicago for the past twenty-five years. In Chapter 18 I will discuss in detail how to organize yourself and your building to enforce your tenants' rights.

Suing the Landlord

We have another tool at hand to use in our tenants' protection. It will not recover any money damages per se but will recover lawyer's fees. Under the Illinois Municipal Code (Chapter 24, Division 13, 31, or 31.1), tenants and property owners within 500 feet of the building in question may sue the owner of the building if building code violations are suspected. If the violations exist, you win. The landlord must make the repairs (or close the building and you lose). If all you wish is to get the repairs done, hire a lawyer and sue. It can be a "rapid" action taking less than nine months. If the tenants win the case against the landlord, the court orders the landlord to refund any lawyer's fees paid by the tenants.

Finally, you have tenants' rights as citizens. You can go into civil court and sue for breach of contract; for damages for things which have happened to you because of your landlord's actions or inactions; and for the cost of suing your landlord. Sue the landlord for *fraud* and *deceit* if he promised you things and didn't deliver. Sue him for *negligence* if he was responsible for something which damaged you or might damage you (loose steps, falling plaster, lead in paint, lack of heat, unrepaired almost anything). Sue him for *willful negligence* if you gave him notice of problems that he did not properly correct and the problems caused damage, injury, or death. Go into court and request a restraining order or injunction to stop him from doing something (such as shutting off the heat or utilities, not cleaning up the building, not providing fire extinguishers, mail boxes, or door locks, etc.).

There are many things you can do with your tenants' rights—use them. If the landlord is nice, you can be nice. Of course law suits and other legal actions are last straws. Far better it would be if tenants could sit down with their landlords and work out the differences. A simple call and a short meeting to discuss problems would be the ideal way to deal with a situation. Friendly cooperation is always best, and this cooperation should be a two-way street.

Experience, unfortunately, shows that the landlord is not interested in anything more than talking. The usual history: there have been a few phone calls or even a few complaints made in person at the management office or to the janitor. Promises are made, but nothing gets done. The typical resolution of the problem is you take it the way it is, fix it yourself (if it is something you can do), or move out when the lease is up. It is sad that management is so unresponsive to legitimate requests for solutions to real problems.

Remember how the landlord is when he wants something from you. If your rent is late, he wants a late fee. If you are behind on the rent, he wants you to pay up or move out. If the kids play on the front steps, he wants them locked up. If you have a pet, he'll scream if he doesn't like the animal.

The landlord can make almost any rule he wants and can break your lease for the thinnest of reasons. Either you stand at attention or out you go. I think there should be some reciprocity between landlord and tenant. I believe that if all you get are mushy promises or out-and-out refusals when you ask the landlord for what he is legally obligated to supply, you have a right and duty to stand up to him.

If he is nice, you can be nice. If he is a stone wall, take out your hammer and start chipping.

We have tenants' rights. Even though the system may be stacked against the tenant, if we know the laws and what our rights are, we should proceed to take our rights. The bureaucracies and the courts may not be ready for us, but if we organize ourselves at the building level, maybe we won't need them.

16

Standing Up for Your Rights: The Tenant Versus the World

Taking Action Against the Landlord

In Chapter 15 I discussed what your rights are as a tenant and what you should expect from your landlord. I indicated a number of legal options you theoretically have to enforce your rights. Now I would like to talk about some of the procedures you, as one person, might employ in dealing with the landlord, the city, and the law. *Remember:* It is you against "the system," but the options are worth discussing if not exploring.

Complain to the landlord. The first time something goes wrong, make a phone call or tell the janitor. Do this immediately. Make some arrangement for repairs to be made. Establish a time convenient for you to let the workmen into your apartment. If it is an "outside" problem, establish when the job will be completed. The more severe the problem, the faster it must be remedied.

If the problem is not cleared up satisfactorily, escalate! Call your landlord again, complain, and send him a short letter stating the problem and the facts regarding your two phone calls requesting action. Mail one copy to him, keep a photocopy for yourself.

You could, of course, fix the condition yourself if you have the time, the skills, or the money.

If you are dealing with a serious problem, you can contact the city of Chicago Building Department Complaint Bureau, (312) 744-3420. Depending on what the problem is, an inspector will come out within five days to five months.

Once you get the city involved and/or have any trouble from the landlord about your complaints, immediately contact your local community organization (check Appendix A for one near you).

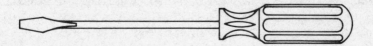

The city has established a routine of working closely with these groups. Most of these groups have clout—by God,—something you need. The community organizations know the inspectors and they also know a lot about building problems. They will probably know about your landlord, news travels you know.

Coordinate your moves with your community group. Perhaps they will make some of the follow-up calls for you. They usually will inspect your building, get expedited service from the inspector, and get hold of your landlord (if you so wish). Later they keep track of the case and will appear in housing court if the case is bad enough to get that far.

You should also call the aldermanic ward office for your ward (the number is 744-6800). Ask for your alderman's office. After a bit of transferring and referrals, you'll get the right person. Make the same complaint to them that you made to the Complaint Bureau and ask them to follow up on it. If they ask, tell them you voted twice in the last election for every Democrat on the ballot. They may refer you to other persons at other numbers—keep at it. This is a good way to get rid of all the frustrations you built up against the landlord. As a matter of fact, this may be the only benefit derived from working with the city. By the way, if you are told to call the Housing (Rent) Complaint Bureau, forget it, it is a waste of time!!

Call the city again (744-3435). Ask for the Building Inspection Department—Conservation, and then state which part of the city you live in: North, South, or West. When you get the wrong number, just keep asking for Building Inspection Department—Conservation (North). Finally someone will answer: "Yes, this is it." Good. Tell them you've made a complaint about your building (state the date) and give them the address. You may get transferred again at this point, but be persistent. They will either ask you what your problem is or what you want from them. You ask them when the inspector is coming out. You should try to meet the inspector at the building. If you don't meet him, your landlord (who receives a notice of complaint and the appointment time for the inspector) will, and that may be the end of your complaint. The landlord will "fix" things up, and the problem will disappear for everyone but you. ASK FOR AND WRITE DOWN THE NAME OF THE INSPECTOR, THE NAME OF THE PERSON YOU ARE TALKING TO, AND THE NAME OF THE AREA SUPERVISOR. Also get the phone number you're connected to. Complain about the situation and ask the city to do something quick. Having the phone number and the inspector's name is like having a little piece of clout for yourself. You can contact the inspector between 8:00 and 8:30 A.M. most days at the phone number you got when you were finally connected. Find out what is happening. Ask him if he's been out and what he saw. Ask him when he is coming back. Find out what action he is recommending. If the city is taking the landlord to court, or Compliance Board, ask him about dates. You should also call 744-3408. Here you can get court docket information, scheduling of your case, a status report, and perhaps what is or what will happen to your landlord's case in Compliance Board.

Follow up on this procedure once every few weeks.

Working with the City

Working with the city is a desperate situation. They inspect hundreds of thousands of structures every year, they haul ten thousand owners into court. The statistics are very poor, but it takes from six to eighteen months to clear up most code violations after the first court hearing; and it takes three to seven months to get a building suit into court. The city figures if 60% to 80% of the violations are corrected, the building is OK and the case is dismissed.

However, it doesn't seem to make much difference if the landlord doesn't care to make the repairs. Fines imposed against owners for failure to correct violations are seldom collected. Some buildings deteriorate to the point where the city orders them demolished. But again, the landlords have a trick. A building will go from housing court to demolition court. The building is ordered torn down if repairs are not made by a certain date. The owner promises to repair, but doesn't. Just before the demolition date, the owner sells or transfers the property for $1.00 to a contract buyer. The new owner comes into court, asks for a stay of the order and requests a year or longer to raise the money and make the repairs . . . and on it goes. In the meantime, people are living in substandard conditions and being thrown out when they complain.

The city, by the way, may not decide to take your landlord to court. They have an administrative procedure called the Compliance Board. The Board consists of building department employees who hold "hearings." These hearings are at City Hall and are not open to the public nor to any complaining tenant or his lawyer. An inspector will find certain problems in the building which violate the code. He will turn his findings over to his supervisor who, in turn, forwards them to the Compliance Board officer. A hearing date is set, and the owner notified to make repairs by that date. (Normally thirty to sixty days is given before the hearing.) The building is reinspected just prior to that date. The owner appears at the hearing. The inspector's report is read by the officer. If compliance of the building codes is not completed, the officer grants an extension of time, usually thirty to sixty days. If after the second appearance the building is not in compliance with the codes, a court date is set for two to six months in the future.

None of the compliance records are available to the tenant who complained and the records are kept secret from the public. You have no idea what problems were found, what situations were corrected and whether, after all the complaints, anything substantial was done. Once the building gets into the city processes, it is nearly impossible to make further complaints about the same or "newer" conditions. In conclusion, dealing with the city building inspection department is a dead-end street. However, if you are going to try and get necessary repairs made, it is still important to go through the motions.

If there is one advantage, it is that you can put pressure on the landlord. If inspectors start coming around, they may come around his other buildings too. There may be some serious violations. Building inspections can get to be very expensive. The landlord may have to spend a small fortune paying off the inspectors (yes, Virginia). He will have to pay his lawyer to come into court (or perhaps Compliance Board). He may even have to pay to take out a building permit to make the corrections and he will be billed certain inspection fees by the city for sending the inspectors out to the site. In some cases, he might actually have a building shut down. The city will act swiftly if you can convince them that people are about to freeze or die because of some other danger that the landlord has neglected.

Following Your "Case"

Use the telephone to keep track of your "case" after the inspector comes out. In addition to the inspector, talk to his supervisor. Ask for the file number of your case. If they ask you who you are and why you want it, tell them you are the complaining tenant and that you have testimony to give. Call 744-3707 and ask for the Compliance Board. Ask to speak to the supervisor. Find out the hearing date and try to get the charges. Ask if any work has been done. Take his direct phone number and his name for future reference. Call 744-3408, the office of the Assistant Corporation Counsel. Ask the person who answers to tell you the status of your case. Give the address and the file number. Tell them you want to be in court to testify and you need to know when and where the court hearing will take place. Ask the name of the lawyer assigned to your case. The actual court hearing will be in a courtroom on the 11th floor of the Civic Center, Clark and Randolph Streets.

You now have information. Use it in your best interests. If work isn't done, complain to the inspector and the Compliance Board, and show up in court. You can also call various other city departments and complain. Use your imagination!! Use the Appendixes to assist you. The trick is to get the name of an inspector and his direct in-dial number. The more inspectors that come around, the more likely the owner is to shape up. It is possible to have the water or gas or power shut off if violations are extreme. In these cases you may have to move out, but your lease would be broken and you might have legal recourse to sue for damages. If a building is shut down, it could cost the owner far more than if he just fixed up what he should have done in the first place.

The procedure I have just described is "attempted democracy in action." The problem is that nothing is likely to get done unless everybody who has a complaint is very persistent. A high-ranking city spokesman, who asks to be shielded, indicated to me that the city cannot handle the volume of complaints it receives. He stated that the last thing the city wants is for a complaintant to call a second time to find out what's happening. The city has a computerized system to keep track of the complaints and could actually give us a status report, but that would probably mean that we could find out what inspectors were on the take, and how slow and uninterested the city really is in caring for its citizens.

The city is supposed to issue a written answer for each complaint received, but usually does not do so, even when it is requested. If enough of us call and complain and complain, the city would finally have to respond with action instead of bureaucratic stumbling. Maybe that is a job for the Rent Complaint Bureau.

A few simple suggestions as you follow your case through the city departments: always try to be present when an inspector is due at your building. Get his name and phone number. Show him everything you know that is troublesome. Follow up later by phone. Ask him when the court date is, and what room the hearing will be in. Go to court. Most court calls are for 9:30 A.M. at the Civic Center. Go early. When you enter the courtroom ask the court clerk if your case will be heard today in this courtroom—sometimes there are changes. Then ask who is the Assistant Corporation Counsel handling the case for the city. Speak to that person. Tell him or her you have testimony. Be prepared to give specific problems: "There is no heat," "the water does not work," "he won't put locks on the doors," "the windows fall out," "he shut off the electricity," "the rats are everywhere" and so on. Bring pictures of the conditions.

When your case is called, go up to the bench and stand behind and to the left of the city attorney—stand away from your landlord or his lawyer. If you get the chance, tell your story to the judge. Be courteous but firm. Listen to what is said. If you have questions, wait until after the "call is cleared" (the end of the morning's cases) and then ask the judge what happened. So few tenants go to Housing Court and talk to the judges that the judges do not even consider the fact that there are human lives being played with by a couple of lawyers and a cheap or stubborn landlord. Let the judge know how it hurts.

Don't Fight Alone

Well, so much for democracy in action. You want something done now, today. Your landlord wants nothing done, ever, and the courts take years to get anything started, let alone completed. What can you do?

In this chapter, I will continue to discuss the mechanical options that you or your group can employ.

Let's make a first premise: you can do very little by yourself. Alone you are the lamb in a wolf's mouth. You really must work in concert with other tenants. Chapter 18 details how to organize a tenants' union and how to work as a collective group in dealing with that mean ole' wolf, the landlord.

Assume, and it's a good guess, that nothing much is happening because of the city inspectors or the courts. Assume that your landlord is crying like a baby to the judge, promising any complaining tenant that he is working on the problem, and evicting any person he thinks is protesting too loudly. In the meantime, nothing gets done. What is next?

Prepare for battle.

You could, I repeat, make the repairs yourself, as in *Spring* v. *Little*. This assumes you have the money for repairs or the skill and time necessary. If you want your money back, then you should go through the procedure mentioned in Chapter 15 to write a letter to the landlord detailing what is needed and how much it will cost him. You need to get one written estimate from an outside supplier, the company you have selected to do the job. Your landlord has the right (a courtesy the courts advance to him) to refuse your bid and find his own supplier. However, if he doesn't do the job before the deadline you've given him, you should go ahead with your workmen and assignment.

Common law allows that work done on a building is done for the property. If the workmen are not paid, they can sue the landlord for the money owed and put a mechanic's lien against the building. The lien legally ties up the property and can make it hard for the landlord to borrow money or sell the place. *The landlord need not have requested the work*, by the way—you can have it done if the need is justified. If you work from this direction be prepared to show a court that:

1. *The city inspectors had cited the building for violations that these repairs corrected.*
2. *The landlord had refused a reasonable request to perform the work in a reasonable time.*
3. *The repairs were necessary to protect the health, safety, welfare, or the life of the tenants.*

You should also be prepared to be evicted by your landlord and possibly sued by him or the workmen for the cost of the work performed.

A "legal" variation on this theme is to have the work performed and pay for it yourself (instead of billing the landlord or having a lien placed against the property). Then you negotiate with the landlord for repayment, rent credit, rent rebate, or rent reduction. If your landlord is still refusing, you have four options:

1. *Forget it.*

> 2. *Sue him in Small Claims Court if the bill is under $300.00 ($1,000 with the aid of a lawyer). (I will discuss the procedure in Chapter 17.)*
> 3. *Deduct the amount spent from your rent.*
> 4. *Withhold your rent.*

If you deduct part of your rent, you may get an eviction notice. You will be summoned to Forcible Entry and Detainer Court (Eviction or Renters' Court) and you can try to fight it through. With a lawyer and a jury trial you may win, but it will cost a fortune. Without a lawyer, you won't win.

You could simply withhold your rents without making repairs. (Remember public aid recipients can hold their rents for three months and then deduct 20% of the first ninety days rent as a penalty but must pay the rest over.) The landlord may take you to Eviction Court. You will need a lawyer, a strong case of desperate conditions and the hope that some officer will hear a case containing the words *"Spring* v. *Little."* Slim chance, however.

If things are bad enough that either they get fixed or you will move out, you have another alternative. The legal term is *constructive eviction*. It refers to conditions so bad that it is impossible for you to live with "quiet and peaceful enjoyment." A landlord who harasses you, or shuts off the utilities or heat, or won't make repairs, can be trying to evict you through "constructive means." Also the physical building conditions can be the cause of a constructive eviction. The key is that the building is uninhabitable for one reason or the other. (Other "constructive" problems could be the landlord's failure to properly protect your building against burglars, noise from neighbors which the landlord can but will not control, roaches and mice which the landlord will not or cannot control, etc.) Consult a lawyer, however, before trying to break a lease on the grounds of constructive eviction.

To move out, give your landlord 30 days notice and state in your letter that certain specific conditions have gone uncorrected and that the presence of these conditions makes the situation impossible. You will need to have copies of your letters of complaint made to your landlord at the time things first were noticed. Be sure to date your letters.

Your landlord may accept your breaking your lease without penalty, may penalize you for breaking the lease, or may refuse to let you break the lease. Move out at any rate. If you are called into court you will use as your defense the fact that the place was unlivable. You will verify this statement with copies of letters sent to your landlord complaining about the conditions, photographs, copies of inspection reports (subpoenaed from the city) and witnesses who have seen or heard what made you move out. You will need a lawyer and a lot of money, at least $250 and as much as $1,000.

If you move out early, you have a way of recovering your security deposit (assuming you did not go after the apartment with a claw hammer). You could send your landlord a letter "granting" him your "permission" to apply your security deposit to your last month's rent (see Appendix M). Then do not pay your last month's rent; it is not quite "legal" but it sure works!!

I repeat, again, that individual actions such as these just covered do not go to the core of our problems, nor can one small sheep resist the crushing force of the wolfish system.

Remember: You are a sitting duck when you make complaints by yourself. You cannot win if either the city or the courts get involved. The law is designed to protect "them" and not you. Next step is a tenants' union, Lincoln Park, or the funny farm. Organize!!

17

Suing (and Being Sued) in the Courts

Civil Court Procedures

Well it happens, you know. There are eviction notices, law suits, and housing court actions. What are they all about? What can happen to you? What should you know about these things?

The courts you will be involved with are *civil courts*. They are Courts-in-Chancery or the Municipal Division of the Cook County Circuit Courts. It is doubtful that the criminal courts will be involved (unless somebody is arrested by the police). The courts have the power to evict you, order you to pay back rents and court costs. You can also use the courts to force the landlord to bring the building up to code, break your lease, collect security deposits or repair monies, or stop bothering you. At a more escalated level, you can sue your landlord for damages caused by his negligence or broken promises, or because of his violations of the city codes. The courts can also grant you the specific right to withhold your rents, get a rent reduction, or receive rent refunds.

The five types of courts you will mostly come in contact with are Forcible Entry and Detainer Court (Eviction or Renters' Court), Pro Se Court (Small Claims Court), Municipal Court (Housing and Demolition Court), Chancery Court (for Injunctive Relief) and Law Division (Regular Civil Court). A sixth court, criminal court, is a possibility if you put a peace bond on the landlord.

Most of the courtrooms are located in the Civic Center in downtown Chicago. The Civic Center is located at Clark and Randolph Streets. Rooms 1502 and 1508 are the usual courtrooms for Eviction Court. Housing Court cases are heard in the odd-numbered rooms on the 11th floor, and other actions take place in assigned courtrooms or judges' chambers. If you are served papers, it will indicate where to appear.

This chapter is not a how-to-be-your-own-lawyer instruction sheet. With the exception of Small Claims Court and Housing

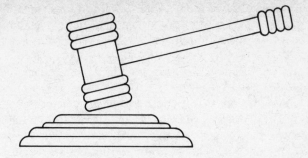

Court you will need a lawyer if you want to win. A lawyer charges $35 to $50 an hour. In Eviction Court, a lawyer may not be necessary depending on what you want to have happen to you.

Eviction Court

The most common place for a tenant to end up is the Eviction Court. The most common reason for being evicted is non-payment of rent. The second most frequent reason is not moving out after the end of your lease. There are two basic types of leases: *term of years* (usually written) and *month-to-month* (usually oral). A written lease is not broken unless the tenant breaks the rules or doesn't pay his rent. An oral lease requires no reason to break and only 30 days written notice to vacate.

The general procedure for eviction following nonpayment of rents is simple. Under most cases, the landlord must serve you or a person living in the apartment (by posting on the door) with a "Landlord's Five Days Notice." This notice gives you five days to pay whatever rents you owe or face eviction. If you pay the landlord within five days, there is nothing else to be done. You cannot be evicted until the end of the term of your lease. However, if you are on a month-to-month lease, the landlord may simply cancel your lease arrangement.

If you do not pay the rent within the five-day period, the landlord can go into court and sue you. Your court date will be at least two weeks after the landlord goes to the Civic Center to formally file for eviction. A summons to appear in court is served by the Sheriff. If the summons is dated before the Five Days Notice has expired, or before the rent is due, the case will be thrown out if you point this fact out to the judge.

If you receive a Ten Days Notice, it is for a "violation" of your lease. You should write a response to your landlord stating the facts, or correct the condition if that is possible. If you want to stay in your place, take a lawyer. If not, wait until you are served with a court summons and go to court. Try to make a case if you can, if not, play out the game.

Assuming the summons papers are correct you will have to "file an appearance" by the "return date." That means you have to go down to the Cook County Circuit Court Clerk's office, Room 602 of the Civic Center. Take your summons notice to the "Forcible Entry and Detainer" (rent cases) window. You will be told what date to appear in court.

Your court date will be one week later than your return date. If you did file an appearance, your courtroom will be 1508 in the Civic Center. If you failed to file an appearance, go to room 1502 one week after your return date. The court call is for 9:30 A.M. in both courts. Bring to court, along with the summons, your lease, rent receipts, pictures, and any other papers you can produce. You will see from 30 to 100 other tenants with similar notices and pieces of paper, so come early because there are seats for only about 50 people.

If you wish to hire a lawyer or bring in evidence or witnesses, go immediately to the court clerk and tell him or her you wish a continuance in order to make your defense. The clerk will help you to make arrangements.

If you want to get the agony done with, just wait your turn. After time passes, your case will be called. You will approach the bench as will either the landlord, his agent, or their lawyer. If you do not appear, the case will be decided against you, you will be ordered to pay back rents and move out within fourteen days. If "they" do not appear the case will be dismissed at the end of the court session that day.

When both sides appear before the judge, he will ask to see the Landlord's Notice. He will ask you if you owe the amount of money the landlord demands or if you broke the lease. If you say no, then you will have to explain. Produce either rent receipts, cancelled checks, or witnesses. It is *assumed* that you are not trying to invoke *Spring* v. *Little* or any other defense. If you do owe money, tell the judge what the circumstances are. By the way, partial acceptance of rent for any particular month may constitute rents paid-in-full for that month. You may successfully argue that you have been paying a reduced sum and now the landlord has changed his mind, or the eviction was for a breach of a lease rule and the rule was ridiculous. Good luck.

After hearing all this (in about two minutes) the judge will find that you owe money or that you did break the lease and that you should be evicted. If you have told the judge about the terrible conditions in the building and how the landlord is crazy and bites small children, and so on, the judge may decide to set aside some or all the rent you owe. He may simply order you to vacate within fourteen days or before the first of next month, and forgive the rents. You almost certainly will be tossed out, however.

Usually the landlord is asking for a "joint" action: he wants your money in and you out. He may tell the judge how terrible the conditions are in your apartment, how noisy you are, and how much extra water you use. The judge may award him back rents and court costs in addition to your eviction. The judge will order you to set up a payment schedule with your former landlord.

The actual amount of time you have from first not paying the rent until you are on the street varies. It is at least two months, however, and it could be longer. Whether you actually pay the landlord is also questionable. The judge is going to be more "kindly" to you if you are a decent sort down on your luck and/or with children. He may not order you to pay back rents if you promise to move out during the period of time he has stated. You may be ordered to pay back rents and current rents if you overstay.

Current rents owing are seldom counted in an eviction case unless they are part of the Five Days Notice. The suit is almost always for back rent. If conditions are bad in the building, the judge may forgive the rents. If you, the tenant, seem to be at fault, the judge may give you a short notice to vacate, collect all the rents owing, and assess the court costs against you. Rarely does one get to stay in his apartment after an appearance in Eviction Court.

After the judge enters his order it is up to the landlord to see to it that you obey the order. If you overstay, the landlord can request to have the Sheriff come out. He can also summons you back to court if you still own him money.

If you still don't move, the landlord tells the Sheriff to move you out. By this time three months have probably passed by. Now is a very good time to move, pronto. The Sheriff, when he does arrive one week to one month later, will remove the doors from your apartment and move the apartment contents out to the street. Not very nice.

If you have been through the court process and have been ordered evicted, you can find out if your landlord has requested the Sheriff to throw you out. Call 443-8195 and ask if you have been scheduled for physical eviction.

If you are being evicted, you are not alone. A total of 5400 eviction cases are filed on the average month in Cook County, most of them in the city. That averages out to 9.6% of all tenants yearly!!! Approximately zero tenants are allowed to stay, meaning there is about a 100% win rate for the landlord.

When the judge tells you to leave, he issues a "writ of restitution" on behalf of the landlord. If you don't move out, the landlord takes the writ to the Sheriff's Office and makes arrangements to have you put out. (The Sheriff receives 900 eviction requests each month). The landlord must pay a $50.00 advance deposit. This money is used to pay men hired by the Sheriff's department to actually move your stuff to the street. It will cost your landlord between $100 and $200 to set your belongings out.

The Sheriff must send you a notice stating that unless you are out by a certain date, "the boys will come over and fix ya'." Most people move before the boys arrive. To interfere with the moving is a criminal offense and the city police will arrest you. If found guilty of interfering, it could cost you $500 or six months at Cook County Jail.

You have twenty-four hours to move your household off the street. If not, the city sanitation department is called and they move it to the nearest dump. There are no evictions during the Christmas season, or when the temperature drops below 15 degrees. Bad weather delays evictions occasionally.

If you are evicted, call your nearest community organization, the Salvation Army, or an Urban Progress Center of the city Department of Human Resourses. They will find temporary housing for you.

If you owe money you should pay it. The judge may ask the landlord to send him a letter telling him that you have paid the landlord the money you owe him. The judge may set a court date requiring you to appear if you don't pay. The payment letter cancels that court date.

If the judge does not set another date, then it is up to the landlord to collect the rents or come back into court on a motion to attach (seize) your bank account or other types of property. You are supposed to be notified of the time of the hearing on the motion to attach. You can make your defense if you are present, but the judge may or may not accept your argument. The judge issues an order to your landlord allowing him to take the money out of your bank account. This order is served on the bank and the money is withdrawn in favor of the landlord. You don't have to lift a finger.

Sometimes a landlord will try to skip the courts altogether with what is called a "self help remedy," that is taking the law into his own hands. This type of action is in lieu of filing for eviction and is based on an old Illinois law. Legislation is now in the works to outlaw this practice completely.

In the meantime, while you remain in the building the landlord may get a bit itchy. He might cut off your utilities, padlock the front door, or call you every hour on the hour. If he does, you should call the cops and complain. Tell them your landlord is interfering in a court matter. GET A PEACE BOND AGAINST HIM. The next day go down to court, ask to see the eviction judge, and tell him what is going on. (Go at 9:00 A.M. or 1:30 P.M.) Your landlord is in contempt of court because he is interfering with the judge's order allowing you to stay for 14 days (or whatever) before the eviction. The court assumes you to be ignorant of the law, but knows your landlord is supposed to be smarter (that's why judges and lawyers are landlords and make all the rules). Your landlord can be fined for his foolishness.

If you go into Eviction Court with a lawyer, it means you want to stay in your current apartment. Your lawyer will make an "appearance" for you on the first date. He will request, and receive, a hearing or trial date. His strategy may be to appear only in front of the judge, or in front of a six-man civil jury. Your lawyer will pursue the case for you. The time-in-court process may take several weeks to several months. You will have to spend several days off work and in court. You will almost certainly come out ahead morally with a jury, but be far behind in cash.

It is possible for your landlord to enter your apartment and seize most of your property (clothes and other personal objects cannot be seized). He does not need your permission to enter if you are not present. If you are present, he will need the Sheriff before you have to let him in. He can seize and hold your property until you pay the money you owe him. This action of "distraint" is rarely used, fortunately. Even the Cook County Courts seem to frown on such landlord methods. The police have been instructed to ignore your phone calls for help, by the way. Your best bet is to call a lawyer immediately and try to get an emergency injunction against the landlord as well as an order restoring your property to you. After six months he can sell the property for back rents and return the "change," if any, to you. This sale usually requires a court order.

Holdover cases (staying longer than the term of the lease) come out about the same as nonpayment cases. You pay rent for the time you holdover (but maybe not double rent) and still you'll have to move. Under certain circumstances a trial will get you a lease extension and other corrective measures, but you need a lawyer and a good case of retaliatory actions by your landlord from the start. CONCLUSION: STAY OUT OF EVICTION COURT. These days, without *Spring* v. *Little*, it is a losing battle from the beginning. Eviction Court is "Landlord's Court." Find another battlefield with better odds, and organize.

Housing Court

The other territory of the landlord is Housing Court. You cannot sue in Housing Court, only the city has that power. This is where the city "enforces" the building codes. I have already described in bloody detail the criminal neglect which takes place in the Housing Courts. Your role is that of witness. If you have pictures or evidence to present it is best to go with a large group. Hook up with a community group—they know the ropes and have clout. This way the judges, who are sometimes very nearsighted, will be more likely to see you. Having a representative from your alderman's office is very helpful. Maybe your lawyer's presence would be of assistance. You have a slim chance of getting relief by yourself when appearing in Housing Court.

A large, well-organized group, backed by the community, an honest building inspector, evidence, and a good lawyer can get action, or maybe control of the building. It has been done!

Basically, you have to prove that the landlord has neither the desire nor the money to fix the place up, but that your group has the time, experience, and money necessary. The judge may award the building "in receivership" to your group. You then become the landlord and temporary owner. *Receivership* is a process where control of the property is taken away from the owner by the court. The court appoints a "civilian," usually a lawyer buddy, to oversee the business of the building. The receiver receives not only the property but a nice percentage of the rents. The receiver is supposed to pay off the debts, fix up the building, and keep up the mortgage payments. Usually only the receiver "makes out" (he gets his fees off the top).

Groups on the North, West, and South Sides of Chicago have taken over their buildings in this manner and have made deals with the banks to buy the properties. This type of takeover requires full-time participation from several people. If receivership is contemplated, retain a lawyer to work out the details. The idea of everybody owning their own, collective building is exciting.

The other purpose of Housing Court is to put pressure on the landlord to get the job done. If you dog the landlord every step of the way, he will learn it is much easier to comply with your requests and the building code requirements, than be constantly pressured by his tenants in front of the court and the building inspectors. If tenants are diligent and follow through, it becomes very hard to allow continued payoffs to the inspectors. It is hard to explain a good inspection report with a dozen tenants.in court to complain. Go to Housing Court, but be prepared for a long, frustrating wait. There may be a pot of gold at the end of this particular rainbow, but it is a long hard trip and just one leg of the journey.

Suing the Landlord in the Chancery and Law Division Courts

There is an alternative to the Housing Court route, but this requires your affirmative action. You must sue the landlord and the city of Chicago. As a resident of the State you may sue under the Illinois Municipal Code (24-13-31).

Step one is to take a building survey (see Appendix I). Then get the inspectors to come out and go through the building with them. If nothing happens within sixty days, call your lawyer. He will institute suit against the landlord and the city (if the city hasn't moved fast enough). The lawyer will request an injunction or temporary restraining order from the court. This type of order requires your landlord to do certain things, and/or stop doing other things. Basically, the suit asks the court to order your landlord to bring the building up to code specifications, stop mistreating the tenants, and comply with all other laws related to construction, landlords, and tenants.

You will have to be very specific on what needs to be done. The records from the building inspector will be important but may not cover all the problems. You will need witnesses, photographs, perhaps plaster scraps, dead roaches, or other sorts of physical evidence. Your lawyer will have to have a good case-at-law establishing your standing to sue. You need not prove that there is some special or unique damage in order to win your case, but having such evidence may be helpful.

The lawyer files his suit in Circuit Court at the County Clerk's office. The Sheriff (usually) serves a copy of the suit and a summons into court on the landlord. (It is very important that the owner also be sued, or you may have to start all over again.) If all goes well, the judge will hear the request for a temporary restraining order at the first hearing date. Sometimes the judge will give the landlord a period of time (from five to thirty days) to make a written answer. After the answer is made your lawyer has a chance to make a written reply. Sometimes, particularly on a temporary or emergency request, things go much faster. The judge will hear two types of arguments. One has to do with the "legality" of the lawsuit. This has to do with the form of the suit (how you are proceeding) and not the contents or merits of the case. If the form is correct then the judge will listen to the problem.

Judges are very happy to throw out requests for injunctive relief because of improper form, thus saving themselves the trouble of making real decisions or being held up as bad examples if the case is later appealed.

Assuming you have a good lawyer and the judge agrees to hear the case, he will first hear your side and then your landlord's side. If you convince the judge that there are serious problems, he will request that your lawyer draw up an order. He may tell all parties in the case to go into a conference room (at the rear of most courtrooms are two small conference rooms) and work out a compromise on what needs to be done and by what dates the work is to be completed. Then the judge will set a date for a progress report. It may be during the period of time work is in progress or it may be on the date all work is to be completed. Your landlord must do the work. He cannot put it off as he does in Housing Court. You perform the role of witness. This temporary order, however, usually covers only the most serious problems. Another hearing date is usually set for the main part of your suit. However, in a few months, instead of a few years, you can usually take care of most complaints.

The law provides that your lawyer's fees have to be paid by the landlord if you can prove that the landlord was in violation of the building codes. You will probably have to pay your lawyer, and the landlord will have to reimburse you. The award of lawyer's fees may not cover all the expenses, but it should cover most of them. You also will not receive damages or other punitive money in this type of suit.

The ultimate step in aggressive pursuit of your landlord is a full-fledged lawsuit for damages and restitution of other inequities. Again, you will need a good lawyer and a very good case. The strongest case is to combine the citizens' suit (outlined above) with a request for money damages for specific acts, inactions, injuries, and losses. Damages can be collected for repairs you had to make to the apartment and on any appliances your landlord originally supplied you with, including bills from plumber's, electrician's, plasterer's, exterminator's, roofer's, furnace repairmen, appliance repairmen, hardware stores. If the repairs were necessary (and particularly if the repairs were required by the building code), you should recover the costs of these repairs. Save the receipts. Receipts usually are *prima facie* (self-evident) evidence that the repairs were necessary.

Damages can also be collected because you had to spend money to correct a condition caused by the negligence of your landlord, including getting sick because of inadequate heating; property damage from broken water pipes; lead poisoning from lead-based paints; having to move out because of unlivable building conditions; unhealthy heating gas or sewer leaks; injuries caused by poor lighting in the common areas; ruined clothes from faulty landlord-provided laundry facilities; or, any type of personal physical injury or wound due to faulty construction (loose steps, falling plaster, protruding nails, broken handrails, falling siding). If you had doctor's bills or if you lost time from work because of these types of injuries, or if you had to spend money to replace the damaged losses, you can sue to recover your expenses. You may also sue for an additional amount because the landlord was at fault for allowing these conditions to exist.

If there is a fire in the building caused by faulty equipment supplied by the landlord, or if the landlord allows faulty equipment to be in the building (for instance, a space heater or stove belonging to a tenant), you may be able to prove that the landlord was negligent in his job because he didn't make repairs or order the faulty equipment removed. If there are "security" locks on the front and back doors, and these locks do not work and a burglary results, your landlord may be liable for the losses sustained in a burglary.

Then there are the broken promises. The streets of Chicago are paved with the sharp slivers of shiny broken promises. If your landlord promised you that your place would be ready by a certain date, and it was not, and because of this you either had to move into conditions not suitable for habitation, or had to store your belongings and live in a motel or with friends, or lost money or time from work because of your landlord's failure to be ready, you can sue for damages. If you were promised that certain repairs would be made, appliances replaced, or services made available and the landlord did not deliver, you can sue. If he promised to have the place repainted but didn't do it, and if you have a good case on a lot of other counts, then sue for decorating also. You might sue for recovery of money spent on improvement, for general damages because he cheated you, and for fraud and deceit because he lied to you.

Your case is much stronger if you originally had a specific list of promises attached to and made part of the lease. The Universal Tenants' Rights Rider would also help your case. If you signed your lease without these written protections, you must make your case much stronger, but you do have a chance. If you have a lease coming up soon, think about the riders to protect yourself in case you must go to court.

For the general conditions of the building and the general performance of the landlord, you can sue for a rent abatement (reduction) and for recovery of a percentage of back rents based upon how much the value of the rent was reduced by the acts or neglect of your landlord.

In addition to damages, you can also gain certain nonmonetary advantages. You can get a lease extension at a fair rent, written agreements concerning maintenance, building upkeep improvements, and decorating. You can get recognition of your tenants' group, can rewrite your lease, and maybe get a new management company. If the damages are substantial and the owner/

landlord is small, you may even gain control of the building.

Such lawsuits are expensive and time-consuming and the results may not make you rich, even if you win. The law takes a dim view of little common folk complaining against the privileged classes. The cost of such a suit will range from $2000 to $5000, and either your losses have to be substantial or you must have a very strong case. Your lawyer's fees are usually part of the final settlement.

The procedure in such cases is orderly but filled with delays. Your lawyer will require several weeks to draw up a suit. The complaints will be based upon interviews with all the participants involved and you may have to give a sworn statement (an affidavit) to your lawyer concerning the facts. You must have good records: receipts, doctor's letters, correspondence between yourself and the landlord, evidence of damage (spoiled clothing, scars, photographs, witnesses).

When the lawsuit is filed, the Sheriff will be sent out to serve the landlord—the *defendant*. You are called the *plaintiff*—the plea-er or pray-er. After all the defendants have been served, they have thirty days to "answer" the complaint. This answer is their lawyer's legal response. They will usually deny everything and claim you have no legal grounds to sue. Actually, it will take more like three or four months before the answer is filed. This is a delaying tactic. Your lawyer can file for a default (they lose automatically) if the defendants do not file the answer within thirty days, but the judge will invariably extend the due date and ignore the default request.

The defendant will usually request that the plaintiff be "deposed" before the defendant answer is filed. A *deposition* is a legal proceeding designed to gather facts. The plaintiffs, usually one at a time, are questioned by the defendant's lawyer. A court reporter is present to take the testimony. The plaintiff's lawyer is also present to protect the plaintiff, but he does not ask questions. Later, at another time, the roles are reversed and the plaintiff's lawyers ask questions of the defendants.

You, as the plaintiff, must appear and must answer the questions. If there are several defendants and several different law firms, each might try to depose you. If there are a number of plaintiffs, it could take months and months before everybody questions everybody else. In the Boy Scouts we called this a daisy chain. This is a great delaying tactic. Sometimes your lawyer can request the court to order the defendants to stop stalling, and sometimes the court will listen.

After the depositions are taken and the defendants answer, and the plaintiff depositions are taken and the plaintiffs answer the answer, and the defendants answer the answer to the answer, and so forth, a trial date is set. This date is from six to twenty-four months hence. In the meantime the legal bills rise and negotiations commence. At some point it will seem simpler and easier for one side to give in and stop losing money. The landlord, collecting rents as he does, may have the upper hand. Large real estate firms have a lot of staying power so you must be dedicated.

Once started, a lawsuit of this nature can take many turns. You may be willing to settle for a lot less than you are suing for. Your lawyer should have some tricks up his sleeve to force the real issues and bring about a solution. The reason for such suits is usually some grievous errors and mischief on the part of the landlord. Removing the major problems may salve over the loss of some money or time.

I would suggest that the first thing your lawyer do is to request that a temporary restraining order be issued making the court the receiver of the rents due the landlord. You, as a tenant, would still have to pay the rent, but the court would receive the funds instead of the landlord. The court may decide to pay the landlord the rent (every month) if the landlord shows adequate progress correcting some of the grosser problems. Occasionally the court might hold the rents until the work is completed. Suing in a joint count (Municipal Code, Chapter 24, Division 13, Sec. 31) and for damages, you could also recover the lawyer's fees.

If you can't tie up the rents, the next request is a temporary restraining order forcing your landlord to do the work (as previously discussed). If the landlord is ordered to do the work and then defaults, you can request rent withholding or summary damages (without that long wait for the trial on the main suit).

As leases expire and the landlord refuses to renew the leases of plaintiffs, your lawyer can go into court asking for a restraining order prohibiting the landlord from taking any retaliatory action of any sort and also extending all leases until such time as the case is resolved.

If the landlord starts cleaning up his house, and taking care of the code violations, and making good on his promises, you may consider negotiating the rest of the suit.

In any event, you'll want to recover actual cash losses, lawyer's fees, and protect yourself from retaliation. You'll want written agreements about what is settled, and you may want official recognition of the tenants' organization, a lease extension at a fair rent, and maybe the new refrigerator you were promised. All these things are negotiable. If you are satisfied with the way the building is being taken care of, and don't want to spend more money for lawyer's fees, now is the time to cut bait. If you think other things are important (and are prepared to spend time and money on these items) full speed ahead. If you can settle for something in between, do it. If you have a strong case, there is always that trial—a couple of years and a couple of thousand dollars from now.

An organization of tenants will defray the costs, give mutual moral support to each other, and also have far more powerful tools to use in the battle against the landlord. I am saving a discussion of tenants' groups for the next chapter because I want to cover other court avenues here. The courts, with you as the affirmative initiator, may be very helpful on an emergency basis, but in the long run, the only winners will be the lawyers who collect the fees. We, as tenants, could be broke and forced to move before the case comes to trial. There are better ways, as we shall see in Chapter 18. By the way, after many months of such legal activities against the landlord, the Franz Kafka story, "The Trial," becomes frighteningly real.

Small Claims Court

Small Claims Court (Pro Se Court) is useful for recovering security deposits and money spent for repairs. It is a route best used for disagreements concerning minor damages and money claims. The limit that can be recovered at any one time is $300.00. You can use Small Claims Court no more than three times in any one year, and you can only sue your landlord once during that time.

In Small Claims Court you are your own lawyer. Only individuals may sue in Small Claims Court, but you can sue anyone, including businesses and corporations. The person or company you sue has the right to have a lawyer present (but you may not). It is possible that whomever you sue will countersue, but such are the joys. The process takes at least forty-five days and could go several months.

To initiate a suit in the Pro Se Courts, go to Room 602 in the Civic Center and ask to see a Pro Se (pronounced pro-say) advisor. He or she will help you fill out the necessary forms. You should bring with you your lease, any receipts or estimates you have for the money claims, $30.00 cash and any other correspondence you have with your landlord or concerning your case. You must also know the amount of money you are asking, have the correct names and addresses of those individuals or companies being sued, and know if any corporations are involved. It will cost you $12.00 to file the lawsuit which the advisor will fill out with you.

The papers are given to a clerk in the Clerk of the Court office. After being properly stamped and numbered they must be served. Either the Clerk's Office will send the papers certified mail (return receipt requested) for $2.25 or you will have to pay the Cook County Sheriff to make a personal delivery. The Sheriff's office is in Room 701 at the Civic Center. His fee is $12.00 plus $.30 a mile to each place of service from the Civic Center. You must serve corporations by process of the Sheriff, while individuals can be served through the mails.

Knowing who to sue is very important, no matter what the court. You must sue the "beneficial owner," that is, the person who actually enjoys the profits from the building. It is common for the owner of a building to be hidden by a series of trusts. (These are arrangements with banks who hold the property in the name of the bank, but actually do not own the property.) It may take several trips into court and several court orders to discover who the actual owners are, so when you sue, sue the manager, the management company, and the owners. If the ownership of a building has changed, sue all the parties, before and after the change. When things get this complicated, you really do need a lawyer.

You can do the preliminary research on ownership or you can hire a title search company. For a modest fee of $8.00 to $15.00 you can get the legal description of the land, the name of the current owner or bank holding the building, the amount of money paid at the time of the last sale (if it is not in a trust), and the name of the previous owner. You can also find out if there are any outstanding lawsuits against the property. Your title search may also include information about the assessed value of the property and the amount of taxes paid and who paid them. If you have the time and spirit, it is fascinating to do your own title search. Go to Room 803 in City Hall and ask a clerk to look up the legal description of your apartment building. The fee is less than $1.00. Take the description to the Cook County Recorder's Office and ask for the title search section. Ask a clerk what book you need. In a bunch of dusty old journals you will see the history of the building in an abbreviated form. Write down the last document numbers and go to the microfilmed document section. Here you will see deeds, court orders, and other official documents. The documents may well tell you who owns the property.

Go also to the Cook County Clerk's Office and tell them you want to see the tax records for the building. Give them the street address and legal description. They will get you the information.

But now, back to court . . .

After you give the Clerk or the Sheriff your complaint and summons, you wait. The summons has a "return date" noted. This requires the defendant (the party you are suing) to make an appearance at the Clerk's office before a certain date twenty-eight to forty-four days after the date of the complaint. Do not go to the Clerk's office on that date; go several days after the return date and ask if there has been a return on your case. Bring your copy of the summons. If the appearance was made by the return date, all is good. Your court trial is scheduled for 14 days after the return date. The actual date will either be written on your complaint or should be obtained from the Clerk's office when you check to see if the appearance was filed.

If no appearance was filed, the case could go two ways. In the one instance, it is possible that the summons was not delivered. If the summons was sent through the mails, there should be a return receipt from the post office; if the summons was served by the Sheriff, there will be a sworn statement. Both are on file with the Pro Se Clerk in Room 602. If the summons was delivered, and there is no appearance filed, you may have won your case. Go to court on the assigned date (Room 1308 in the Civic Center). The time of your call will be on the summons.

If, on the other hand, the summons was not served, you will have to send the Sheriff out again and pay him another fee. You will also have to wait until the next return date to see what happened.

You must gain service before you can have your day in court. If somebody is ducking the Sheriff and the mailman, consult with the Pro Se Court advisor. While you are at the Civic Center, go up to

Room 1308 and watch the proceedings. Most cases are called for 9:30 A.M., others are called for 2 P.M. This is a good way to prepare yourself for your own trial.

Between the time your summons is served, and the date of the trial, your landlord may try to settle with you. He may make a deal to pay part of the money owed, or reduce the rents, or replace that old, broken-down refrigerator. If it sounds like a good deal, put the offer in writing, have him sign it, and wait for him to deliver. Go to court on your date and tell the judge you are in settlement negotiations and request a continuance in the case for two weeks in order to complete the settlement. DO NOT DROP THE CASE. If you gain a settlement you are satisfied with, go back into court on that second date with your written agreement, show it to the judge, and ask that the case be dismissed in favor of the settlement.

On the other hand, your landlord may be very unhappy about what you have done. If you are a tenant, your landlord may threaten to evict you if you don't withdraw the suit. This is harassment and perhaps a retaliatory act if it concerns repairs made because of code violations. Tell the judge.

Your landlord (or former landlord) may countersue (counterclaim). He may claim you did more damage than the amount of your security deposit and sue you for $300.00. He may claim back rents or insist that the repairs you made ruined something or were unnecessary. The judge will listen to both sides of the story and make a decision. If there is a counterclaim which is not served on you but handed to you, or simply "announced" to you at the trial, immediately request a continuance for the purpose of understanding the complaint and making an answer. If your landlord is "springing something" at the trial, this will give you time to check the facts and make a defense.

Your case may take several turns from this point:

Assume that your landlord does not make an appearance and does not show up in court on the trial date; assume also that the records indicate he was served. When your case is called, tell the judge that the defendant is not in court and ask him for a default judgment in your favor. This is an order, issued by the court, for your landlord to pay up. In other words, you win.

Or, assume you are in negotiations or that your landlord has offered you a settlement. As I suggested before, tell the judge the status of your case, but do not drop the suit. Ask for a continuance. If you drop the suit before your landlord pays up, you may have to start the suit all over again with the filing fees, the service, the long wait, etc. Keeping the suit alive keeps you safe. You can always haul the landlord before the court if he stalls or doesn't deliver.

Or, assume your landlord countersues and serves you with the claim prior to the trial date. Assume you have enough time to make a defense against his claims by finding witnesses, receipts, pictures, leases, or whatever. When you appear in court, you will have a chance to tell the judge your side of the story and your landlord will tell his side of the story. You will then have a chance to refute the landlord's case. If you are countersued, you may hire a lawyer, if you wish.

The judge will ask most of the questions, but for the purpose of eliciting more information, you may ask your landlord some questions, in fact, be prepared to do so. The court is not a gymnasium, and a trial is not a boxing match. Be calm, cool, use clean language, and no punching below the belt. The judge will be very hard on whoever tries to jive him, or upset the decorum of the court. If the judge says to calm down or stop asking a line of questions or stop interrupting, do it. You'll lose the case on personality points (even though that's got nothing to do with the law).

A few tips: Come to court early, before the call time. If you have a motion to make (for a continuance or if your landlord has been hassling you), tell the court's clerk. He or she will tell you when you should tell the judge or where you should go to file your motion. If you have witnesses make sure they come to court with you. A witness is someone who *actually saw* the damages you had to repair, or was present when you paid the rent or security deposit, or heard the landlord promise or threaten you. Letters and sworn statements from anybody not in the courtroom are no good. The judge says he cannot question a piece of paper and usually will not accept anything but "live" testimony.

If you have not prepared your case before the court by making a simple outline of the problem and/or organizing your evidence, you could lose. The judge may throw the case out because you were not ready. Or the judge might order a continuance until you are ready. In either case, it's better to be ready the first time.

After all the testimony has been presented, the judge will render a decision. Sometimes he will order both parties to the conference room to iron out the differences between the amount of money on the counterclaims, or to establish a payment schedule. Sometimes he will render a decision outright. In the case of security deposits, there is a specific procedure your landlord is obligated to follow (see Appendix F and Chapter 15). Even if you are from a small building, your landlord still has a legal obligation to return your money to you within a reasonable amount of time.

If you had to make repairs that you asked your landlord (in writing) to make, and he didn't, and if these repairs were related to the Chicago building code ordinances, then you have a good chance of recovering your money. If you sustained damages or injuries related to broken pipes and faulty equipment, and can prove that your landlord was at fault, then you should win your damages. If, in defense or as part of a counterclaim, your landlord claims that you broke your lease when you repainted the ceiling purple, or hung a dozen plants from the walls, then there may be mitigating circumstances and you will have to settle for less, unless you can prove that decorating is not part of the lease (remember normal wear and tear is excepted from damage claims, and decorating is something the landlord has to do every few years anyway, regardless of the color of the ceiling).

Well, assuming after all this that the court awards you most of your security deposit (and maybe the court costs if the landlord is a real s.o.b.), you still have to *collect* the money. The court does not make collections. The judge usually will ask the landlord if he has the money. If the landlord says no, then the judge will give him a date by which he must pay. You and your landlord can agree on the date or even the method of payment. The judge will set a court date to correspond to the time all the money should be paid. Usually the judge will ask that a letter be sent by you to the judge indicating that the money has been paid. If payment is made and the letter is sent, the judge will cancel the next hearing date and close the case.

If the letter is not received, then both parties are obligated to be in court on the next date. If you, the plaintiff, do not show up, your case is dismissed and you lose the chance to collect the money. If the landlord does not show up, he can be held in contempt of court. He will be ordered to appear at the next hearing date (which would be a few days after this second hearing). The Sheriff will serve him with a notice.

You can call the landlord and tell him to be in court. You might inform him that if he doesn't appear, his fun will be just beginning. If he does not show up again, the judge can order a body attachment and Mr. Sheriff arrests him and brings him into court at the next hearing date. *Or*, the judge can order a garnishment of his bank account. The Sheriff serves his bank with an order and you can get your money. If you don't know where his money is hidden, the judge will ask the landlord where it is when he comes into court on one of these supplementary proceedings. You will have to fill out all sorts of papers, but the Pro Se advisor in Room 602 will help.

Small Claims Court is a real court following real law. If you do your part correctly, you have a chance of getting what you want. As with everything involving the courts, however, this court route takes time. If the money is important, and you have the time to spend, the Pro Se Court will be good for you. It is a pity that the maximum suit is not $1000.00—it would make it worth the effort, particularly since security deposits can now exceed the $300 limit. In Chapter 18 I will explain how, as a group, you can use Pro Se Court for a larger claim.

Landlord Harassment

Occasionally, your landlord will cut off your utilities or disturb you with workmen or prospective tenants at all times of the day (and night). He will call you on the phone trying to throw you out or collect the rent. What can you do? If you have a lawyer, call him immediately. If your case is currently in the courts, you can go to the Civic Center and see your judge. He may advise you to see a lawyer or see the Legal Assistance Table in Room 602. If you are not currently in the courts, you can try some other innovations. Change the locks on your doors. It may break the lease, but it should stop the unauthorized visits. Call the police if the landlord is threatening you. Tell them you need an officer to sign a complaint against the landlord for threatening you and disturbing the peace. If you are a member of a tenants' organization it is much easier to deal with these problems (see Chapter 18). As an individual you can also contact the Legal Assistance Foundation. You must go in person. Call 341-1070 for proper times and closest branch location.

If you sign a complaint with the police, you will have to go to a branch court (these are criminal courts outside the Criminal Courts Building, usually in police district stations). It will take all morning. The judge will ask what is going on. If you can convince him your landlord is threatening and frightening you, he will require the landlord to post a performance (peace) bond. This bond will be forfeited and the landlord arrested if he violates the terms of the bond. Usually the bond means he must stop harassing you in any manner. If he continues, all you have to do is call the police. They will collect him and take him back to court. You must appear, spend another morning, and tell the judge what happened. If the landlord was nasty enough, zap, into the slammer for a few days. If the police at first refuse to help you, try, try, again. Eventually they will come out if you persist, however, the situation has to be pretty bad.

Even though the laws are on the books protecting you from being harassed, locked out, or cut off from services, the Chicago police have issued an order to officers not to arrest landlords for such actions. The police have been instructed to tell you that what the landlord has done is a civil matter. In point of fact, what the landlord is doing is breaking the law, but the police won't protect you. Use a different tactic. Ask to sign a complaint for disturbing the peace. You can and do have the right to make such a complaint. If the police refuse this request ask for the section sergeant or the district lieutenant. You do have the right to sign such a complaint for disturbance of the peace. When you sign a complaint the police arrest the landlord. He might also ask to sign a complaint against you. You may then both spend the next few hours in the back of the same squad roll, in the same cell, and at the same court call. Not pleasant, but at least somebody in authority will hear the complaint.

If your utilities are cut off by the landlord, and the landlord is paying for them, call the Building Department Complaint Bureau, your alderman, and the Department of Human Services. If you are paying for the utilities, call the utility companies and the Illinois Commerce Commission if your landlord cuts them off. In both cases, call your lawyer or make arrangements with legal aid.

Bucking the landlord is a tough business. At the drop of a rent check, he will try to throw you out, or countersue you for damages. It is not an easy situation, but the time has come to put a stop to these unbalanced legal scales. We have to start standing up for our rights. Even if it takes time and money, we, as a group, will be much better off when we demonstrate that as tenants we will not be pushed around. The courts are supposed to belong to the people. When the judges see that we, the people, are serious about our rights, and are willing to flood the courts, the courts are going to crack down on the landlords. When this happens the landlords are going to cooperate. Until then, it is an uphill battle.

If you can avoid the courts and lawyers, avoid them! Lawsuits are expensive and more often than not the lawyers win, not the litigants. A lone individual in a lawsuit is a sitting duck. If you are taken to Eviction Court, you will be evicted. Neither the laws nor the courts were conceived on our behalves. These are the bastions of the "other" side. So-called rights and justice are myths crushed and exposed when we get involved in the courts. Avoid the courts and organize to find alternative methods of gaining your rights.

PART SIX

Putting It All Together and Making It Work

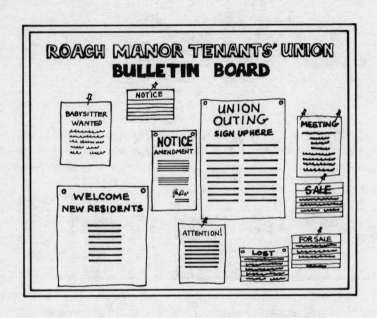

18

Organizing a Tenants' Union

Up to this point the discussion has been what you, as an individual, can do about protecting your rights as a tenant—finding the proper apartment setting, getting a good lease, protecting yourself in and from the courts and the landlord. The battle is a tough one. Alone, the tasks seem almost overwhelming, and sometimes they are. As tenants, we need help. If we have money, a lawyer will help. If we have time, a David and Goliath struggle may save us. If we have friends, maybe they can influence the outcome or comfort us. If we have some cunning cleverness, maybe that will pull us through. But generally, the tenant will lose, and the landlord will win. The repairs will never be made, the promises never kept, the heat never enough. And if we complain, we'll get thrown out.

Organizing together with tenants in similar struggles will give us the strength and mutual support needed to overcome the obstacles. Organizing pits the wills of all the tenants in a particular building against the limited powers of the management: singly we are discrete particles and the landlord is a hammer, smashing us to powder. As a unified, collective structure we become as sintered metal, fused together and harder than hell to crack.

There is not a lot of case law for tenants' organizations in Illinois. Other states, notably New York, recognize the rights of tenants to organize. Legally, any group can organize for any lawful purpose, and in that regard tenants' unions are lawful. To be on the safe side, it is advisable to incorporate or register with the state (discussed later in this chapter).

A successful tenants' group needs several elements. It needs the dedication of a few people who can keep the spark lit when the going gets rough. It needs good organization, bylaws, and a hard-working group of officers. It needs to draw upon the experience of other tenant groups (there is no sense in reinventing the wheel in every six-flat and high-rise in the city). Most importantly, it needs to have clear-cut goals. There must be strong reasons for formation and these thoughts cannot later be lost or set aside.

Meetings have to be open to all residents and closed to all management employees. Meetings need to be somewhat regular between crises and frequent during crises. The membership should be kept informed of what is happening via newsletters and posters. An esprit needs to be generated and fostered.

Primarily the goal of a tenants' organization is to affirmatively and forcefully represent the tenants of the building to that building's management or ownership. In addition to using the power of people involved through picketing, petitioning, and publicity, the tenants' association also has the power of money, big money.

Tenants are afraid to organize because they believe the landlord will "get them." This has always been true. The landlord has been able to focus all of his resources on a particular tenant. The effect is obvious and overwhelming. One tenant cannot resist—he either shuts up or is forced out. An effective tenants' union prevents this from happening. The landlord can no longer deal with one tenant at a time (his venerable game of divide and conquer).

And what is the magic which protects the tenants? It is the unity of all the tenants to support each other through collective action. The ultimate, most powerful, fearful, and successful action is to strike. A rent strike, a rent withholding action. Mutiny of the bankbook!

It should be clearly understood and accepted that a tenants' organization is stronger than the landlord. Tenants have the power to put the landlord out of business and very quickly, and landlords know this. They have been playing a game of bully and blough for a long time. They have been waiting for the second shoe to fall. The jig is up, the cat is out of the bag. Just look at the facts.

1. The rents paid by tenants in your building every month amount to big money. Figure out how many occupied units there are in your building and multiply that by the average rent. If there are twenty-four apartments and each pays an average of $250.00 per month, that's $6000.00 a month. Between the mortgage, utility bills, and the office staff, your landlord needs most of that money to keep from going broke. Let's say your organization withholds the rents. How is he going to pay the mortgage? If you withhold for several months, what can he tell the bank? He needs your money.

2. Rent withholding per se is not a truly "legal" way of getting the landlord's undivided attention, but it works. Assume he is foolish enough to fight you, what can he do? Legally he can evict everybody who hasn't paid their rent. We've already established that

eviction can take two to three months. So we have now tied up
$18,000 (no sense in paying rents if he is going to evict everyone).
He will have to spend money to file eviction notices against each
person. He will have to hire a lawyer (as you will, of course), but the
cost of your lawyer is split among all the members, he has to bear
the entire burden himself. Each eviction case is separate, and for
each and every case you can request a jury trial. At a jury trial,
when the facts come out, he will have to lose. You and *Spring* v.
Little will win. When an entire building is withholding rents, there
must be some severe problems!!

3. Even if he did succeed in evicting individual rent withholders,
he would have to spend months trying to collect back rents (if they
were awarded). He probably would have to employ a collection
agency or pay for supplemental court actions which would chop
at least 25% from his rents and he probably can't afford those kinds
of fees.

4. If the landlord empties his building, he will have to fill it
again—and that will take many months. He cannot afford to lose
that kind of revenue for six to eight months.

5. If he tries to selectively evict people, the entire union continues to withhold rents. Retaliatory evictions will not save him. If
he later refuses to renew leases, the threat of another withholding
action is sufficient to stop that type of slimy practice.

Are you convinced? You have the power! It is the ultimate
weapon. The courts will take notice of what you're doing, and if
buildings across the entire city are doing this, you will have victory
just at the mere mention of rent strike. Your landlord knows what I
am talking about. Do not be afraid.

This is where we have been heading—organization. In numbers, we are very strong. With organization we can make ourselves
heard and felt. We can deal with the landlords, the city, and the
courts. We can regain our lost rights.

The landlord wants to deal only with one tenant at a time. He
can bully us, he can promise us, what happens is between a few
people. If the landlord doesn't keep his promises to one tenant,
what can that tenant really do? Nothing. We can move out if we
can break our lease, or we can put up and shut up. If the landlord
wants to throw the lowly tenant out, the landlord can do it. If he
wants to keep the security deposit or not pay the security deposit
interest, he can get away with it. The landlord uses the rents of
everybody in a building to hire lawyers to go after one person. As

long as the landlord can keep each of us separated from our fellow tenants, he has all the power and we have none.

If we organize, we are stronger than the landlord. One person complaining is a small voice in the void, but all the tenants, speaking in unison are a mighty shout. Our collective voice is powerful enough to crack the foundations of landlord dictatorship and bring down the walls of the lordly bastions. We can do it.

A tenants' organization is real democracy in action. It uses the politics of the street, the power of the people. In defending our tenant rights, the tenants' union is the first step. Organization must come before the courts, before the lawyers, before the official complaints.

A tenants' group can pool the resources of its membership. It can hire a good lawyer, it can bring pressure on the city to keep the landlord straight. It can make a strong impression on the judge when its membership is present in court. It can meet, en masse, with the landlord and pressure him into action. It has many eyes, ears, and hands. It can keep track of the landlord. A tenants' group can wield the ultimate weapon: the rents. A tenants' association withholding rents has an unprecedented amount of power over the landlord.

The landlords know that if the tenants ever rise up, the whole game of landlord/tenant relationships will have to have new rules. The landlords do not want a new game. They like the old one. Collect the rents, pay off the inspectors, throw out the complainers, let the buildings run down, make their profits. The game is too one-sided to be called a game, it is a farce. Well, the time is now.

When and How to Organize

The first step in organizing a tenants' union is to decide if there is a need for one. If there are general building problems or if the landlord is giving you, personally, a hard time, you can assume the need exists. Landlords do not single out particular tenants. If they are nasty to one, they'll be nasty to everyone if given the opportunity. Analyze your own situation. Go through your apartment and take an inventory of physical conditions. Look at your lease and evaluate some of the additional clauses. Think about the condition of the building: is it clean, the halls well lit? How about the hot water, the heat, the water pressure, the security system, the front and rear door locks? Do you have fire extinguishers, smoke detectors, screens, storm windows? Are there major promises made by the landlord but not kept? When something goes wrong does it get fixed right away? Are the rents being raised out of sight?

If you come up with a list of problems, you can bet everybody else can make a similar list. Are the conditions bad enough to merit a tenants' union? Well, that depends! Rent raises are one good reason to organize. The landlord sits in his office some place and squeezes the bank accounts of hundreds of families, but what is he giving us in return for high rents? We deserve what we are paying for. If conditions are not up to snuff, if rents are too high, if the landlord harasses us, we need the tenants' union.

The actual reasons for organizing vary: loss of heat or hot water, a policy of not returning security deposits, never delivering on pre-move-in promises for appliances or decorating, run-down conditions, failure to repair and maintain the building, the plumbing, the electricity, capricious evictions. You get the idea.

If you think you have the necessary ammunition, start the process. Go to as many occupants in your building as you can. Knock on the door and ask if you can speak to them about building conditions (or the rent raise, poor heat, or what have you). Tell them you are upset about this or that and ask them if they would like to get together with some of the other residents in the building to talk about the problem, or any other problems they might have. Mention a preset time and place (your apartment, early evening, during the week). If your building is too large to get to everybody, select people on each floor or section. Later, those who attend the first meeting can help recruit others living near them. You will need ten to fifteen residents to have a good foundation to kick off your organization. In small buildings you need all the tenants. It is possible to organize a six- or eight-flat. I have done it, and it works.

If your apartment will hold all the people you recruit, good. If you get an overflow crowd, meet in the lobby, or in a common area. If your building has meeting rooms, reserve or occupy one. During the summer, meet outside on the front steps or in the courtyard. This way you will also get the attention of others you have not contacted. If the management sees what is going on, that's just fine. This is only the start of the psychological warfare which will exist until everybody understands the purpose of your association.

If there are employees of the management present at your meeting, invite them to leave. This is your meeting, not your landlord's.

As a matter of common sense, your association should not have any employees of the building as members. No janitors, part-timers, or superintendents. The reasons are threefold: (1) being a member might jeopardize their jobs, (2) being an employee and a member is a conflict of interest which may result in attempts to deflect the goals of the group, and (3) being an employee could very well mean being a management spy.

The first meeting is a very informal discussion group. You, as organizer, can speak first. Introduce yourself and explain why you have called the meeting: to discuss common problems of tenants in the building. Tell the group that if enough interest exists, you would like to form a tenants' association.

You may wish to invite somebody from another tenants' group or community organization to discuss what a tenants' union is. After the briefest discussion about organizing, tell your story (how long you've been in the building, what problems you have, what the promises were). Tell the rest of your neighbors how manage-ment has treated you. Tell them what your rent is and how long your lease runs. Ask everybody else to introduce themselves and tell their stories. If there is a special crisis, compare notes on that crisis, but also find out what else is going on. You will be amazed to hear similar stories from most of the tenants—complaints about roaches, bad plumbing, flaking paint, unkept promises, and rent raises like yeast bread in the oven. If most people agree that some-thing has to be done, ORGANIZE.

The next step is to set up a committee to draw up a simple set of rules, to select a temporary chairman and secretary for the next meeting, to contact everybody in the building, and to propose a few alternatives for organization names. The reason for the com-mittee is to get a *group* of people involved. This helps share the burden of work and distributes the enthusiasm. Your organization must not be run from the top by a couple of "leaders," it needs grass roots participation and a sharing of the leadership roles. This is very important.

The organization committee should meet as soon as possible. The committee shouldn't be larger than seven people, so if you have more talent, divide the committee into sections. One should be responsible for rules and the name, the other for publicity and contacting the entire building. In a very small building, perhaps fewer folks can work up the bylaws and do the publicity. By taking care of these procedural goals at the beginning, you free your tenants' meetings for discussion of major goals, problems, and action.

At this first meeting, you should collect a couple of dollars from each person to cover the initial expenses of organizing. Money will be needed for printing up meeting notices, or duplicating the bylaws, or making a pamphlet or brochure outlining what problems exist or the how and why of a tenants' union. Later you will need to collect dues on a regular basis.

Call the second general meeting as quickly as possible. Have teams go from door to door in the building. Give residents a meeting notice and tell them that twenty-five people have gotten together to form a tenants' association. Invite everyone to come to the meeting, air their grievances, and join. If your management tries to stop this meeting, ignore them. Meet wherever you have to, or can. It is your Constitutional (First Amendment) right to have a meeting. Do it.

At the second meeting, explain to the newcomers what is going on. The chairman should lead the discussion. Find out what general things need to be done: stop the rent increases, get maintenance for the building, get the heat working, and soon. Draw up a list of emergency demands. Appoint a negotiating committee of three people to contact the management and ask what they are going to do about the emergency problems. Your committee must meet with someone for management who has the authority to make decisions. This will be either the owner or the "downtown" office manager, sometimes it is the resident manager. A tiny management company or a secretary fronting for the owner is not good enough.

It is also a good idea to distribute an apartment condition survey (see Appendix I). This survey will help each tenant make a list of the problems in his or her apartment. The group should appoint a "housing committee" to prepare a report. This report will be shown to the building inspector, the Housing Court judge, and your lawyer if you have to go to court.

At this second meeting you should also elect a permanent chairman, secretary, and treasurer. These people can serve for several months, but do determine length of tenure in advance. A board of directors can also be chosen. These directors represent the group as a whole and "oversee" the executive officers. This helps keep a balance of power away from some "elite" leadership. Choose a name and hear what else the organizing committee has to report. Dues should again be collected. The amount of dues depends upon how many people join the group and what your anticipated expenses are to be. Make a list of who joins and how much they pay. Later the permanent treasurer will issue receipts and membership cards. If you are going to hire a lawyer his retainer will be $500.00, so start saving money. Have the membership authorize the officers and directors to make plans and take actions as needed. A decision should be made on what form of official recognition you desire: incorporation or name registration. You need one or the other.

Incorporating Your Union

Incorporation or registration of the group is desirable. The total cost of incorporating under the laws of the State of Illinois is less than $60.00. The application papers will be mailed from the Secretary of State's office in the Loop—just call 793-3380 and ask for incorporation papers for not-for-profit groups. The forms are simple to fill out. You need to have officers, an address, and a purpose. Your category is Civic Improvement Association.

Or, you can register the union under the Assumed Names Act at the Cook County Recorder's office. The actual registration costs are less than $10.00 for listing the names of the officers plus $2.00 for each additional name in the union (*this* can be expensive). Your major cost is in placing an ad in the *Daily Law Reporter*. This is an "official" newspaper containing legal notices. The law requires you to publish your assumed name in the paper. The ad could run from $40.00 up, depending on the number of names you list. It may be sufficient just to list the officers—choose whichever is cheaper for you.

Also check with the Internal Revenue Service office at 219 South Dearborn for the federal tax exemption status requirements.

The advantage of some sort of official registration is to force the management company to accept your organization's existence when it comes to negotiating and signing agreements. If you incorporate, you may also protect yourself personally from a counterclaim or lawsuit. As a corporation you will have to submit a financial statement to the state and a tax report to the federal government, but the forms are simple and you do not need to be an accountant. Your corporation, by the way, can contract for work to be done on the building. The corporation can also buy equipment (washing machines for the building, water heaters, screens, fire extinguishers, etc.).

Whether you incorporate or simply register with the county, you will need to open two or three bank accounts. A checking account is needed for your operating funds: dues, special assessments, proceeds from fund raising. From this account you can pay your bills. Another account is a savings account to hold rent monies. Into this account can go regular monthly rents and withheld rents. Out of it comes rents paid to the management and funds paid to firms and suppliers whom the group has hired to make repairs to keep the building safe and within the building codes. If you will be making building repairs from the withheld rents, use a checking account, otherwise, an interest-bearing savings account will earn money for your group (perhaps enough to pay the lawyer's fees) while you are withholding the money. A savings and loan association "NOW" type checking account would be a good way to go.

You are also advised not to reveal the location of your rent-holding account to your landlord. If you are collecting rents and depositing them, buy a cashier's check to make the monthly rent payments. Keep the identity of your banks secret as long as you can. This may mean having two separate banks: one for the operations account and one for the rents. Our association would buy a cashier's check from a different bank every month to keep the landlord in the dark. (Don't forget that he may try to attach your account.)

The Functioning Union

The duties of the officers should be made part of the bylaws (see sample tenants' union bylaws in Appendix J). Before the third meeting each officer should do some homework. The chairman should call meetings of the executive committee and the board of directors to coordinate the work of recruiting members and publicizing the association. He or she should keep track of the housing committee and their survey and report. He will want to keep in touch with other tenants' groups, community organizations, and "advisors." It would be a good idea to shop around for a lawyer, too. Perhaps one should be invited to the third meeting.

The secretary will be busy getting papers from the state or the county. He will also prepare a report for the tenants to be distributed at the third meeting that contains the bylaws and any communications to and from the landlord. His research assignment will take him to a title search company or to City Hall to find out what the records show about ownership, taxes, titles, liens, and the price of your building. He may have to go to the Department of Housing and Urban Development (HUD) to get information. Perhaps a visit to the inspectors' floors at City Hall will gain information.

The treasurer will affiliate with a bank, get the necessary papers and endorsement cards filled out and signed, obtain bankbooks, and establish a set of accounting books. He may shop around for an accountant who will donate services to bless the books. The treasurer will purchase money receipts books for each of his accounts, and get membership cards printed.

The real work of the tenants' group will start with the third meeting. The committee appointed to meet with the management to discuss the emergency problems will have a report. The treasurer will have money in the bank, the housing committee will have a report on the general conditions of the building, and the secretary should have received the incorporation application from the state and a complete report on building ownership and financing.

If my guess is correct, the negotiating committee will report that: (1) management refused to meet with the committee, (2) management set up a meeting for the future, (3) the committee met with a lower-echelon management type who said he would "see what he could do," or, (4) they met with the landlord who promised to look into the situation and take care of things "as soon as possible." In short, my guess is that nothing was achieved.

Now is the time for action. Draw up a formal list of complaints, requests, and demands. The list should be in the form of a letter to the landlord. It should list emergency repairs, general repairs, lease changes, grievances, a recognition request for the association, a no-retaliation warning, and a collective bargaining rights request. Under repairs, each apartment should be listed detailing specific problems—what in which room needs what. The same is true for the general building, be very specific. (See the examples in Appendix L.) You should request an immediate written response from the landlord, and his response must have *completion dates for each entry on the list*. You should also request a meeting for the purpose of negotiating your collective bargaining agreement. You should demand a general meeting between all tenants and the landlord. This meeting can take place anywhere *except* the landlord's office. The letter should be signed by the officers and contain a list of the names of your membership. The secretary should prepare the letter and have the board of directors approve it before it is transmitted. A copy of the letter should be sent to each tenant in the building.

The type of organizing done so far, and the work involved may seem detailed, but you are fighting a tough battle. You must start from a firm basis and you must be strong. You have to be legally solid, and you have to have the support of the tenants. You have to know the facts. When your association can demonstrate it has the ability and the guts to fight for what is right, you will reinforce the attitudes of the membership and be able to recruit more people into the group. Remember, you are in for the long run and early preparation is important.

Your next step is to hold another negotiating meeting with the landlord and have a general meeting between the tenants and the landlord. Call a general membership meeting as soon as you have a negotiating committee report. If the report is that management is still unresponsive, press for a building meeting with the landlord. The landlord will usually want to come to "calm things down." These meetings demonstrate to management that the tenants are unhappy and mean business. The general consensus is that tenants feel a lot of solidarity when such a meeting is held. They get to gripe at the landlord and put him on the spot. Landlords seldom deliver on their promises at such meetings, unless a signed agreement is made during the meeting, but be prepared with your bargaining agreement and the list of needed repairs with completion dates, just in case.

If the landlord refuses to come to a meeting, there are some methods you can employ to encourage him to cooperate. One is to set up a picket line in front of the building. It is perfectly legal, however, you must not block the sidewalk or prevent people from entering or leaving. You can pass out literature, but you are required to pick up any literature that people discard. You can sing or chant slogans as long as they do not disturb the neighbors. If the police come, be quiet, march in a single file on the sidewalk, and smile. You will not be arrested if you are orderly and obey the law. You do not need a permit.

The picket signs should contain only true statements of fact.

"Our XXX Management Co. building has roaches." "XXX Management Company will not negotiate with our tenants' union." "XXX Tower mistreats tenants." "Our Landlord, XXX, permits building code violations to exist in the building." "We have no heat." These statements are not libelous because they contain the truth. Don't, however, call the landlord a slumlord or an s.o.b.

If the landlord won't come to you, go to him. Find out where he lives and visit his home on Saturday morning when the rest of the neighborhood can see what is going on. Leaflet his neighbors, or simply knock on their doors and tell them what conditions are like where you live. Explain that the landlord, their neighbor, won't fix things. Do not slander the man, just tell the truth. Try the same thing at his church, his club, even his grocery store. He may get a court order against you to stop, but by that time you will have made your point.

You can also file complaints with the licensing officials at the county and state levels. Check to see if the landlord (if he is a company or corporation) is registered with the proper bureaus. All persons doing business in any name other than their own name must be registered with the Cook County Clerk under the Assumed Names Act. Call the Clerk's office to verify registration. If *Inc., Corporation,* or *Limited* follows a name, call the Illinois Secretary of State's Office to determine whether the company is legally registered. If your landlord is a real estate broker (or his company is engaged in real estate sales) call the Illinois Department of Registration and Education to verify whether he is properly licensed to be in the business. When you find discrepancies, notify the Illinois Attorney General's office. For a landlord who is a registered broker, contact the Department of Registration and tell them you wish to file charges against the landlord for malpractice or malfeasance. Don't bother to call the City Revenue Bureau (the department that issues retail licenses)—the city requires licenses for balloon peddlers but not for landlords.

Of course there is always the press. Call every newspaper in town and tell them about your organization. Tell them how the landlord allows code violations to exist and refuses either to fix them or meet with your membership. Tell them when you will be picketing or what happened when you did picket. In this day of rising tenant consciousness what you are doing is big news. Try it. If you picket on the weekend tell the TV stations—they can always use filler on Saturdays and Sundays. Contact other tenants' groups and ask for their support. They may send picketers around, or perhaps make a few phone calls on their own to the city, the papers, or even your landlord.

Try a phone-in where everybody calls the management offices on Tuesday to demand repairs be made. And they keep on calling every day until the work gets done or the landlord meets with you. Have everybody make appointments to see the landlord. Insist that the appointment be immediate and after work—it is your right and his obligation. Set up call-in and visit-in days for the whole building. You'll stop all other work in the office or drive the landlord away from the building. In either case, you'll make your point. By this time everything is on the table. The landlord is not really responding, and the tenants are united and ready for a fight. The fat is in the fire.

Declaring War

There are many things your association can do to pressure the landlord into cooperation. The group can go the city inspector route: contact the Complaint Bureau of the building department; send a copy of your letter to the mayor's office and the chairman of the Building Commission (see Appendix B); contact your aldermanic office and request that they inspect your building; send a copy of your complaint letter to the alderman.

Become a funnel for the rents of your membership. Rent collection is tricky, so be ready to consult your lawyer. Your treasurer must issue a rent receipt as each member turns over the rent to the association. Cash is undesirable because it is difficult to handle. Checks or money orders should be employed instead. There are several ways to handle the rents but the easiest is to have the tenants make their checks payable to the management company. Your treasurer collects these checks, on behalf of your membership, for transmittal to the landlord. When the treasurer presents the checks to the management, request a written receipt for each rent check. The purpose of this type of collection is to show management that the union has the power to collect money from the tenants, and indicates the relative strength of the group.

Far more desirable is to have the tenants make their checks payable to the tenants' association. The treasurer, in turn, endorses them over to the landlord. If money is collected far enough in advance these checks could be deposited in the union bank account and a single check issued to the landlord from the union. Again, individual receipts from the landlord are required. The advance collection of rents for deposit is hard, so endorsing the checks over to the landlord is much easier to handle.

If the landlord still is uncooperative even after you have proven your association's power to collect the rents you will have to plan for rent withholding. Rent checks will be issued in favor of the association and the association will collect and deposit these checks in that well protected second bank account.

IT IS IMPERATIVE IN ANY RENT WITHHOLDING ACTION THAT THE MONEY BE COLLECTED AND SET ASIDE. It is not good enough that everybody withholds the rent money. There are two important reasons. In the first place if the tenants' association actually has control over the funds, the members know that they have real power and are accomplishing something important. The association can demonstrate power over the landlord and the association also knows who is supporting the action and who is not. The second reason to make sure the money is actually collected is that eventually it will have to be paid to somebody. The association may be ordered to pay a bank, a receiver, or the landlord the back rents, or there may be creditors who have performed services for the association who are to be paid out of the rent account. If the association appears in court and cannot produce the rent monies, its whole case could be lost. The biggest crises of rent withholding actions come when everybody is supposed to come up with four months back rents and all those people, instead of socking it away or paying the union, spent it!!! You do not need that kind of publicity and that kind of defeat. Please, collect the rents and *keep them safe* until they are needed.

A word of warning about collecting checks in the name of the union, either for withholding or simply for passing along to the landlord. Be sure there are sufficient funds in the union account to cover if one of your member's checks bounces. Your landlord may come back to you with eviction notices—be prepared. It is not the purpose of the association to pay for people who cannot pay their rents, and this is an unfair burden on the group that could destroy it. Please explain this to your membership. (If money is a problem, place that member in touch with a community organization who can help them find a cheaper place or a job.)

The landlord is obligated to take the tenant association checks for payment. He cannot refuse the source of the money because anybody can pay the rent for anybody. If the landlord refuses the rents on this basis, tell him that his refusal removes any further obligation from the people attempting to pay the rent for that month, and that the month is thereby free. He knows it already, it's the law. But for him to see thousands of dollars of rent money made out to the tenants' association is frightening. Anytime the membership votes the action, rents can just as easily be withheld and he knows that too.

It may be, by this time, that the landlord understands it will be better to cooperate than face a full-fledged rent strike. He will have inspectors all over the building; the tenants will show them every violation they can find; the alderman's office is keeping track; a large group of tenants is ready to go into housing court in a few months if things are not repaired. The association has gotten be-

tween the master and his money. He may have even read this book
and discovered to his horror what can happen to him if he doesn't
shape up, now.

While all this is going on, your union is holding meetings, sending out reports and flyers, collecting rents, and talking to everybody in the building.

Your goals are recognition, a collective rights agreement, repairs, maintenance, fair rents, security deposit refunds, heat, security devices, followup of the landlord's promises to individual
tenants, and prevention of retaliatory actions against union members.

What other work can or should your association be doing regarding the landlord? Primarily finding out as much about him
and his operations as possible. Do a detailed estimate of his rent
collections. Find out if he can afford to do what you are demand-
ing he do to repair or maintain the building. Learn where he has
loans on the building. Try to determine what his monthly costs are
including the number of employees and costs for utilities. Someone in your union will have to become an expert on these things
(see Chapter 14). Also make a list of his major suppliers and a list of
his other buildings.

You need to know these things for several reasons. One is to be
able to contact his creditors and his banks to "inform"
them that dangerous and illegal conditions exist in the building.
The banks will be particularly interested. Send them copies of
your complaint letters. Banks holding mortgages or construction
loans on the building will want to know what is happening to their
investment. The banks may also hold loans or loan applications
on other buildings run by your landlord. They are going to think
more carefully about these other loans on the basis of your actions. Another reason to find out who the bankers are is to let them
know about your rent withholding action. They may want to get
"involved" in cleaning up the problems. Depending on strategies,
some day you might take the building in receivership and will
want to be on good terms with the banks. If your landlord is
financially "brittle" or stops paying his bills, your association may
have to make payments to the utilities or the bank to prevent the
building from being shut down.

The landlord's other suppliers and creditors probably don't
care what your problems are, but they will be annoyed if you call

and tell them they are doing business with a man or company who is mistreating residents. (Do not use the word *slumlord* unless you can prove it or can pay a hefty libel or slander suit award.) Their annoyance will be passed along to the landlord. The landlord will not like the world to know he has problems.

If you go into rent withholding, be sure and inform all creditors and suppliers. They may start putting a credit squeeze on the landlord. They may ask him for cash payments or insist he bring his accounts up to current. They are not about to lose money because the landlord doesn't know how to manage his building. If you are withholding rents, and work or supplies are needed, you can always deal directly with these people (although you might have to pay cash on delivery).

It might also be helpful to know the names of workmen and former employees. These folks can become resources of information if you have to start "unburying bodies" for a court case.

If you have succeeded in starting a tenants' union in your building you can succeed in helping people in your landlord's other buildings do the same. When the landlord is small and your building is small, you can always use more bodies and more leverage. Remember, rent monies are real cash. If his cash supply from 50% of all tenants in ten buildings is cut off, he is in deep trouble.

Complete your research on the addresses of the other buildings your landlord runs or owns. Someone in your group has to become a master sleuth. Talking to workmen is helpful, also talking to the office employees. You might have a "shill," someone unknown to the management company, come looking for an apartment. If the landlord shows him several buildings, those buildings are the start of more tenants' associations. Carefully make contacts in those other buildings and see if you can organize them. Such branching strengthens the large unions' power, but it is important to let each small union or association recruit its own members and run itself.

If all else fails, go to court. Your lawyer may advise you to take the initiative and not try to withhold rents without court permission. When you have the entire building backing up a lawsuit, you have a chance of success. Your lawyer should be able to prove the code violations, gain restraining orders allowing the court to supervise rent collections, force the landlord to make repairs, and win the lawyer's fees from the landlord. Under such court actions you should also get protection against retaliatory acts. In the course of the proceedings, you must keep the pressure on the landlord to recognize your union.

The enforcement of the court order is really up to your union. It will be your lawyer who will tell the judge about the landlord's progress, or lack of it. If the landlord is not cooperating either in repairs or in negotiations, you can sue him for a reduction of rents and damages caused by his negligence or stupidity. You might also sue for receivership. These suits are discussed in Chapter 17.

Because your group represents many people you can share the costs of such suits and the weight of your numbers has to make its point to the judges and the juries. The fact is that your landlord does not have the time or energy to keep up this type of battle. Even the largest of the management companies in the city cannot sustain this type of onslaught. For one thing, the publicity is killing. No one wants to move into any building where the management's reputation is bad. With large management companies, when one of their buildings gets into court or the papers, the other buildings may very well follow suit. For them, it makes good sense to settle quietly and fast.

Watch Your Back

A few bits of general advice: Keep constant contact with all tenants. Report any type of harassment to everybody and your lawyer. Start a master file of letters, notices, and memoranda. Ask all tenants to keep notes of what they hear and see, they will be needed for court cases. Hold meetings frequently to keep up the group spirit. Keep close follow-ups on your lawyer, the city, and the landlord. Do not let your lawyer drag his feet.

If retaliations start, give warning to the management to cease or the building will go on a rent strike. Remember, you have the upper hand. It is cheaper for a landlord to be a nice guy than to be stubborn and lose the building.

Compromise where it is fair, and fight like hell when it isn't. Your ultimate goal is a negotiated lease based upon a collective bargaining agreement. The reason you need this agreement is to protect yourself from the type of rip-off management practices that caused the trouble in the first place. You must keep the landlord in line. It is a jungle out there, and if you don't keep walking the path, the weeds will grow up again and swallow you.

A few bits of warning: There are bad tenants as well as bad landlords. Your association should attempt to keep its membership in line. There are legitimate reasons for evictions. Evaluate each case on its merits. Fighting, property destruction, filth, hard drugs, these things are not the cause célèbre of your union. If you get involved in these types of diversions, the whole credibility of the organization will be lost. It is also a very good idea NOT to get involved in political campaigns unless your candidate is a champion of tenants' rights. Your goal is to protect the tenants from rip-offs, not save society.

Additional Union Advantages

Tenants' associations also fill other roles for their membership. You can start a food buying (co-op) service, or organize baby-sitting clubs. You can charter a bus or a plane. As residents of a building learn to know and like each other, a real feeling of community exists. People actually help each other. When suspicious strangers are in the building, they are watched. If a stranger enters an apartment and a neighbor notices, the cops will be called. In a non-association building, no one does anything because no one knows anybody or cares.

Your tenants' group can also sponsor parties, sports teams, gardens and clean-up groups. You can buy and operate a co-op laundry facility. There are dozens of important and useful "other" things. When a tenants' association operates in a building the nasty parts of city life are reduced. It really does seem a little more like "home." This is true.

You, Too, Can Succeed

Do tenants' unions really work? Yes. In New York City the tenants of an apartment complex called Coop City (the name had to do with the financing of the building) struck to the tune of 30 million dollars. They were protesting rent raises and uncompleted construction. The strike lasted 2 years and the tenants won!! In Chicago, a high-rise apartment on South Lake Shore Drive was organized after the tenants complained that the place was going to hell. About one-third of the 150 tenants withheld rents for four months. The union held close to $40,000. The owner of the place was hurting for mortgage payments. He did not evict. He signed a long-term collective bargaining agreement, agreed to a grievance procedure, replaced the building manager, and promised to work with the residents to solve a number of other problems.

All the tenants in a six-flat on the North Side formed an association to force the landlord to complete construction on their re-converted six-flat. It took a rent slow down (paying the rent on the last day of a five-day notice), three trips to housing court, and three lawsuits. The landlord knuckled under and the construction was completed. On the South Side, a tenants' union organized by a community organization forced a group of buildings into the courts. When the landlord failed to make repairs, the union was granted receivership of the buildings, and now owns them.

On the North Side, a tenants' organization was formed in a fourteen-flat. The landlord failed to come around. They went to court, gained receivership, and then ownership of the building. On the West Side a twenty-four-flat organized and went on a rent strike. The landlord took union members to eviction court. No rents were paid for eight months. The landlord refused to make repairs. The court, after the eighth month, ordered the building closed and forgave the rents. The tenants were able to keep almost two thousand dollars each in unpaid back monies. Even when a building is closed, or the union does not succeed completely, there are still victories.

If you think about the real alternatives with and without the organization, you can see how a tenants' association opens up the choices. Without a union you have to take it or leave it.

Have a lawyer available for advice BUT avoid court and *be prepared to ignore your lawyer's advice as it relates to rent strikes*. What is legal and what is effective sometimes are far different things: you want results, not shiny halos.

A tenants' association is our only strength.

APPENDIXES

APPENDIX A

Community Organizations: Addresses and Phone Numbers

There are hundreds of community groups and organizations in Chicago. I have culled what seems to be the most important groups into this list. Names change and the groups move to new addresses and get new phone numbers. Such directories of community groups tend to fall out of date, so use this list as a starting point. Choose which groups to contact on the basis of their names and their locations.

Alternatives, Inc.
1126 West Granville
Chicago, Illinois 60660
973-5400

American Indian Center, Inc.
1630 West Wilson
Chicago, Illinois 60640
275-5871

ASPIRA of Illinois
2316 West North Avenue
Chicago, Illinois 60647
772-8866

ASPIRA of Illinois
3432 West Diversey
Chicago, Illinois 60647
252-0970

Back of the Yards Neighborhood
    Council
1751 West 47th Street
Chicago, Illinois 60609
523-4416

Bickerdike Redevelopment Corp.
535 North Ashland Avenue
Chicago, Illinois 60622
666-2575

Brainerd Community Action
    Committee
9421 South Ashland Avenue
Chicago, Illinois 60620
881-3793

Chicago Housing Tenants
    Association
Tranquility Memorial Community
    Center
539 West North Avenue
Chicago, Illinois 60610
337-0218

Chinese American Civic Council of
    Chicago
2249 South Wentworth Avenue
Second Floor
Chicago, Illinois 60616
CA5-0234

Christian Action Ministry (CAM)
3932 West Madison Street
Chicago, Illinois 60624
826-9300

Coalition Against Rent
  Exploitation
Tranquility Memorial Community
  Center
539 West North Avenue
Chicago, Illinois 60610
337-0218

Community of United People
  (COUP)
1019 South May Street
Chicago, Illinois 60607
666-5683

Community Renewal Society
111 North Wabash
Chicago, Illinois 60602
236-4830

Community 21 Planning Office
  East Humboldt Park
1400 West Chestnut
Chicago, Illinois 60622
486-8445

Edgewater Community Council
1112 West Bryn Mawr
Chicago, Illinois 60660
334-5609

El Centro de la Causa (Latin
  American Youth Center, Inc.)
731 West 17th Street
Chicago, Illinois 60616
243-8508

Fair Housing Center
116 South Michigan
Chicago, Illinois 60603
641-1035

Fifth City Community
  Organization
3350 West Jackson
Chicago, Illinois 60624
(No phone number available)

Fifth City 40 Block Association
Institute of Cultural Affairs
410 South Trumbul
Chicago, Illinois 60624
722-3344

Garfield Organization
Suite 708
4010 West Madison
Chicago, Illinois 60624
533-5900

Greater Lawndale Conservation
  Commission (GLCC)
3142 West Roosevelt Road
Chicago, Illinois 60612
826-3030

Greater Roseland Organization
  (GRO)
140 East 113th Street
Chicago, Illinois 60628
995-1172
995-1369

Heart of Chicago Community
  Council
2032 West Cermak Road
Chicago, Illinois 60608
VI7-6679

Hull House Uptown Center
Housing Resource Center
4520 North Beacon
Chicago, Illinois 60640
561-3500

Hull House Association
3179 North Broadway
Chicago, Illinois 60657
549-1631

Hyde Park-Kenwood Community
Conference
1400 East 53rd Street
Chicago, Illinois 60615
288-8343

Illinois Public Action Council
59 East Van Buren
Suite 2600
Chicago, Illinois 60605
427-6262

Intercommunal Survival Center
1222 West Wilson
Chicago, Illinois 60640
769-2087

Institute of Urban Life
14 East Chestnut
Chicago, Illinois 60611
787-7525

Kenwood-Oakland Community
Organization (KOCO)
4618 South Lake Park
Chicago, Illinois 60653
548-7500

Korean American Community
Services
3435 North Sheffield
Chicago, Illinois 60657
248-6226

Lakeview Citizens Council (LVCC)
3410 North Sheffield Avenue
Chicago, Illinois 60657
472-4050

Latin American Coalition of
Lakeview
3410 North Sheffield
Chicago, Illinois 60657
472-6048

Lawndale Association for Social
Health (LASH)
4011 West Ogden Avenue
Chicago, Illinois 60623
277-1740

Lawndale Peoples Planning and
Action Conference (LPPAC)
3324 West Roosevelt Road
Chicago, Illinois 60624
826-8180

Leadership Council for
Metropolitan Open
Communities
407 South Dearborn
Chicago, Illinois 60605
341-1470

League of United Latin American
Citizens Educational Service
Center (LULAC)
4054½ West 26th Street
Chicago, Illinois 60624
522-4400

Lincoln Park Conservation
Association (LPCA)
2373 North Lincoln
Chicago, Illinois 60614
477-5100

Little Village Community Council
Little Village Chamber of
Commerce
3610 West 26th Street
Chicago, Illinois 60623
762-3468

Logan Square Neighborhood
Association
2641 North Milwaukee Avenue
Chicago, Illinois 60647
384-4370

Metropolitan Area Housing
Alliance (MAHA)
1123 West Washington Boulevard
Chicago, Illinois 60607
243-5850

Mexican Community Committee
of South Chicago
2939 East 91st Street
Chicago, Illinois 60617
978-6441

Midwest Community Council
9 South Kedzie Avenue
Chicago, Illinois 60612
826-2244

Native American Committee (NAC)
4546 North Hermitage
Chicago, Illinois 60640
728-1477

Native American Outpost
1368 West Wilson
Chicago, Illinois 60640
271-1900

Near Westside Community
Committee
628 South Racine
Chicago, Illinois 60607
666-8444

Near Northwest Civic Committee
1329 West Grand Avenue
Chicago, Illinois 60622
243-2342

North Austin Council
5758 West Potomac Avenue
Chicago, Illinois 60651
379-7822

Northeast Austin Organization
(NAC)
5057 West North Avenue
Chicago, Illinois 60639
745-0294

North River Commission
3440 West Lawrence
Chicago, Illinois 60625
463-5420

North State—Astor—Lake Shore
Drive Association
1500 North Lake Shore Drive
Chicago, Illinois 60610
943-5128

Northwest Community Council
2905 West Sherwin
Chicago, Illinois 60645
274-3025

Northwest Austin Council
5758 West Potomac
Chicago, Illinois 60651
379-7822

Northwest Community
Organization (NCO)
1109 North Ashland Avenue
Chicago, Illinois 60622
276-0211

Organization for a Better Austin
(OBA)
5903 West Fulton
Chicago, Illinois 60644
287-2702

Organization of New City
843 West Garfield Boulevard
Chicago, Illinois 60621
487-6318

Organization of the North East
(ONE)
1105 West Lawrence
Chicago, Illinois 60640
769-3232

Park Manor Neighbors
Community Council
7105 South King Drive
Chicago, Illinois 60619
783-2850

Pilsen Neighbors Community
Council
1521 West 18th Street
Chicago, Illinois 60608
666-2663

Puerto Rican Organization for
Political Action (PROPA)
Allies for a Better Community
(ABC)
1233 North Ashland
Chicago, Illinois 60622
252-7140

Pyramidwest
3324 West Roosevelt Road
Chicago, Illinois 60624
533-1016

Ravenswood Conservation
Commission
2326 West Leland Avenue
Chicago, Illinois 60625
784-1100

Rogers Park Committee Against
Unemployment and Inflation
1545 West Morse
Chicago, Illinois 60626
465-8931

Rogers Park Community Council
1725 West Lunt
Chicago, Illinois 60626
764-4326

South East Chicago Commission
(SECO)
1400 East 53rd Street
Chicago, Illinois 60615
324-6926

Southeast Community
Organization (SECO)
1610 East 85th Place
Chicago, Illinois 60617
721-2363

South Side Planning Board
77 South Wacker
Chicago, Illinois 60606
225-9776

South Shore Commission
7134 South Jeffery
Chicago, Illinois 60649
667-0790

Southtown Planning Association
811 West 63rd Street
Chicago, Illinois 60621
876-7474

Southwest Community Action
Coalition (SCAC)
1931 West 87th Street
Chicago, Illinois 60620
239-6226

Southwest Community Congress
3506 West 63rd Place
Chicago, Illinois 60629
436-6150

The United Friends (TUF)
1402 North Sedgwick
Chicago, Illinois 60610
337-1310

The Woodlawn Organization
(TWO)
1180 East 63rd Street
Chicago, Illinois 60637
288-5840

United Neighbors in Action (UNA)
4005 West North Avenue
Chicago, Illinois 60639
227-8550

Uptown Chicago Commission
4753 North Broadway
Chicago, Illinois 60640
561-3978

Uptown Peoples Action Program
  (UPAC)
4715 North Broadway
Chicago, Illinois 60613
878-0668

Voice of the People
4927 North Kenmore
Chicago, Illinois 60640
769-2849

Westside Association for
  Community Action
3210 West Arthington
Chicago, Illinois 60624
826-0227

The preceding information is compiled from the following sources:
Community Renewal Society, Community Development Division,
111 North Wabash Ave., Chicago, IL 60602
Directory of Community Organizations. Published by Institute of Urban Life,
14 E. Chestnut, Chicago, IL 60611

APPENDIX B

Helpful Addresses and Phone Numbers for Government Agencies and Consumer Groups

In addition to community groups, there are a wealth of other agencies, public and private, that can be helpful. They range from the city of Chicago to the press. The numbers listed may, alas, change over time, so check the phone book. A word or two of advice: be persistent, particularly when dealing with the city of Chicago. They may try to put you off. You must keep trying, even if you are transferred 10 times, keep at it! Remember also that the phone directory and the Redbook "B" Buyer's Guide (the Yellow Pages) are your best friends. Use them to find additional sources and also Appendix A's community organizations listing to locate other assistance.

City of Chicago Numbers (Main number is 744-4000)

To find out the name of your alderman:
Citizens Information Service
67 East Madison
Chicago, Illinois 60603

To contact your alderman:
Chicago City Hall
121 North LaSalle
Chicago, Illinois 60673
744-6800

Assistant Corporation Counsel
City Hall Room 610
121 North LaSalle
Chicago, Illinois 60673
744-3945 General Information
744-6944 Assistant counsels prosecuting housing cases

744-3408 Housing Court scheduling, docket numbers and status reports

Board of Health
Civic Center
Randolph and Clark
Chicago, Illinois 60673
744-4338 Lead paint reports

To verify issuance of proper building permits:
Building Permit Files
City Hall
121 North LaSalle
Chicago, Illinois 60673
744-3416

Building Department Main
   Number for Complaints
Room 803, City Hall
121 North LaSalle
Chicago, Illinois 60673
744-3420

Building Department Complaint
   Bureau
Administrator-in-Charge
Room 803, City Hall
121 North LaSalle
Chicago, Illinois 60673
744-3484

Building Department
   Commissioner of Buildings
Room 900, City Hall
121 North La Salle
Chicago, Illinois 60673
744-3400

Building Department Code
   Enforcement Bureau
Area Supervisors
City Hall
121 North LaSalle
Chicago, Illinois 60673
744-3405 Ask for Area Supervisor
   for your address

Building Department Information
   Center and Special Complaints
Room 803, City Hall
121 North LaSalle
Chicago, Illinois 60673
744-3431

Chicago Housing Authority (public
   housing)
22 West Madison
Chicago, Illinois 60602
791-8426

Commission on Human Relations
640 North LaSalle
Chicago, Illinois 60610
744-4111

Compliance Board
City Hall
121 North LaSalle
Chicago, Illinois 60673
744-3407 Schedules, hearings and
   results

Consumer Fraud Commission
City Hall
121 North LaSalle
Chicago, Illinois 60673
744-4901

Department of Human Services
Third Floor
640 North LaSalle
Chicago, Illinois 60610
744-4045 General information and
   locations of community service
   centers
744-8111 Commissioner's office

Fire Department Inspector
Fire Prevention Bureau
55 West Illinois
Chicago, Illinois 60610
744-4762

Mayor's Office of Inquiry and
   Information
First Floor, City Hall
121 North LaSalle
Chicago, Illinois 60673
744-5000 To report lack of heat or
   other essential services

Rent (Housing) Complaint Bureau
Room 350
640 North LaSalle
Chicago, Illinois 60610
744-6719 and 744-7320

Water and Sewer Department
Complaints Bureau
1000 East Ohio (Olive Park)
Chicago, Illinois 60611
744-7038 Water
744-7055 Sewer

Cook County

Clerk of the Cook County Courts
Room 601
Civic Center, Randolph and Clark
Chicago, Illinois 60602
General information number:
443-8100
(Return dates, trial dates)

Cook County Assessor
118 South Clark Street
Chicago, Illinois 60602
443-5500
(Tax information about building)

Cook County Board
Office of Inquiry and Information
Civic Center, Randolph and Clark
Chicago, Illinois 60602
443-3390

Cook County Sheriff
Civic Center, Randolph and Clark
Chicago, Illinois 60602
General information number:
443-6426
(Service of summons and
complaints)
Eviction information: 443-8195

Cook County State's Attorney
Civic Center, Randolph and Clark
Chicago, Illinois 60602
General number: 443-5500
Fraud and Complaints
Department: 443-8425

Renter's Court Information
Room 602
Civic Center, Randolph and Clark
Chicago, Illinois 60602
443-8166

Small Claims Court
Room 1308
Civic Center, Randolph and Clark
Chicago, Illinois 60602
443-7868 (For Pro Se Clerk, Room
602)

State of Illinois

Attorney General
160 North LaSalle
Chicago, Illinois 60601
General information number:
793-2512
Consumer Protection Bureau:
793-3580
Fraud and Complaint Division:
443-8425

**Department of Registration and
Education**
160 North LaSalle
Chicago, Illinois 60601
341-9810

Illinois Commerce Commission
Consumer Protection Division
160 North LaSalle
Chicago, Illinois 60602
793-2887
(For illegal utility cutoffs and
disputed utility bills)

**Illinois Human Relations
Commission**
160 North LaSalle
Chicago, Illinois 60601
793-2893

Office of the Governor of Illinois
160 North LaSalle
Chicago, Illinois 60601
Governor's office: 793-2121
"Action" office: 793-3433
Consumer Advocate: 793-2374

Secretary of State
Corporation Division
188 West Randolph
Chicago, Illinois 60601
793-3380
(To apply for not-for-profit
   incorporation for tenants)

Legal Help and Referrals

Chicago Bar Association
Lawyer Referral Service
29 South LaSalle
Chicago, Illinois 60603
782-7348

Chicago Council of Lawyers
53 West Jackson
Chicago, Illinois 60604
472-0710

Chicago Volunteer Legal Service
19 South LaSalle
Chicago, Illinois 60603
332-1624

Legal Aid Bureau
64 East Jackson
Chicago, Illinois 60604
922-5625

Legal Assistance Foundation of
   Chicago
343 South Dearborn (main
   location)
Chicago, Illinois 60604
341-1070
(Generally only for those who are
   on some sort of public aid or
   could otherwise not afford to
   hire a lawyer)

"Action Line" Services

Chicago Tribune
"Action Line"
435 North Michigan

Chicago, Illinois 60611
(Send letter regarding problem
   plus two stamped envelopes,
   one addressed back to you, the
   other addressed in care of the
   landlord or management
   company you are complaining
   about.)

Chicago Sun-Times
"Action Time"
401 North Wabash
Chicago, Illinois 60611
(Send letter plus two stamped
   envelopes as required by
   Tribune.)

WBBM Radio
"Direct Line"
630 North McClurg Court
Chicago, Illinois 60611
787-3000
(Call between 9:30 A.M. and 12:30
   P.M. Monday through Thursday)

WLS Television
Action 7/Seven On Your Side
190 North State Street
Chicago, Illinois 60601
263-0800

Other Press Services

Associated Press
188 West Randolph
Chicago, Illinois 60601
781-0500

Chicago City News Bureau
188 West Randolph
Chicago, Illinois 60601
782-8100

The Chicago Defender
2400 South Michigan Avenue
Chicago, Illinois 60616
CA5-2400

Chicago Reader
Box 11101
Chicago, Illinois 60611
828-0350

Walter Jacobson
WBBM Television
630 North McClurg Court
Chicago, Illinois 60611
WH4-6000

Keep Strong Magazine
1222 West Wilson
Chicago, Illinois 60640
769-2087

Mike Royko
Chicago Sun-Times
401 North Wabash
Chicago, Illinois
321-3000

WTTW Television
News Center
233 North Michigan
Chicago, Illinois 60601
565-0850

United Press International
360 North Michigan
Chicago, Illinois 60601
781-1600

A Few More Generally Helpful Numbers

Chicago Public Library
425 North Michigan Avenue
Chicago, Illinois 60611
Information Center: 269-2800
(Instant over-the-phone reference
    service)

Chicago Transit Authority (CTA)
Merchandise Mart
Merchandise Mart Plaza and Wells
    Street
Chicago, Illinois 60654

Schedules and routes: 836-7000

The Chicago Tribune Map of the City
Tribune Public Service Office
435 North Michigan Avenue
Chicago, Illinois 60611
($1.50 at the desk; $1.85 by third
    class mail; $2.10 by first class
    mail)

Commonwealth Edison Company
1 First National Plaza
Madison and Clark Streets
Chicago, Illinois 60690
Service North: 588-9000
Central, Loop, and West: 379-5000
South: 382-1100
Corporate offices: 294-4321

Illinois Bell Telephone
225 West Randolph
Chicago, Illinois 60606
New service: 372-9100
Existing service changes: (see front
    of White Pages for correct
    number)
Corporate offices: 727-9411
Name and number service:
    796-9600

City of Chicago Municipal
    Reference Library Service
City Hall,
Room 1004
121 North LaSalle
Chicago, Illinois 60602
744-4992
(Questions about city ordinances,
    etc.)

Peoples' Gas, Light, and Coke
    Company
122 South Michigan Avenue
Chicago, Illinois 60603
Customer service: 431-7000
Gas leaks and emergencies:
    431-7001
Corporate offices: 431-4000

APPENDIX C

Landlord's Application and Warranty of Habitability Statement

1. Name of management company (lessor)_____
2. Address_____
3. Phone number_____
4. Name of owner_____
5. Building and apartment_____
6. Name and number of resident manager_____
7. Owner of building and address_____
   _____
8. Date of promised apartment availability_____
9. Monthly rents_____
10. Name of apartment applicant (lessee)_____
    _____
11. Address and phone number_____
    _____
12. Type and registration number of city license_____
13. Type and registration number of state license_____
14. Are there any conditions in the building that require repairs (roof, new plumbing, or wiring, replacement of the rear porch, new heating system, etc.)?   Yes   No   Explain_____
    _____
15. Is the building involved in housing court or building code compliance hearings?   Yes   No   What is the reason?_____
    _____
16. Are there roach, mice, or rat problems in the building?
    Yes   No   _____
17. Is there a regularly scheduled extermination service provided?
    Yes   No   By whom?_____
18. Have there been any burglaries in the building? What are the details?
    _____

19. Has the building had any fires in the past several years?
    Yes   No   What happened?_____
    _____

20. Is the building up for sale?   Yes   No   If so, can lease be
    cancelled?   Yes   No

21. Is there regular building cleaning?   Yes   No   How often?
    _____ By whom?_____

22. What repairs will management make and what repairs will the tenant
    have to take care of?_____
    _____

23. How are maintenance problems reported?_____
    _____
    How long does it take for repairs?_____

24. Will the management company reimburse tenants for parts and labor
    if tenants make their own repairs?   Yes   No

25. Is storage available?   Yes   No   Where?_____
    How safe is the storage against theft and moisture or dirt damage?
    _____

26. Is parking available in the area?   Yes   No   How much will
    it cost?_____

27. Who should be contacted in case of emergency?_____
    _____
    24 hour phone number_____

28. Does the management maintain fire and accident liability insur-
    ance?   Yes   No   What are the details?_____
    _____

29. Are there any special conditions of tenancy placed upon residents in
    the building?   Yes   No   Please state_____
    _____
    _____

Warranty of Habitability

Lessor and/or agent for lessor states, warrants, and covenants that
the above apartment unit and building comply with all applicable
city, county, state, and federal regulations including the building
code ordinances of the city of Chicago. Lessor or his agent states,
warrants, and covenants that the dwelling is habitable, is available
on date promised, and that the lessor and/or his agent will maintain and/or improve said apartment and building and keep it at all
times in habitable, clean, safe, and sanitary condition and convey

all services required to do same for the period of the lease as required by the lease, attachments to the lease, and all applicable ordinances, codes, and statutes, now and in the future.

Lessor and/or his agent affirms that all statements contained herein are true and correct.

Applicant (lessee) shall have ten days from notice of acceptance of his application for a lease (by lessor) to review and verify statements contained in this Landlord's Application. If landlord or building should prove unacceptable during this period, the applicant's (lessee's) full application fee will be refunded within five working days.

This Landlord's Application and Warranty of Habitability Statement supercedes conditions to the contrary in the "Application for Lease" and is made a binding part of the lease.

_____   _____
Applicant for Lease   Date   Landlord and/or   Date
   (Lessee)   Landlord's Agent (Lessor)

_____   _____
Additional Signature   Title

APPENDIX D

I. Apartment Conditions and Exceptions Report Form

Use this list to summarize the physical condition of your apartment when you sign your lease and then make a new list just after you have settled in. Getting a written document of conditions could save you a lot of grief and/or money later. Both you and your landlord should do the inspection together and both of you sign the list.

Check One: Pre-check-in (before signing lease)
     Check-in (first ten days after move-in)
     Check-out (before or after move-out
     and/or key return)

Condition of Apartment Checklist/Exceptions Report

For apartment _____, at _____
_____ to be made a rider
to lease and attached and made part of lease dated
_____ for the above-described premises.

Intercom system		Legend
Front door lock		Acceptable:
Rear door lock		A-excellent/new
Front door		B-good/normal/clean
Rear door		C-marginal/OK
Refrigerator		
Stove		Not acceptable:
Air conditioner		X-marginal/minor work
Furnace		needed/dirty
Kitchen sink		Y-defects require
Toilet		sufficient attention
Tub/shower		Z-major defect/filthy/
Lavatory		significant rework
Dishwasher		or replacement required
Disposal		

	Walls	Woodwork	Flooring	Ceiling	AC Outlets	Windows	Storm	Screens	Radiator	Doors	Paint	Carpeting	Lighting	Fixtures	Closets
Hallway															
Living room															
Dining room															
Kitchen															
Bedroom #1															
Bedroom #2															
Bedroom #3															
Bedroom #4															
Bathroom #1															
Bathroom #2															
Porch															
Storage room															
Garage															

Exceptions

List each problem separately by room, item, and condition.

_____

_____

_____

_____

Are there any apparent building code violations? List each separately as above.

_____

_____

_____

_____

I have inspected the above apartment on _____ and concur with the evaluation as marked, with the following exceptions:

_____

_____

_____

_____

_____

_____
Lessee   Date

I have inspected the above apartment on _____ and concur with the evaluation as marked, with the following exceptions:

_____

_____

_____

_____
Lessor (as agent)   Date

Please compare this report with pre-check-in, check-in, and check-out condition reports.

APPENDIX D

II. Sample Rider to Lease Regarding Promises Made and Permissions Granted

You will have to make up your own list based upon specific conditions. This is just an example in a proper form.

Rider to LEASE to be attached to LEASE and made part of LEASE proper for premises located at_____
_____
between LESSEE_____
and LESSOR (owner, manager, and/or agent)_____
_____

1. Apartment will be repainted by LESSOR prior to start of LEASE period. The bathroom walls will be painted hard enamel white, the kitchen walls will be chrome yellow, the kitchen ceiling will be white. The east wall of the living room will be sky blue pink and the rest of the apartment will be mauve.

2. The LESSOR will repair the kitchen stove and will install a new 14-cubic foot refrigerator prior to start of LEASE period.

3. A doorbell/buzzer/intercom system will be operating prior to start of LEASE period.

4. Front and back door deadbolt locks will be installed by LESSOR, and all keys will be changed from those of the previous tenants'.

5. LESSEE will be allowed to install shelving on walls. LESSEE will restore walls to original condition filling and sanding screw holes or LESSOR will accept shelving supports to remain after termination of LEASE.

6. Indoor hanging plants and outside window boxes are permitted. LESSEE will fill plant hanger holes or allow hooks to remain at termination of LEASE. LESSEE will stabilize outdoor plant boxes so they are not in danger of falling.

7. LESSOR permits picture hooks, curtain rods, door chains, and pot hangers to be installed by LESSEE.

8. LESSOR will supply disposable air filters for furnace three times a year in January, May, and September.

9. LESSOR will supply and install storm windows, weather stripping, caulking, and screens for all windows.

10. Installation of a burglar alarm is permitted including installation of small gauge wires and detector mechanisms.

11. Storage in the basement is included as part of LEASE.

12. Permission is granted for LESSEE to install a portable dishwasher in the kitchen.

13. Permission is granted for LESSEE to install air conditioners in windows where LESSEE so desires to install them.

14. LESSEE is granted permission to wallpaper ceiling in bedroom. LESSOR will be given approval power as to wallpaper. Paper will be permanent addition to apartment and LESSOR will not require its removal at termination of lease.

15. Three new electrical circuits will be installed in LESSEE'S apartment. LESSOR will provide electricians and materials. The new circuits will be located as follows: one 20-amp circuit in kitchen over counter; one 15-amp circuit in large bedroom near window (for 110-volt air conditioner); one 220-volt, single-phase circuit in living room near north window (for air conditioner). Cost of such work will be split 50%-50% between LESSOR and LESSEE. LESSOR will pay for all costs and LESSEE will reimburse LESSOR. Cost of work will be approved prior to start of work. Work will be performed within first 30 days of lease period.

16. LESSOR will pay for repairs of stove, refrigerator, garbage disposal, and furnace.

17. Permission is granted for LESSEE to park MoPed next to back door.

18. All work to be performed (excepting wiring) will be completed prior to commencement of LEASE. Failure to comply with this agreement may result in cancellation of lease by LESSEE, and the return to LESSEE of all monies advanced plus other damages to LESSEE.

19. As the terms herein change and modify the LEASE, this agreement shall hold force and be in effect and the other clauses so effected are considered null and of no force.

_____   _____

Tenant (lessee)   Date   Lessor (or agent)   Date

APPENDIX E

I. Universal Tenants' Rights Rider to Lease (Short Form)

If you are one person (not a tenants' organization) and you do indeed care to protect yourself against some of the worst provisions of the landlords' standard leases, I suggest that you submit the following simple rider. It is clear and not imposing, but very practical.

Rider to LEASE to be attached to LEASE and made part of LEASE proper for premises located at_____

_____

between LESSEE(S)_____

_____ _____

and LESSOR_____

(1) LESSOR warrants, covenants, and guarantees: that the above-demised premises are habitable, safe, and secure; that there are no latent or potential defects which may affect habitability; that the premises are in substantial compliance with the building codes of the city of Chicago and all other applicable regulations of all jurisdictions; that LESSOR will maintain building and premises in a like condition for the entire term of the lease, including all essential services.

(2) LESSOR will maintain and repair the stove, refrigerator, and all other equipment he supplies as part of this lease, in working order provided defect is not a result of willful negligence by LESSEE.

(3) As the laws of the State of Illinois, cases-at-law, and the ordinances of the City of Chicago now in force modify this lease, the lease shall be considered modified to that extent.

(4) In the case of reassignment or subletting of LEASE by LESSEE, LESSOR shall not unreasonably refuse a prospective tenant.

(5) Entry to premises shall not be unreasonably denied provided that LESSOR make advanced arrangements for entry to apartment.

(6) Right to notice and process before suit or action is guaranteed mutually to and by both LESSOR and LESSEE.

_____   _____
Lessee   Date   Lessor (as agent)   Date

Lessee   Date

To attach to LEASE dated_____ running for a term of _____

years from_____ to_____ .

II. Universal Tenants' Rights Rider to Lease (Long form)

This is also a sample of a suggested rider. Even though this rider can be tied to almost any lease, the lease should be read for sleepers that need to be countered. Also, read the landlord's riders and attachments because he may put in some very hard-to-live-with rules.

Rider to LEASE to be attached to LEASE and made part of LEASE proper. For premises located at_____

between LESSEE_____

and LESSOR (owner, manager and/or agent)_____

_____ .

(1) LESSOR warrants, covenants, and guarantees: that the premises described above are habitable, safe, and secure; that there are no latent or potential defects which may affect habitability; that the premises are in compliance with the building codes ordinances of the city of Chicago and all other applicable regulations of all jurisdictions of city, county, state and federal agencies; that LESSOR will maintain building in a like condition for term of LEASE.

(2) LESSOR warrants that LESSOR, his agents, and assigns will maintain and repair all appliances and equipment which LESSOR conveys as part of LEASE. The LESSOR will maintain the premises in a healthful, clean, safe, and sanitary manner and cause others to do likewise. LESSOR will maintain and operate and cause to operate properly all essential services including all plumbing, heating, electrical, and water-heating equipment in building, and repair same immediately. LESSOR will supply extermination services on a regular basis and will control all vermin.

(3) LESSOR will issue a written rent receipt for each and every payment of monies tendered as payment for LESSEE's rents. Receipt shall be issued at time money is tendered. No monies shall be owing if issuance of a receipt shall be refused.

(4) LESSOR holds harmless LESSEE for damages occurring to the above-described premises when damages are caused by LESSOR's poor materials, improper workmanship, or incorrect applications or installations. LESSEE is further held harmless in the event of damages caused by unknown third parties or circumstances beyond LESSEE's control.

(5) LESSOR will grant a rent set-off if LESSOR fails to maintain building in compliance with the building codes; fails to maintain adequate and sufficient essential services; fails to maintain the habitability of the premises at least at the level established at the time the lease commenced; fails to make improvements in accordance with other attachments and agreements to the LEASE. The set-off will be determined by the decreased fair market value of the premises.

(6) LESSOR will grant LESSEE a rent credit in the form of a rent set-off as reimbursement for any and all payments LESSEE makes on behalf of the LESSOR in order to maintain essential services including water, gas, oil, coal, and electricity; and to make repairs necessary to maintain premises habitability conditions including, but not limited to: repairs for furnace, water heater, stove, refrigerator, toilets and all other plumbing, windows, storm windows, screens, doors, door locks, floors, walls and ceilings. LESSEE will inform LESSOR in advance of repairs as to problems and cost of repairs. If LESSOR does not respond, LESSEE will take all necessary actions.

(7) The attached LEASE may be cancelled prior to the termination date on the face for the following reasons: (a) LESSEE is transferred to a new work location further than 15 miles from above-described premises; (b) LESSEE dies; (c) LESSOR fails to maintain essential services or repair major appliances promptly as necessary; (d) fire and/or any other conditions make premises unsafe, untenable, or uninhabitable. Notice of cancellation will be as follows: Transfers—a two-month (60 days) written notice is required, the termination date will coincide with the end of a calendar month; Death of Lessee—forty-five days notice to take effect at end of notice period; Fire—to take effect immediately upon receipt of notice; Unhabitability—five days from date of notice to make repairs or cancel LEASE. (e) LEASE may also be cancelled by either party when the other party substantially violates any agreement of the LEASE or of the attached riders. Costs and damages may also be recovered by either party through action at law if the LEASE or attachments are breached.

(8) LESSEE (tenant) absolutely does not grant any power of attorney to LESSOR or his assigns. LESSEE does not waive any rights of notice nor does LESSEE confess judgement. LESSEE does not agree to pay any court

or other legal costs on behalf of LESSOR unless these are assessed in open court. LESSEE will not limit his remedies for damages as they are set forth within the body of the LEASE but will retain full rights to action at law in cases of breach or damage against LESSEE.

(9) LESSOR will not unreasonably refuse or reject proposed tenants if LESSEE wishes to reassign LEASE before termination. It is understood that LESSEE will advertise, screen, and show the above-described apartment and these shall be LESSEE's sole costs and duties regarding reassignment. All other fees will be borne by reassignee and/or LESSOR.

(10) LESSOR warrants that the above-described premises will be delivered in a completed and habitable condition and conveyed to LESSEE on the first day of the term of the LEASE. LESSOR will pay cash damages for all lodging, food, moving and storage expenses, and lost income caused by failure to deliver premises on time. If premises is not delivered within 10 days of start of LEASE, LESSOR will pay all the above expenses plus the difference in rent for another apartment if another apartment of similar type is not available at the rent on the face of the LEASE here attached and LESSEE cancels this LEASE under clauses 7-c, d or e of this attachment.

(11) The attached LEASE shall remain in force until the termination date on the front regardless of change of ownership. The security deposit shall be transferred and conveyed to any new owner or agent and the new owner or agent will have the control of same.

(12) The attached LEASE is renewable at the end of the present term. The amount of rent for renewal shall be reasonable and in keeping with the fair market value of the services and housing offered. Failure to renew LEASE because of lawful complaints, tenant activities, or actions filed by LESSEE against LESSOR for breaches of the LEASE or applicable codes, ordinances, statutes, and regulations is prohibited. LESSEE shall have recourse to recover damages including reasonable lawyer's fees and moving expenses. If building is sold, or converted to condominium, or no longer habitable, this clause does not apply.

(13) The tendering of rents to LESSOR is absolutely conditional upon proper performance, by LESSOR, of all covenants of LEASE agreement, this Universal Rider, and all other agreements herein attached. The LESSOR's duties shall not be mitigated by any alleged breach by LESSEE, which shall be considered independently.

_____   _____
Lessee   Date   Lessor (or his agent)   Date

APPENDIX F

A Clause-by-Clause Analysis of Landlord Leases Numbers 12R, 15, and L17, Plus 30-day and Oral Leases

There are four current apartment lease forms in use in Chicago. Two of them are copyrighted by the Chicago Real Estate Board (CREB), a not-for-profit organization of real estate operations. We cannot reproduce the texts of any of the leases in this book.

Almost every owner, landlord, and management company uses one of these forms. The forms are printed, legal-size paper ($8\frac{1}{2}'' \times 15''$) with print covering both sides of the form. Of the three "landlord's" leases exact wording differs, but not significantly. The most dramatic proof that a landlord's lease is a landlord's lease (regardless of specific preprinted content) is to watch Eviction Court proceedings at the Civic Center. The judges never look at the leases. They simply look at the notice to pay up or move out. The simple truth is, the lease is a hook and you've been caught. If you have not read Chapter 7, read it now, and then come back here.

Each of the three landlord's leases is analyzed here. I will start with the most comprehensive lease, Chicago Real Estate Board Lease Number 15.

Basically, these leases are indeed the same. Some are more specific than others, but these leases cover the same ground. They are all written by legal types bent on obfuscating the lease contents. There is a cross reference analysis for the other leases following this analysis. Lease number L19, the Chicago Council of Lawyer's lease, is covered in Chapter 7. This lease is radically different than the ones studied here because it is balanced and fair to both parties, and it is written in understandable language. If you have or can convince your landlord to substitute L19 for one of these unfair leases, do it. If you have L19 as a lease, you are on much safer ground as a tenant.

Come, let us demystify together.

Top Matter—Generally the same for all leases.

Apartment Lease (not furnished, not heated)

This is a lease for a period of time (usually one or more years) for an apartment. There will be no furniture and you will have to pay for the heating and the hot water in addition to utilities. Usually the landlord will supply a cooking stove and a refrigerator but you had better make sure by seeing the appliances.

Date of Lease

What date was the lease signed? Make sure the date is filled in correctly. Later, you may need to prove that conditions had changed between the signing time and move-in.

Term of Lease

Make sure the term of the lease (when tenancy is to begin and when it is to end) is correct. It is common practice to date a lease for a one-month term (instead of for one or two years). If this happens, then the landlord can throw you out after one month. This happens more often than you would believe. Do not sign a lease which does not have the proper dates on it.

Monthly Rent

The amount of rent you owe each month excluding utilities (and/or parking).

Security Deposit

The amount of money you have to put down against damages. The amount of security deposit ranges from one to two months' rent, and is payable in advance. The security deposit is supposed to be kept in a separate account. If the building you live in has twenty-five or more units, you are supposed to receive 5% interest yearly, payable every twelve months in cash or as a rent credit. *Warning:* do not expect to get your full security deposit returned. This money is seldom put in a special account and is often "lost" by the landlord (more about this in the body of the lease).

Tenant

This describes the address of the apartment and the names of the people living in the apartment. Landlords make a nice fringe benefit by charging you if you change part of a tenant party. I saw a lawsuit recently where the landlord sued to evict a family who listed only three names on the lease. A second child, a girl home for the summer from college, was said to violate the terms (more about this in the body of the lease). It is highly questionable, however, what right a landlord has to dictate to a tenant who can live with that tenant as long as criminal and housing codes are not violated.

Lessor

The name appearing here is usually the "agent" for the owner of the place. That person (or company) has the responsibility for the day-to-day operations of the building. Illinois law does not require that you know whom you are renting from. In one of those strange (yet predictable) turns of law, the agent has little legal responsibility for you or the apartment. The real owner is usually cloaked in hidden trusts through banks or other financial institutions. The institutions will not tell you who owns your place. When you sue, or the city sues for lease problems, it takes months to go through the subpoena process to find the owner. The management agent (usually the culprit) sits pretty the whole time.

In Consideration, Etc.

You agree to the terms of the lease. In consideration for your monthly payments and your continued abiding by the clauses of the lease, the lessor grants you the opportunity to try and live in the apartment you've rented for the time specified. And good luck.

Additional Covenants and Agreements (if any)

A Pandora's box of atrocities. The additions can be anything. Usually they will state who is responsible for utility payments or heat.

They also may grant parking. They may state a fee for late payment of the rents after a certain date each month. It may contain a cancellation clause after a certain number of days notice. You may have to pay real estate taxes!!! Pets may be outlawed, or it could be your in-laws. The added agreement may state that tenants are responsible for repairs to appliances and/or the apartment. You may have to prove you have tenant's insurance. These clauses may state what the noise limits are or when you can use the front stairs during the rainy season (oh yes!). Some may contain a limit to the amount of hot water used! Read these special restrictions or additions very carefully. If you don't like them, change them now, or don't sign the lease. Additional clauses may also be contained in a rider or attachments (other pieces of paper) fastened to the lease (paper clip or staple) and signed at the same time as the lease (or later). These become binding parts of the lease. Sometimes, they are printed forms. *Read them very well*.

Signatures

This is the proverbial dotted line. When you sign, you are obligated to the lease. You must pay the rent. The landlord is supposed to similarly be obligated to the agreement. He is supposed to provide you with a livable apartment. DO NOT SIGN until after you have made sure the lease contains a workable arrangement between you and the landlord. DO NOT SIGN until after you have made a final inspection of the apartment and determine it is ready. If *anything* needs to be done (decorating, repairs, appliances, cleaning)—anything at all—have the landlord sign, as part of the lease, a clause stating specifically what he is going to do *before* you move in, and have as part of the clause, that the landlord will be responsible to pay *cash* for damages caused if you cannot move in. See the Universal Tenants' Rights Rider in Appendix E, and the special rider in Appendix D. I strongly recommend that if an apartment is not ready at the time a lease is ready to be signed, that the lease not be signed and your money be returned to you. Find yourself a finished apartment. The horror stories of unfinished apartments make a carnival side show a normal way of life, and besides you wouldn't like it, believe me! Remember: *the landlord rents the apartment as is.* He cannot be held to promises he makes about things he is going to do later unless you make a contract with a damages clause. All he needs is your signature.

Later you may need a lawyer, a psychiatrist, and a personal loan to get out of the situation. Finally, sign all the additional agreements first, sign the lease last. Get signed copies of the lease and addenda and put them in the same safe place you keep your rent receipts.

Now on to the body of the lease. When you sign, these sweet treats are what you have agreed to live by for the term of your lease. Oh yes, the courts will enforce most of these clauses (after all, nobody forced you to sign). Landlords will also selectively enforce the clauses to get people out of the apartments for any reason.

What follows is an analysis/commentary on lease #15. It is too bad we could not print the actual lease text side by side with this. Take your copy of the lease and follow along. If you have lease #12R or #L17, they follow this analysis at the back of this appendix.

Apartment Lease Number 15

1. Rent

You must pay your rent in advance, on, or before the first of the month (or whatever date the rent is due). You must pay all of it. If you don't, your lease can be cancelled and you can be evicted. If you are more than five days late, your landlord charges you $5.00 to cover "his additional costs for late payment." More than ten days late, the landlord will charge you $10.00 over the rent. You are supposed to take the rent to the landlord, or mail it. The postmark is considered the same as the date paid. By the way, it is best to pay by personal check and receive a signed rent receipt at time of payment. Money orders or bank checks are OK if you can trace them later in case you have to prove payment. Cash is least desirable from a tenant's standpoint. *Always request a receipt.* I heard a judge tell a landlord that if the landlord would not give the tenant a receipt for the rents, the tenant should not pay his rents until a receipt is available. *Do not leave the landlord's office without a receipt.* Do not let him tell you he will mail it to you. *No receipt! No rent!* The payment of the rents is called the "essence" of the lease. In a sense, this is true. With no payment of rent money, the lease "dies." While the lease requires you to pay rent no matter what (as we shall see in subsequent clauses) it does not require the landlord to do little more than offer you the "opportunity" to live in the apartment for a period of time. On the face of the "essence" statement, the landlord can evict you and is no longer obligated to the terms of the lease if you have violated the agreement through nonpayment. This is not true. You have some very legitimate reasons for not paying your rents. (Slum conditions, no heat, no water, no power, leaking roof, to name a few.)

Through a series of recent court decisions, the Illinois courts (as well as other states' courts) have established that the landlord is required to warrant (promise) that what he rents is habitable. This means that the apartment meets the local building code requirements. Under some circumstances, it is legal for you not to pay your rents until he makes repairs to bring the building up to code. Practically speaking if you don't pay rent, you probably will be summoned into Eviction Court where a judge will tell you that you do not have to pay back rents, but that you will have to leave. At the same time, the landlord cannot cut off your water, heat, or power, nor can he lock you out. Only the courts can order you out, not the landlord.

The real rip-off in the rent "essence" is that only the renter is tied to the lease, but for all practical purposes the landlord is not. Subsequently, when the landlord fails to perform, it is almost impossible to get satisfaction (or even break the lease). In terms of rent law reform (which is desperately needed) there must be an equitable way of holding a landlord to a lease. The rent clause, which is an independant clause (nothing else depends upon required rent payments), should be made an interdependent clause. In this way, you pay the rent as long as the landlord adheres to the lease arrangements. When the landlord fails to live up, you withhold part or all the rent (depending on the breach) until he honors the lease. What's fair is fair.

2. *Possession*

If, at the time your lease starts, the apartment isn't ready or available for occupancy, you may cancel the lease after waiting ten days. (Or you can send the landlord a letter within fifteen days after the start of the lease and say you'll keep the place and move in when it is ready.) If you cannot move in within ten days from the start of the lease, the landlord has only to give you back any money you have paid him. "This is your sole remedy." You cannot collect damages such as furniture storage and motel costs, or extra rents charged by your previous landlord as a holdover fee, or double moving costs like trucks and movers, or restaurant costs (if you go to a motel to "live" while waiting for the place or another place). It is a one-way game. You owe the rents on the lease whether you move or not, but the landlord doesn't even have to have the place ready for you and owes you nothing in return for your troubles. Finally, if the "decorating" isn't completed, that's too bad, because decoration is not a condition "precedent" to possession, meaning that if the place isn't painted, papered, plastered or "touched up" before you move in:

1. *you cannot refuse to move in (you still owe the rent),*
2. *don't expect much more to be done,*
3. *if any more work is done expect to have workmen disrupting you, getting dirt and paint on the rugs, moving all the furniture (and not replacing it), and coming and going as they please through your place with no regard for your time schedules or problems.*

I repeat: *do not move into an unfinished apartment.* The rental agent simply wants to get revenue as quickly as possible from the place. It is irrelevant whether the apartment is livable or not, or who suffers.

3. *Application*

The application is made part of the lease. If it contains false or incorrect information, the landlord can cancel the lease with a thirty-day notice and throw you out. This is supposed to protect the landlord against "undesirables." Practically speaking, it prevents you from taking another roommate, changing roommates, or allowing more people to live in the place than you originally applied for. It also forces you to tell the landlord all he wants to know about your finances, your job, and your past life (while it doesn't require him to tell you a thing about himself, his business, the owner of the building, or the condition of the building). This clause is a convenient way to get you out. By the way, if he does throw you out, that's tough. He doesn't have to compensate you for moving or for any other damages that might befall you. If you pay your rent, and if you treat the apartment and other occupants of the building properly, and do not perform criminal or dangerous acts in the apartment, there should be no reason why you should be evicted. Your way of life, religion, sexual preferences, and ethnic background are none of his business. Who lives with you is none of the landlord's concern as long as the apartment is not overcrowded (as defined by law). Although the application is supposed to screen out the "undesirables" the truth is that a landlord will rent to almost anyone who can pay the rent. This clause is a ruse.

4. *Promise of the Parties*

Only written additions, changes, and modifications to this lease, signed by both tenants and lessor are binding. There is no such thing (states this clause) as a verbal promise. *Nothing is binding that is not put in writing.* Repeat this sentence 100 times until you have memorized it. More tenants are taken to the cleaners when they try to get that new stove, or wall repaired or toilet fixed or the carpeting cleaned. Generally, if you sue on a verbal promise (and all you have are verbal promises), you will lose. Don't think you can hire a plasterer, or buy a stove and deduct it from your rent, or bill it to the landlord. The judge will say you did it on your own without written permission from the landlord. You will have to pay for it. And if it is a permanent repair or item, it will have to stay with the apartment. You lose—ha! ha! gotcha again!

5. *Security Deposit*

The lessor holds a security deposit to ensure the "performance" of all the parts of the lease. He can use the security deposit to make necessary repairs for which the tenant is somehow responsible (damage to the building, walls, appliances, plumbing, etc.). The landlord does not have to tell the tenant about the repairs, however, until after they are completed. Then the landlord presents the tenant with a bill (and receipts or estimates) and orders the tenant to pay this amount back into his security account. The landlord has to notify the tenant within thirty days of the time the landlord makes the repairs. The tenant must pay the landlord immediately (the landlord usually doesn't pay his suppliers for sixty to ninety days, by the way). The security deposit is not the limit which the landlord can spend on "repairs" and charge the tenant. He can spend more and charge you for it. The security deposit can also be used when the landlord collects "damages" (read that penalities but "penalties" as such are not legal in this lease, so the lawyers call them "damages" instead). These damages are spelled out in the lease elsewhere, but include failure to let the landlord inspect your apartment, and holding over longer than the term of the lease among others.

The security deposit is not supposed to be used to pay rents. The money is being held for the "performance" of the lease and to pay for damages only. However, if you don't pay your rent, the landlord may seize the deposit and collect it for "damages," ironically because you didn't pay your rent!

The security deposit is supposed to be returned to you within thirty days after you move out at the end of the lease, if there is any money left in the account after making repairs or the collection of "damages." If after thirty days you do not get your money back, the landlord owes you two months rent money. However, if during the same thirty days, the landlord sends you receipts and estimates of repair work, he only owes you the difference between the deposit and the cost of work. If the building is sold, or the management changes hands, the new owner or manager is supposed to be given the security deposit by the old owner or manager. Good luck. What really happens and what is supposed to happen are usually quite different. The landlord is supposed to hold the security deposit money in a special account and if you live in a building with twenty-five or more units, the state requires that the management pay you 5% yearly interest. State *law* requires (in buildings of ten or more units) that he pay back the deposit within thirty days after termination of the lease, unless there are repairs to make. Then he must submit to you within thirty days of termination an estimate of the work to be done. He must actually complete all work within sixty days of termination or he owes you that two months rent as damages.

Landlords will do almost anything not to give you back your deposit. Towards the end of the lease, they will hassle you by trying to show the apartment at inconvenient times or by marching workmen through the place. If you bar him or his people, he will collect "damages" for your failure to cooperate. After you move out, he will claim the place was a mess and he had to hire a cleaning crew to come in. He will say he couldn't rent the apartment until extensive cleaning and repairs were made. He will claim he lost rent because the place wasn't rentable. He will tell you each picture hanger hole cost him $7.00 to patch and $3.00 to paint. He'll say it took a special trip by an exterminator to kill all the bugs that remained after you removed your plants. He'll complain about the condition of the kitchen sink and the bathtub. There were holes in the screens and the backdoor lock needed to be replaced. He'll tell anyone who wants to listen that you used too much water and the sewer bill was twice as high. He'll complain that a plumber had to come out and clean all the drain traps because you poured grease down the sink, unmentionable items down the toilet, and allowed hair to accumulate in the tub drain. Because of the work and the dirt, he couldn't rent the apartment for a month, so he had to double the advertising and lose three months rent.

Kiss your security deposit good-bye the day you plunk it down unless you are ready to go to court. Go to Small Claims Court if you have to go to court, but there is another way to get part of the deposit back. Don't pay your last month's rent. This may be in violation of the lease, it is illegal, but it is sure effective!!! If you have paid more than one month's rent in a deposit, forget the second half, but it is a good bet you wouldn't get any of it back, so what the hell.

Don't be afraid!!! The eviction procedure is much longer than the 30 days you need to move. The landlord cannot legally lock you out. If he does, call the cops and break down the door. It is a crime. He cannot legally cut off the heat, water, or power. If he does, call the city and the cops. And for good measure, call the State Attorney's office. You might try calling your landlord at 3:00 A.M. at home to complain also. It does wonders.

The self-recovery process works like this: On the thirty-first day before your lease expires, send your landlord a letter instead of the rent check. See Appendix M for a sample letter.

If you do not have any damages, you should have no problems about sending such a letter. If you do have damages, your landlord may haul you into Small Claims Court. In any case, be prepared with photographs and witnesses to defend yourself. Refer to Chapter 17 where I discuss in detail how to operate within the courts (and how to sue to get your deposit back if you pay your last month's rent). In any case, you have a better chance of getting your money back by releasing your security deposit than by paying the last month's rent. Although my advice is to be aggressive, it would not hurt to sound out the management company or landlord about whether you are going to be charged for damages, and when, if, and how you will get your deposit back. If it looks chancy, be strong and protect yourself. Don't pay the rent.

By the way, a security deposit cannot be raised during the term of the lease. Only at the beginning when a new lease is signed or when an old lease is renegotiated.

6. *Lessor to Maintain*

The lessee (the tenant) accepts the apartment and the building AS IS, and finds the place to be in good shape. There are no promises about making any changes or repairs except those made in writing. What you see is what you get. You cannot break the lease later because things are not quite what they seem to be, or because the landlord didn't do something he promised verbally.

If there are written promises, the landlord promises to finish the work within sixty days from the start of the lease. The lessor promises to maintain the building properly, make all repairs necessary, keep the place clean, safe, and within building code requirements including sanitation requirements. He must provide heat (if the building is centrally heated), water, and make sure plumbing and wiring is safe and working. If he supplies appliances and other equipment, he will repair them. He will also make sure the locks work, and so on. The clause (a long one) reads like the long-awaited Bill of Rights for Tenants, it isn't. The landlord has as long as he wants to make those repairs without offering you any rent abatement or adjustment to your lease. It may take him "forever" to get around to the needed work with no danger of penalizing himself. The rest of the clause reveals that it is almost impossible to enforce the promises or the warranty.

The clause continues to state that although the landlord would like to do all these things, he may not be able to do them. The reasons are simple. The repairs may be too expensive, or the tenants are responsible, or he didn't know about the conditions, or the tenants wouldn't let his workmen fix the conditions, or outside problems like strikes or material shortages prevented him from doing the work, or he "tried" to fix the conditions but couldn't. For whatever reason, the landlord's failure to make repairs or fix the place "shall not" breach the lease. The tenants will still have to pay the rent. All the above reasons for not doing work are "absolute defenses" against any legal action. The tenants cannot sue, ask for damages, nor can they request a rent deduction. Clause 6 is a fraud. It contains in legal, formal language, every excuse known to dribble out one side of a landlord's mouth. Basically, the lease tells you that the landlord does not care about you. He cares only for his money. The fact that you cannot tie rent payment to landlord performance has allowed for the deterioration of housing in this city. If landlords had to keep their buildings in good shape to collect rent, we would have 25% more available housing in this city, and the rents would be a lot more reasonable.

7. *Utilities*

Unless otherwise written as an amendment (in this lease anyway—some leases state on their face whether heat and/or hot water is supplied), the tenant is responsible to contact the utility companies for service, and pay the companies directly. You may even have to pay for water.

8. *Tenant's Use of Apartment*

The tenant is not supposed to conduct any business in his apartment, just live there. He can have guests in "reasonable numbers" but no one can stay there longer than three weeks in a year. The tenant and his guests are not supposed to do anything destructive, illegal, disturbing, or damaging to the reputation of the building. This is part of the "Bad Tenant" part of the lease. It also is supposed to keep out more roommates (or girlfriends and boyfriends). Nobody, not listed on the lease, is allowed to "reside." Only newborn babies or adopted children are allowed if they are not listed on the lease (you cannot let your college-aged child, or brother or sister, live with you during their vacations).

9. *Tenant's Upkeep*

Generally speaking, the tenant is supposed to keep his apartment clean, safe and sanitary. He is not supposed to allow in his apartment furniture or plants that have bugs or mice. He is supposed to take out the garbage regularly and throw it in the trash collector. He is supposed to keep dangerous and flammable materials out of the building. He is not supposed to deface, destroy, or damage any part of the building including the floors, walls, fixtures, etc., in his own apartment. He is supposed to stop other people from doing destructive things. The tenant will have to pay for damages and is responsible to keep the apartment in "good repair" (whatever that means). At the end of the lease, the tenant is required to turn over to the landlord the apartment in the same way he found it when he moved in, "reasonable wear excepted." This is the other half of the "Bad Tenants" part of the lease. Between these two clauses, you can be kicked out any time and you can lose your security deposit. You may also find out that you are responsible for repairing the stove and door bell. It is obvious, I hope, that the tenant is not going to be willfully destructive of the apartment that he lives in.

10. *Alterations, Additions, Fixtures, Appliances, Personal Property*

This is a preforfeiture of your security deposit clause. You are prohibited from making any alterations or additions to your apartment without written permission. This could include painting a wall a different color, or adding mirrors or tiles, hanging plants or new light fixtures. It also prohibits you from installing a dishwasher, clothes washer, freezer or second refrigerator without written permission. You cannot attach things to the walls, floors, or ceilings. Well, that's a pretty tough clause to abide with. How do you put up pictures, curtain rods, closet bars, or shelves? Whatever you do will come back to haunt you, if the landlord so pleases.

This clause states that any security device (lock, peep hole, burglar bar) and all other additions (which the landlord likes) becomes the landlord's property. If he doesn't like the change or addition he can make you remove it. Well, it is ridiculous to ask permission of the landlord each time you hang a picture or put up a mirror. I am sure you have no intention of leaving a $100.00 tiffany swag lamp or a wall shelf unit when you leave. Before you move, patch the holes and pull out all your own property. If the landlord wants something, let him buy it if you want to sell. Leave the apartment the way you found it. Take photographs and be prepared to go to Small Claims Court for your money. Remember you are supposed to return the apartment in "Like condition, reasonable wear excepted." Remember also that decorating (painting) is part of the landlord's usual preparation before rerenting. A landlord who keeps your security deposit because he had to "wash and repaint the walls" is looking for a court summons. Give it to him.

11. Access

This clause grants the landlord permission to enter your apartment for making repairs and inspections. Within 90 days of the end of the lease, the landlord can show the apartment to prospective tenants. The landlord must send you a written notice before he can start showing the apartment. Then he can come any day from 8:00 A.M. to 9:00 P.M. with 15 minutes warning. The repair and inspection hours are Monday through Saturday from 7:00 A.M. to 7:00 P.M. You can make a different arrangement with the landlord as to when he can come. You also have the right to request a 24-hour advance notice before you have to admit the landlord (or his workmen). If you refuse your landlord's entrance (with his 24-hour notice or his ninety-day warning), you can be fined two months rent. If your landlord fails to keep his appointments or comes at unauthorized hours, you can collect two months rent from him.

Always insist on advance appointments when the landlord comes to call and try to be present. Refer to this clause when requesting repairs in your apartment. Ask when the workmen will come. If your landlord is the type who has no intention of fixing the problem, he will usually mention some vague day or time. Pin him down and send him a note confirming the appointment. If he doesn't cancel in writing and he misses the date, inform him that he owes you two months rent. It is a great incentive to make repairs when they are requested.

12. Subletting (Breaking Your Lease)

Your lease says you can't do it. If you want to move out before the end of your lease, you are still obligated to pay the rent (except under certain circumstances, see paragraph 23). If you can find, by yourself, somebody else to take over the apartment and the lease you will:

(a) *have to guarantee the full amount of the rents until the end of the lease,*

(b) *have to pay for any redecorating or repairs,*

(c) *have to pay the "administrative costs" of checking out the new tenants.*

The landlord can refuse anybody you propose if they don't meet his standards. The new party may also have to sign a lease extension before he is accepted. There is no way you can sublet the apartment yourself. The process has to be through the landlord. It makes it tough for you to get "key money" if you have put in expensive improvements. The only good ways of breaking the lease are to sue your landlord for contract breaking, be evicted, or just move out and claim "constructive" eviction (see paragraph 23). This defense in court states that the landlord failed to keep the place in habitable condition, or that he did things that made it impossible for you to stay. Get a lawyer before you move out on a claim of constructive eviction. Some valid reasons for leaving are no heat, no hot water, failure of the landlord to keep the building safe and secure (especially if there have been burglaries in the building or neighborhood), building code violations, landlord harassment, excessive noise in the building. But you better have a strong case.

13. Abandonment

If you are physically absent for ten days and owe any rent, the landlord can declare that you have abandoned your apartment and seize *all* your property (this is contrary to Illinois law, but landlords still do it). Or if you remove most of your belongings, even if the rent is paid, the landlord can take what remains. This "abandoned" property can be claimed by the landlord as his own and he owes you nothing for it. At the same time, he can still try to collect rent from you and charge you for redecorating and rerenting.

If you decide to move out because of constructive eviction, do it all at once. If you move out just before the end of your lease, and want to have a few days or weeks to finish the move and clean up the old place, better let the landlord know. If he is a bastard, he could grab half of your belongings and then try to collect a security deposit because you left the apartment a mess.

14. Fire and Casualty

In case of fire or other method of destruction of the apartment (or apartment building) and the apartment is only *partially* destroyed and remains "livable and habitable," and if the landlord makes all repairs within sixty days, you still must pay the full rent and your lease remains in force. Habitable means meeting building code standards.

If the apartment is uninhabitable, or it is illegal to remain in the apartment (because of building department or court order), or if the landlord does not make the necessary repairs within sixty days of the destruction, then you can move out "free and clear." You must send your landlord written notice within five days (of the fire or of the expiration of the sixty-day repair period). Tell the landlord you are exercising clause 14 of the lease. Your lease is terminated, and the rent stops on the day you move out. Any unused rent and all the security deposit must be returned to you. The definition of what is livable may be in dispute, but if you believe the place is unlivable, send your notice and move out at once. There is no insurance provision for your own losses or damages (moving costs, alternative accommodations, medical expenses, property losses, time off from work). Before you sign anything from any insurance company, adjustor, or from your landlord, call your lawyer and prepare for a lawsuit.

15. Termination and Return of Possession

The landlord must notify you within forty-five days of expiration whether he will renew your lease, and at what price. If he does not make any notification, you may remain in the apartment on a month-to-month basis after expiration. If you are notified that the lease will not be renewed and you do not move out, the landlord has several tools to use. He can go into eviction court and order you out. He can also charge you a total of THREE TIMES the monthly rent, prorated for each day you stay after the lease expires. Possession of an apartment is defined as still living in the place, still storing belongings, or still holding on to the keys. If you are moving out, turn in the keys! Any offers or deals should be put in writing before you agree to stay past termination. A lease can be extended simply by writing in a statement "This lease extended to (date) at a monthly rent of ($)." This should appear on both copies of the lease and signed by the landlord and you on both copies. If a place is in good condition, and the management good, stay where you are. A modest rent increase is much cheaper than moving, and a lot less hassle! If you are moving out, be sure to check paragraphs 5 and 9 of the lease. If you move out at any time, take everything that you wish to keep (see para. 13).

16. Eminent Domain (Condemnation)

If your building is condemned by the city for building violations or by any state body because the building is in the way of some sort of construction, you will have to move out. Your rent continues until the actual day the state or city takes possession. Your landlord will receive damages or payment from the state but you are not entitled to any restitution for your troubles or loss. A lease should be just as binding on the landlord as it is the tenant. If your landlord breaks his lease because he can no longer rent to you, you ought to be able to receive damages to cover the costs and trouble of finding a new place, and moving, plus the differential between what you currently pay for rent and what a comparable new place costs.

The landlord always has all the answers when it comes to his business problems, but when you get into financial trouble, he throws you out. It ain't fair! If your building is condemned for violations or taken under eminent domain, move out as soon as you can find a good substitute place. If your landlord objects, ask him to pay your moving bill and the rest of the required expenses. If he objects, tell him he defaulted on his part of the lease and talk to your lawyer if he wants to pursue the matter. Sauce for the goose, sauce for the gander.

17. Lessor's Mortgage

Basically, the lease can be overridden by the provisions of the mortgage on the building. If the building goes into default, you would have to wait until the mortgage was settled before you could sue the building. It also means that if your building is sold, your lease can be cancelled immediately. This happens to a lot of people when a building converts to a condominium, or when a new owner wants to raise all the rents, or empty a building to do construction work.

Make sure that *when you sign a lease*, you *add a provision that your lease will run for the entire term regardless of whether the building is sold or changes hands*. If your apartment is sold out from under you, make a gentlemen's deal with the old owner that you'll go if he pays for the moving and rent differential, or you'll sue him for damages for breaking the lease. You could also refuse to go until evicted. It might save you several months rent, and it will cost him almost as much as if he had paid for the move in the first place. Tenants are people too, and should demand to be treated as such.

18. Lease Binding on Heirs, etc.

In the case of death, the heirs of the landlord become landlord. In the case of death of a tenant, if that tenant was only one of one, or one of two (or it could be argued the "principal" tenant because he or she paid the rent), the lease can be broken with written notice at least forty-five days before the actual break, but no more than 120 days after the death of the party. The lease would end at the end of a calendar month following notification. It seems in a way a bit ghoulish to demand someone stay on another two months if they want out, but landlords are landlords and at least they will allow the lease to be broken. Prior to this change, one was always responsible for the rent for the entire duration of a lease, dead or alive.

19. Notices

Any sort of "official" notice must be in writing and served by either delivering the notice in person or by mailing both a regular and certified copy. The notice is considered delivered on the date it is mailed. Anyone 12 years of age or older, who happens to be in the apartment at the time, may legally receive the notice. Any office employee of the landlord may also be served a notice addressed to the landlord. These notices are usually some sort of warning or order issued by the landlord. It could be a Five Days Notice to pay up or move out, or a renewal notice, or a complaint. Notices from tenants are either complaints or renewals. Notices from the courts must be served in person or through the mails with a certified return receipt. Although not tested in the courts, the use of a Mailgram is a very good way to get the attention of your landlord when you wish to complain. Ask for a confirmation copy for yourself when you phone in the Mailgram. If you receive your copy, he received his. This is usually good enough to prove that your notice was sent.

The problem with this clause is that it is possible to transmit the Five Days Notice so that you do not receive it until after the date of expiration.

It is likely that a mailed notice will not arrive until the fifth day (especially during holiday periods or when mailed toward the end of the week). It is equally possible that the notice is "lost" when it is posted on a door. I suggest changing this clause to read that notices are effective only when they are actually received (not mailed), only when they are personally delivered (not stuffed under the door), or only after three attempts have been made to deliver a notice on three separate dates when the receiving party would be likely to be available.

The stories I have heard about receiving an eviction notice without a Five Days Notice, and then watching the landlord lie in court about service, and also the trick of backdating the notice could fill another chapter.

20. *Rules and Regulations*

The rules and regulations contained at the bottom of the lease are made part of the lease. The landlord can make other rules and regulations, later, after the lease is signed, but these new rules cannot substantially change the lease. This is another tenant buster. Under proper circumstances almost all the rules can be broken by the best of tenants. Rules are made to be broken. That is one reason they are in your lease. The landlord hopes you will break a few of them just to give him ammunition if he needs it. The tougher the rules, the easier it is to break them, the more power the landlord has over you. "I will overlook the breach, *this time*, but you had better toe the line from now on." Putting up picture hangers is a great way to get a lecture. The rules, of course, are "differential." "No sign, light, lettering, or equipment shall be exposed at any window" states the rules, but how many tenants are evicted for Christmas decorations or Democratic party election signs? Very few. Try the same window trick with a picket sign complaining about roaches or heat and see what happens. By the way, be careful with red lights, they may be misinterpreted. Read the rules carefully—"no dishwashers; no deliveries or groceries through the front door; no air conditioners; no door chains or door knockers; no disturbing noises." Rules are designed partially to protect tenants from other tenants' abuses, they are also designed to protect the landlord from doing certain things such as improving his wiring to accommodate new modern electrical appliances. While he does not want tenants to put security devices on his doors, he probably does not want to do it either (see para. 6). In the case of complaints of disturbing noises, it is best to find out who is complaining if the landlord comes to you and says "I have had complaints about the noise," or whatever. Ask him to identify the complainer. If he won't, and he wants you out, let him try to take you to eviction court—no witness, no eviction. Anonymous complaints are an old and tired ploy often used by landlords. Don't be afraid to fight complaints, but you may need a lawyer.

21. *Resident to Insure Possessions*

The landlord takes no insurance responsibility at all for any sort of personal or property damages to the tenant or his guests for any reason (except the landlord's willful misconduct—whatever that might be). The tenant must insure himself for property and personal loss and liability. The landlord is not responsible for any sort of damage caused by the failure of the heating system, the pipes, the sewers, the roof, or the plague from rat bite. You name it, he is not responsible *and that includes fire*. He further won't vouch for any other tenant. Fortunately, the laws of the State of Illinois protect you. They prevent you from signing your rights to self-protection away, even if the landlord makes you sign clause 21 with the rest of the lease. Your landlord is *liable* for some things that go wrong in the building. The degree of his liability is for the courts to decide. If you are burned out, and it is because his heating system is inadequate or a stove blows up, sue your landlord. If the pipes burst, don't shake your landlord's hand when he reads paragraph 21 to you, bust his arm! If you trip in the hallway on a nail, or on a bad step, or on loose carpeting, or because it is too dark to see—go after him. He has a legal liability to maintain a safe premises. If he neglects his duty and you are damaged, you have a right to recover. Next time he says he won't shovel the snow off the steps and walks of the building, remind him that it is cheaper to throw salt and buy a shovel than it is to pay a damage settlement. To be on the safe side, it is a very good idea to have your own Tenant's Insurance Policy which covers theft, vandalism, fire, other types of property loss, medical and personal liability.

There are some things that you must protect against. It is very wise not to sign any insurance forms after a loss until you have had plenty of time to discuss things with your agent (not a "claims adjuster"), a lawyer, and your friends. DO NOT SIGN ANYTHING your landlord may hand you without clearing with your insurance agent and your lawyer. You will not know how much you lost until you can take a careful inventory of what is remaining, and then realizing what is gone. *Sign nothing* for 10 days after a fire. Don't let anyone rush you, they will be trying to cheat you.

22. *Remedies Cumulative, Nonwaiver*

Your landlord can sue you for each separate breach of the lease and for each time a breach occurs. The lease clauses are all enforceable unless you have a written agreement to the contrary. Even if you pay your back rents or "damages," your lease is still voided and you cannot move back. Even if your landlord takes the money, you lose. During the time of any lawsuit by either party, you must still pay the rent. No matter what notices you receive from the landlord (Five Day, Eviction, Termination), you still must pay the rent until the lease is terminated.

If you are sued, get a lawyer. Petition the court to set up a holding account for your rents if your nonpayment has something to do with building conditions or a lease breach. Try not to pay your landlord rent which he can then use to pay his lawyer to use against you.

23. *Tenant's Remedies*

Under certain circumstances, the tenant may break his lease and move out. If the landlord fails to maintain the apartment, or fails to perform repairs, renovations, or decorating as set forth in paragraph 6 of the lease, and if the tenant has sent the landlord written notice about the conditions and if the landlord doesn't correct the problems within thirty days, or send the tenant a letter telling him why he can't cure the problems within thirty days, then the tenant may send his landlord a letter notifying the landlord that the tenant will exercise paragraph 23. Send a notice to the landlord within ten days of the end of thirty days indicating that the tenant is terminating the lease. Move-out date must be specified, cannot be less than ten days from the date of the notice, and must be at the end of a calendar month. If the landlord fails to provide heat, hot water, or essential services within five days of notice of the problem, then the tenant may start the lease-break process at the end of the fifth day. Prepaid rents not used and security deposits are to be returned at the time of the move out.

Paragraph 23 is not the answer to a tenant's problems. You are still forced to pay the rent and stay at least a month, a landlord has a month to come up with a set of excuses already set out as "absolute defenses" in paragraph 6. So, even though you can break the lease for cause, it may be very difficult to convince your landlord or a judge that you had "cause," under paragraph 23.

The tenant may also sue the landlord under Illinois Municipal Code, Chapter 24, Division 13, Sec. 31 (see Appendix H and Chapter 15). This is an action to force the landlord to make repairs required by building codes. You can sue but you have to stay in the building to benefit. The only gain from Illinois Chapter 24 suits is to recover reasonable fees for the lawyer and an order against the landlord to repair things to building code specifications. This type of suit needs the support of the residents of the whole building to get results.

The lease basically offers you the chance to put up or shut up. It is the old line, If things are so bad, why don't you just get out? If they are not so bad, what are you complaining about? This clause is an aspirin. What is needed is some good doctoring. Why must we be forced to move out or suffer? Why can't we force the landlord to quick action? See discussion in paragraph 12 "Breaking the Lease/Constructive Eviction." Paragraph 23 is a rip-off excuse to deny tenants the right to a decent place to live. A landlord has the responsibility to maintain the place we live. If we are forced to move out, then we should receive compensation.

The answer to a building code problem or a lease breach is not just to have the right to move out. This simply throws the problem on the next tenant and it leaves you to deal with similar problems at your next place. The landlords will keep collecting the rents, not fixing things up and making lame excuses all the way to the bank. Paragraph 23 is a clever lawyer's clumsy way to circumvent tenants' rights granted by the Illinois Supreme Court. If you are forced to move, sue your landlord for damages and expenses. Don't let him push you around.

24. *Tenant's Waiver*

The tenant owes the rent *independently* of whatever breach the landlord might make to the lease. You must pay the rent until and unless the lease is terminated and you move out. If you win a lawsuit against the landlord, you still must pay the rent even if you can't collect the damages from him. This clause denies the power of the Illinois Supreme Court and the State Legislature. They both have held that rent withholding is legitimate under certain circumstances (see Chapter 15). You cannot sign away your rights, this clause is invalid. *Strike it out of your lease.* Rent should be dependent upon the landlord's performance to maintain the apartment and keep his promises. You can keep your part of the bargain if he can keep his. It should be that simple.

25. *Lessor's Remedies*

If the tenant owes rent money and fails to pay what he owes within five days of receiving a landlord's Five Days Notice, he can be evicted after due process from the courts.

If the tenant breaks another part of the lease and does not take the necessary action to correct the breach within ten days of the receipt of a landlord's Ten Day Notice, the tenant can be evicted through the courts.

The landlord, at his option, may simply throw the tenant out instead of going through eviction proceedings. He may also sue to collect the amount of rent the tenant might owe through the completion date of the lease, even though the tenant has been evicted. He may also collect "damages" and other costs of repairing and redecorating the apartment in order to make it rerentable. Lastly, the landlord can throw out any tenant who declares voluntary or involuntary bankruptcy, or is declared insolvent (broke) by the courts. The landlord can order the apartment vacated within thirty days and then sue to collect damages because the apartment is now empty!

Rent withholding is a legitimate form of action (see Chapters 15, 16, 17). The main thrust of this paragraph is to force the tenant to pay his rent. This sometimes amounts to an attempt by the landlord to get something for nothing. If the tenant owes rent and can't pay it, that tenant had best start packing. If the tenant will not pay rent because of legitimate cause, the landlord had best prepare for court. Properly done, a rent action in a building brings results.

It is interesting to note that a landlord can sue for all his losses, plus all the landlord's attorney's fees and all other court-related costs. The tenant cannot sue for anything except getting the repairs done. Strange that it always is the landlord who wins and the tenants who loses. Not so strange when you figure who wrote this lease in the first place.

The tenant is not a child, the landlord not a parent. We are equal. We deserve and demand equity.

Clause 25 is invalid because it grants the landlord rights prohibited to him by state law. It always takes a court to evict, to determine lease breaches, and to award damages. Strike out everything after clause A-2 on the lease starting with the "unless" in parentheses.

26. Other Agreements

The landlord is not necessarily the owner but can act for the owner. In the case of court actions against the tenant, this agent of the owner may sue in his own name, not that of the owner. The owner can name a new landlord as often as the owner wishes. If storage is part of the rental agreement, the landlord assumes no liability for the stored belongings which must be removed at the same time the lease is terminated. The invalidity or invalidation of one clause of this lease does not invalidate the rest of the lease.

Basically, the lease gives the landlord the right to sue you, but does not give you an equally easy opportunity to sue the actual owner. The landlord, as front man, can cause you grief, but you will have to go through a complicated court procedure to discover who actually owns the building. The law states that you must sue the owner as well as the landlord, agent, or manager. Owners hide behind blind or hidden trusts numbered like Swiss bank accounts (which is just where some of these accounts reside). If you can't find the owner, sue him as John Doe and then go through the lease "discovery" procedure to identify him. If you successfully challenge the lease in court, or a court decision is rendered challenging the lease, the rest of the lease stands. Meaning that you still have to pay the rent even if everything but paragraph 24 is wiped out.

Rules and Regulations

These are obvious. Read them and be prepared. You'll notice that the landlord doesn't state that he'll clean the stairs twice a week or shovel the walks or change the burned out light bulbs in the hall. But, by God, you had best not leave your wet boots in the hallway. Well, justice, you know.

There may be additional rules attached to the lease. Read these with particular care because these are the ones the management will enforce. They are extra because the landlord wants to make a point of singling them out. If you have a problem with these extra rules, get them changed or don't sign the lease. These rules may limit guests staying over, whether you can open your windows during heating season; who pays for certain utilities; or who is authorized to make repairs or install curtain rods, and so on. Beware of the addenda. A clause such as "all rugs and carpeting shall be made part of the premises when such shall be affixed to the flooring by glue, tape or tacks" or "All carpeting supplied by the lessor shall be professionally cleaned at time of termination of the lease by the tenant or the costs of which shall be assessed against security deposit," are expensive rip-offs. A friend of mine had to pay $75 to have a $50 piece of carpeting cleaned. Others have lost hundreds of dollars of tacked-down carpeting. Read the rules with an eye to changing them. Don't be cowed and don't be afraid to speak up.

Guarantee

If the landlord doesn't think the tenant is good for the rent, he may require that the tenant find somebody financially acceptable to guarantee that if the tenant defaults, the guarantor will pay the rent. Usually the tenant pays the guarantor a token sum (in this case $10.00) to seal the deal.

There are two or other landlord's leases in general use in Chicago. One is number 12R and the other is number L17. Lease 12R was the former standard lease which is slowly being replaced either by number 15 (which I have just discussed) or by number L17. Rather than do a complete breakdown of the other two leases, I will key them back to number 15 and discuss particular differences.

Apartment Lease Number 12R

The topmatter is the same as lease #15.

1. *Rent:*
   Same as paragraph 1 in lease #15.
2. *Security Deposit:*
   Generally the same as paragraph 5 in lease #15 except that the requirements to return the deposit or produce receipts are not included. The return procedure is part of state law and is required anyway, especially if you live in a building with ten or more units.
3. *False Application:*
   Same as paragraph 3 in lease #15.
4. *Condition of Apartment/Upkeep:*
   Combines paragraphs 6 and 9 as in lease #15 but makes no promises whatsoever about landlord maintaining apartment. Tenant may be responsible for repairs in apartment. Get a written clarification in your lease.
5. *Use of Apartment:*
   Similar to paragraph 8 in lease #15.
6. *Assignment, Subletting, Abandonment, Reletting, Termination, Right of Possession, Reentry:*
   Generally corresponding to paragraphs 12, 13, and 15 in #15.
7. *Alterations, Additions, Fixtures, Appliances:*
   Generally the same as paragraph 10 in lease #15.
8. *Access:*
   Generally the same as paragraph 11 in lease #15 except there is a penalty of only one month's rent for each refusal to grant the landlord access.
9. *Heating and Water:*
   The landlord agrees to supply hot and cold running water at all times, and heat from September 15 to June 1 each heating season. Exclusions and excuses relate to equipment breakdowns, strikes, or other causes beyond the control of the landlord. City building codes consider heat and water essential services and do not recognize any excuses from landlords. The landlord must supply heat and water. If there are breakdowns, they must be corrected immediately, not "soon." Call the Building Department Complaint

Department if water or heat problems arise (see the phone list in Appendix B).

10. *Fire and Casualty:*

In case of fire or other destruction, the landlord has 120 days to make repairs or terminate the lease. If the landlord elects to repair, the tenant must move out all of his possessions and pay a reduced rent during the repair time (even though he cannot use the apartment).

If there is a fire that renders your apartment unlivable, move out immediately and notify your landlord of that fact. Ask him for moving expenses and any other compensations required (time off from job, lost property, injuries, medical costs). If he refuses, sue him. At any rate, do not pay for a place that you cannot live in.

11. *Eminent Domain:*

Similar to paragraph 16 in lease #15.

12. *Surrender of Apartment:*

Similar to paragraph 15 in lease #15 with some exceptions. Landlord is not required to give advance notice about renewals or holding over (staying legally beyond the lease). If the tenant holds over without permission of the landlord, the tenant can be fined 20% of the monthly rent for each day of holding over. Always make arrangements with the landlord six weeks before moving day. Be sure whether you are or are not moving, and if you are moving, whether you can hold over if need be.

13. *Waiver by Tenant:*

A. Tenant promises to pay the rent no matter what.

B. Tenant promises to pay the rent even if the landlord is suing him, or tenant is suing the landlord.

C. Even if the tenant pays the landlord a whole month's rent for holding over five days, or all the back rents, the tenant still has to move if the landlord so desires, or the tenant may be obligated to pay double rent for another year (see Appendix H).

D. Tenant waives all notices (warnings, evictions, cancellations). This is not legally possible. All notices must be in writing and delivered in person or some other verifiable method. Evictions and "liquidated damages" (fines and penalties) must be assessed or enforced only by the courts.

E. Settling one dispute between landlord and tenant does not mean that the landlord cannot start another action for a similar reason. Just because rents are paid does not mean that the landlord cannot still evict the tenant because the rents were late, or sue for holding over.

F. Essentially the same as above (E).

G. Landlord and owner are held harmless for any type of damage or injury for whatever cause, except by specific Illinois statute. See your lawyer.

H. Tenant appoints his *landlord* as his "attorney-in-fact" to make any lease alterations as they relate to the mortgage or the building (see paragraph 17 in lease #15 about changing ownership in management).

Strike this entire paragraph 13 out of this lease. It violates Illinois state statute, the state constitution and the federal Constitution. You cannot involuntarily sign away your rights. Your landlord cannot sign your name to any paper. Your landlord is indeed liable for his negligence or for accidents and damages and you can indeed sue him. Rent is due for service received, not by grant of any kind.

14. *Legal Expenses:*

Tenant promises to pay all the landlord's legal fees if the landlord needs a lawyer or the courts to attempt to enforce the lease. Strike out this clause. Let the landlord win his money through the courts. You are not required to supply the rope at your own hanging. The court will award damages and costs as it sees fit.

15. *Rules:*

Similar to paragraph 20 in lease #15. Watch out for rule #14. It prohibits picture hooks without written permission. No court will hold you guilty if you put up pictures, just don't use a claw hammer when the nails go in. If your landlord steams about the pictures, tell him to mind his own business. We, as tenants, do not need a parent or cop-image landlord approving our daily activities or lifestyles.

16. *Binding on Heirs:*

Similar to paragraph 18 in lease #15.

17. *Confession of Judgment:*

The tenant confesses that he is guilty as accused by the landlord (in the case of nonpayment of rent or lease violation). He grants the landlord's attorney the right to plead guilty for the tenant. The tenant agrees that he waives his rights of due process and his right of appeal. He agrees to pay the rents, interest, damages, and lawyer's fees.

This clause is patently unconscionable, not to say unconstitutional and unenforceable—strike it out. The idea of the confession clause is to get a judgment against somebody who skips out on the landlord and can't be found for service or trial. Lawyers don't like it because it has a court-set (and limited) fee. Further, these cases are thrown out if they are challenged because *you cannot involuntarily sign away your rights*. Landlords are not holier than thou, they are "hole-lier."

18. *Rules and Regulations:*

Similar to the rules of lease #15. Read them over and giggle.

19. *Assignment:*

If the landlord sells the place or a new management takes over, the new people become the holders in due course of your lease and you now owe them the money instead of the original landlord. *Protect your security deposit!!* Add the words "and security deposit" after "all rights to title and interest . . ." Normally when such a transfer is made, the rents get raised, the heat gets worse, and the security deposit disappears. It is the old question: which landlord is better, Twiddle Dumm or Twiddle Dumb?

Apartment lease #17 is a revision and simplification of old lease form #12R. Apparently, there were complaints that new lease #15 was both too liberal and too detailed. Lease #L17 is printed in a modern typeface with large letters. She may look beautiful, but she's a real stinker.

Apartment Lease Number L17

The topmatter is essentially the same as lease #15.

1. *Rent:*

Same as #15.

2. *Security Deposit:*

Essentially the same as paragraph 5 in lease #15 except that there is no explicit statement as to when or how the deposit is to be returned. State law requires return of deposit within sixty days. See Chapter 15 (Illinois Revised Statutes, chapter 80.101 and Appendix H).

3. *Condition of Premises—Redelivery to Lessor:*

Lessee accepts apartment *as is.* Lessor makes no verbal promises to repair or decorate, nor any statement as to the actual condition of the apartment. Lessee will turn in apartment keys when he or she moves out, and return the apartment the way it was found—"reasonable wear excepted." The Illinois Supreme Court (see Chapter 15, *Spring* v. *Little*) holds that the landlord is responsible for the conditions of the apartment and makes a promise that everything is OK. Strike the first three lines of this clause. Do not sign away your rights.

4. *Limitation of Liability:*

The landlord claims he is not liable for any damages of any sort for any reason including broken pipes, water or snow leaks, loss of heat or water, or seeping sewerage: ". . . not liable for any damage occasioned by failure to keep premises in repair . . ." Strike this clause. It is incredible that we can be asked to sign a lease obligating us to follow a set of rules, and pay a sizeable amount of money for the privilege of having a place to live, while the landlord tells us we have to take our chances with disaster and damage. Civil law does not exempt the landlord from liability, and neither should we.

5. *Use, Sublet, Assignment:*

Generally contains the intent of paragraphs 8, 12, 13, and 15 in lease #15. There are no specific restrictions as to how long guests may visit, but it disallows taking on roommates without permission.

6. *Use and Repair:*

Corresponds to paragraph 9 in lease #15, plus more restrictions contained in the "Rules and Regulations" section of lease #15. Dancing, singing, and music lessons are prohibited, as is any sort of school or boarding house. You must carry your groceries up the back steps. Also, remember not to "tarry" in common areas, it is a violation of the lease. This is just another prissy parent clause held ready like a club, in case the landlord wants somebody out. Imagine an eviction suit because Mrs. Smith insisted on bringing her groceries up the front stairs. Shame, shame.

7. *Access:*

Tenant will allow landlord access to his apartment at "all reasonable" hours for almost any purpose including putting rent signs in the window. This varies from lease #15 in two ways. One, there is no penalty if you refuse (except eviction). Two, there is no time limit as to when the landlord can steamroll through your apartment. Friends of mine, with this lease form, were awakened several times by the landlord showing prospective tenants a tour of the building. My friends' apartment was not for rent, but it didn't stop the landlord from bringing a group of three or four trooping through a very "busy" occupied bedroom. No notice and no permission were given.

Landlords can enter after they have given notice and then it should be with a legitimate reason such as repairs. Only landlords and their employees or agents should be allowed, not "visitors." The word for this type of activity is called breaking and entering. It is called *burglary* if something is taken. It makes no difference whether your landlord has a key or not. Nobody should be allowed in your apartment without your prior knowledge and approval. Strike this clause and grant access by prior appointment only (except in case of emergency).

8. *Right to Relet:*

Generally with the same intent as paragraph 12 in lease #15.

9. *Holding Over:*

If tenant stays in apartment after the expiration of the term of the lease, the landlord can automatically renew the lease for a year *at double* the present rent, or charge the holdover tenant twice the monthly rent prorated to a daily basis for each day as written into the lease in a blank provided in paragraph 9. The landlord need only announce this after the lease expires, but before 30 days have passed. The landlord can also collect damages from the tenant if he incurs any.

I repeat, *make arrangements six weeks prior to move-out with your landlord*. If you want to hold over for several weeks or months, make a deal well in advance. Do not just sit in the place after your lease expires unless you are willing to be sued for several months rent plus be evicted. On the other hand, a landlord should notify the tenant well in advance if he intends to rerent or cancel the lease when it expires. If he rents to a new party, you must move out. It is well known that there is usually a lapse of time for cleaning, repairing, and decorating and that the landlord's urgency to remove you may be a hype to get damage money from you.

10. *Restrictions on Use:*

More rules and regulations. No pets, period. Nothing is supposed to be put or hung from the outside of the windows (including air conditioners and antennae). No storage in the stairways, hallways, or on the back porch. I would strike this clause. It has no relevance. If you want to keep a parrot, it is none of the landlord's business as long as the rest of the building doesn't mind. If you want an air conditioner, it is none of his business. If the wiring won't handle the load, then he is required by law to upgrade his system.

11. *Water and Heat:*

If the lease calls for the landlord to supply heat and hot water, he promises to do so according to municipal code requirements (see landlord obligations in Chapter 15, under the city codes). This lease states he is responsible for heat from October 1 through April 30. The code requires heat from September 15 through June 1. This paragraph also states that the tenant is responsible for code compliance for any heating equipment that the tenant might supply. What this lease does not state is that the heating and water heating apparatus supplied by the landlord must comply with the code, and must be adequate in their outputs to supply the hot water and heating needs of the tenant and the apartment. If the landlord's equipment is inadequate, the landlord is responsible for repair, maintenance, or replacement. IT'S THE LAW.

This paragraph also states that the landlord is not responsible for heat or water (hot or cold) when the system is under repair or for reasons "beyond the control" of the landlord. When a heating system breaks down, there is no heat. When it takes longer than a few hours to repair the system, there is absolutely no heat. It falls some place between charitable and reasonable when the landlord claims he is not responsible for a failure of the heating system. But if the landlord cannot or will not make immediate repairs, there is no excuse. He must maintain the heat!!! Of such things are rent strikes made. The city has an emergency service that will get the heat (and hot water) back in service, or move everybody to a place where they won't freeze (see Appendix B). When the thaw comes, get to your lawyer and bring your landlord into court.

In summary, this clause is redundant and misinformed, strike it out. Amend it to simply state that: "heat and hot water will be provided at all times as required by city code. The lessor is responsible for property maintaining and repairing all heating and water heating equipment."

12. *Storage Room:*

The landlord is not responsible for anything placed in the storage room. Storage is provided free and not as an obligation to the lease. Comment: strike the proper words in the clause to make the landlord responsible for the storage and an obligation under the lease.

13. *Forcible Detainer and 14. Confession of Judgment:*

These two clauses belong together, in a waste basket. Strike them out. They give the landlord the right to declare that you have violated your lease and then to throw you out without a court hearing! This power you grant the landlord "waives" your rights to due process and trial at law. You also declare yourself guilty of rent nonpayment and allow your landlord's attorney to read your confession to the courts.

The landlord needs due process to evict you. He must follow the laws of the state to give proper notice and have signed orders from the courts. Ignore these clauses after you strike them out.

15. *Rent after Notice or Suit:*

All rents have to be paid even if there is a lawsuit going on or about to start. Further, even if the tenant wins judgment against the landlord (and that judgment is not satisfied), the tenant still owes the rent.

16. *Payment of Costs:*

Tenant will pay all of the landlord's costs in case the landlord has to sue the tenant to enforce the lease. Strike out this clause. The judge will decide who will pay what costs. Further, this paragraph assumes that the landlord will win—this is not necessarily the case these days, my friend.

17. *Rights Cumulative:*

The landlord can sue and sue and sue you.

18. *Fire and Casualty:*

If there is a fire or other disaster, the landlord has two months to make repairs or cancel the lease. If the landlord does not complete the repairs within the two months or if he cancels, the rents apparently are due for these months during the repairs no matter what condition the apartment is in. If the lease is terminated by default to complete repairs or by direct action of the landlord, all rents paid after the fire are to be returned to the tenant (including unused rents paid before, plus the security deposit). I suggest you read my comments on paragraph 14, lease #15. If there is a fire in your apartment and the place is unlivable, move out at once and ask your landlord for compensation for moving, fire loss, and any other damages.

19. *Plurals: Successors:*

See paragraph 18 in lease #15.

20. *Severability:*

If one part of this lease is declared invalid, it does not invalidate any other part of the lease. The idea is that rents are due no matter what.

21. *Assignment by Lessor:*

If the landlord assigns the lease to a new landlord, it is the new man to whom rents are due. To protect yourself if there is an assignment, be sure to add the words *security deposit* on the second line of the assignment: . . . "all right, title, *security deposit*, and interest in . . ." This way your deposit is protected. It is a common practice for both new and old landlords to deny possession of the security deposit when they are hauled into court by a tenant for repayment. Getting this in writing before the time of assignment is important for that reason.

22. *Guarantee:*

Same as "Guarantee" in lease #15.

Oral Leases

There are other written landlord's leases in Chicago, but they are similar. Many tenants do not have a written lease. They remain at the sufferance of the landlord (although I wonder who does most of the suffering). These leases are either month-to-month leases or week-to-week leases. The determination of duration is how often rents are paid. The leases are verbal. There are few rules in oral leases because the landlord is king. Your lease may be cancelled with written notice at any time without requiring a reason for the cancellation. You must be given at least seven days to vacate if you have a week-to-week lease. You must be given thirty days if you have a month-to-month lease. The termination date of the lease has to be either at the end of the week or the end of the calendar month. Conceivably, a thirty-day notice delivered on the third of the month could not be enforced until the end of the next month (about fifty-nine days).

These verbal leases, and all written leases which have expired (hold overs), give the tenant very little protection. Heat is still required to be provided, as well as all other essentials, but it does little good to complain. The landlord will cancel your "lease" and throw you out. The only way for tenants with verbal leases to fight is to form a tenants' union or get help from a community group (see Chapter 18).

It should be noted that some slick operators execute a lease (such as #L17) with a terminating date one month after the commencing date. After that termination date, the tenant is legally a month-to-month holdover. The tenant may not even be aware of the situation. If and when he complains, BANG, out he goes. The courts see this maneuver all the time, and they assist in the removal by ordering back rents, damages, and evictions. Unfortunately, it is very difficult to get a written lease if the landlord does not want to issue one. These landlords are looking for a quick buck and no problems. People who have month-to-month leases probably cannot come up with a security deposit. They may have several children and little income. They may not speak the language or even be in the country legally. Landlords take advantage, take the money, usually in cash, and usually without issuing receipts. These same landlords milk every last dime they can out of the building by not making improvements or even paying real estate taxes. Tenants who complain are ejected. Buildings finally fall down or are condemned. The housing crisis grows, the neighborhood is blighted further, and the landlord walks away with money in his pocket and a tax writeoff. The tenants are considered inferior because they live in slum housing. So who cares anyway? Slum landlords are criminals. Month-to-month leases are tools of oppression.

APPENDIX G

The Chicago Building Code Ordinances

What follows is an excerpted summary of the Chicago building code ordinances. The code itself is available for purchase from Index Publishing Company, 308 West Randolph, Chicago, Illinois 60606. The code is published once a year by Index Publishing Company and costs $17.33 if you pick it up at their office or $18.85 if you send your money by mail. The purpose of this summary is to give you an idea of the kinds of things that are required in buildings. Some of these listings may seem a bit esoteric until you run into a problem, for instance a bathroom that has no window to the outside and no vent fan, but they all have relevance.

The building codes are loved by no one: neither by the tenant who believes the code is not strict enough to protect the tenant and force problems to be corrected, nor by the landlord who believes that the code is much too harsh and is always afraid that the inspector will be coming around. The inspectors seem to be very hard on landlords. One reason that landlords do not like to see the inspector come around is that when the buildings are inspected, landlords must pay fees, at least $25 a visit. Another reason landlords do not like to see building inspectors come around is because building inspectors often have their hands out. It is the lesser of two evils to pay the building inspector a token sum under the table rather than to make the necessary corrections.

You should also be aware that when you do get the city involved if there are really significant problems, and the landlord will not correct them, and it is impossible for your building association to correct the problems, you may find yourself being evicted by the city because of substandard conditions in the building. This is a highly unusual occurrence, but it does take place. So, when using the building codes, plan your strategies accordingly.

The numbers you see listed to the left of the building code entries refer to the chapter and subchapters contained within the building code. The text material is a summarization of what is contained in the quotation as noted by that number.

THE BUILDING CODE ORDINANCES OF CHICAGO
Excerpts, Summaries and Interpretations

39.2   The management firm (whoever collects the rents) is defined as liable for all violations within the building. The city may fine the management firm $5 to $200 for each day of each violation.

39.3, 39.4   There is a $10 to $200 per day fine for failure to obtain and post a building permit when management companies do alterations to a building.

39.5   All contractors are also liable for the same fines when working in buildings without building permits.

39.7   The building department may order the owner of a building to stop all work until the owner has obtained a permit.

39.9   "Interference with officials" allows the building inspector to enter a premises to inspect it at any time.

39.11   The city may order a building closed if that building fails to meet the code and the owner fails to make the corrections.

39.12   The owner can be ordered to bring the building into building code compliance within thirty days of the time an inspection is made if major faults are found. Or the city may go to court and take over the building to make repairs and then sue the landlord for the money. The city may also sell the property if the landlord fails to pay the city for repairs made.

41.6   The building department is required to investigate all complaints.

41.7   The building inspector is required to file a notice of what he sees and is required to order the owner to correct all violations within sixty days. If the owner does not make these corrections the city may order the work done or seize the premises.

43.1   It is unlawful to do major alterations or repairs on a building without obtaining a building permit.

47.2   Alterations defined: Any change or modification or construction or space re-arrangement in any existing building or structure.

Apartment building defined: a multiple dwelling unit for residency of three or more families containing three or more units.

52.1   All new buildings and all *existing buildings* redesigned or converted after 1-1-77 must conform to all building codes effective 1-1-77. (See 52.11.1.)

52.11   Smoke detectors are required in all residential buildings less than 80 feet tall with 6 or more residential units.

52.11.1   Not less than one approved smoke alarm shall be installed in *every* single family residence unit and *every* multiple dwelling unit (Chapters 48.2.2 and 48.2.2 define residences and dwelling units as houses and all places where rooms are rented including all apartment units in buildings less than 80 feet tall.) The detector shall be installed on the ceiling and within 15 feet of all rooms used for sleeping. There shall be at least one smoke detector in each family dwelling unit and at least one smoke detector on each floor used generally for normal living activities.

52.11.2 All apartment buildings must have at least one smoke detector on the ceiling at the top of each enclosed stairway in the building. Normally this would mean a smoke detector at the top of the front stairwell and a smoke detector at the top of the rear stairwell.

78.2 All three-story six-flats and all four-story apartment buildings must have smoke detectors as outlined in 52.11 and 52.11.1. The landlord must provide and install these detectors as of September 21, 1977.

67.4 There must be at least two exits to be used in case of fire or other emergencies from each apartment above the first floor.

67.17.1 Lighting is required at all exits, all fire escapes, and all stairwells at all times when natural lighting would be insufficient to allow someone to safely exit a building or to use the stairway.

78 Chapter 78 covers all existing buildings and specifies all the code requirements that these buildings must comply with.

78.2 Smoke detectors: see under 52.1.

78.3 Every existing building must be kept and maintained so as to eliminate conditions hazardous to the public health and safety. The city may order the owner to hire licensed architects or structural engineers to inspect the owner's building and make a report on the structural condition of that building. All buildings must comply with building codes in force at the time of the building's construction and all alterations to the building must comply with the building code at the time the alterations are made.

78.3.d.1 Registration of the building's owner or trustee must be made with the Commissioner of Buildings.

78.3.d.1 a and c Every building must have a manager or agent. His name, address, and phone number must be listed with the Commissioner.

78.3.d.4 The owner or manager of the building must state how many units are in the building and how many people can live in each unit and in each building.

78.3.d.5 The owner must post an official sign in each building as to who manages the building and how they may be contacted (phone number and address).

78.4 The building must comply with all fire protection requirements including fire extinguishers on every floor and smoke detectors at the top of all stairwells and in each apartment (see 52.11).

78.6 Every building shall be structurally sound.

78.8.5, 6, 7 Alterations and changes to the building must comply with the current building codes.

78.8.8 No more than 25% of a roof may be repaired or replaced within a twelve-month period unless the entire roof is made to conform with the current codes.

78.11 *Regulations for Buildings Used for Housing in Chicago:*
The purpose "of this ordinance is to protect the public health, safety, comfort, morals, and welfare of the city of Chicago," to retard and prevent blight. It requires: (a) minimum standards for health and sanitary equipment necessary to promote health, suppress disease, protect the safety of the occupants of the building, and the neighborhood in general; (b) facilities for ventilation, light, space, and means of egress which promote health and safety; (c) common sense from residents and landlords as to what is safe, healthful, and good for the welfare of the building and all concerned.

This code applies to all buildings where people live.

78.13.1 and 2.3 Every apartment must have a separate bathroom with a flush toilet, a bathroom sink, and a bathtub or shower except that two two-room apartments may share the same toilet facilities.

78.13.5, 6 Every apartment must have a kitchen sink in good working order.

78.13.7 Every apartment must be capable of being heated to at least 65° F during the day when the outside temperature is -10° F. Even if the owner requires the tenant to provide heat, the owner is responsible for the heating if the tenant is unable to keep the apartment at minimum temperatures required by this clause. Use of stoves are not permitted as a source of heat.

78.13.8 If the owner supplies heat, it must be available from September 15 to June 1 during the heating season. The minimum temperature of the rooms heated are as follows: 6:30 A.M. temperature must be 60° F; 7:30 A.M. temperature must be at least 65° F; 8:30 A.M. until 10:30 P.M. the temperature must be at least 68° F; 10:30 P.M. until 6:30 A.M. the temperature may not fall below 55° F.

78.13.10 and 11 All sinks and shower tubs are to be provided with hot and cold running water 24 hours a day. The hot water must be at least 120° F at all times.

78.14 Each room (except a bathroom or closet) where people live shall have a window big enough to let sufficient light into the room. Essentially the window should have an area of approximately 10% of the floor area of the room.

78.14.2 and 78.14.5 Every room people live in should have natural ventilation equal approximately to 5% of the floor area. The windows must also open at least that wide. If ventilation cannot be natural or is impractical, then mechanical ventilation is acceptable where most of the new air being brought in is fresh and the old air is being expelled from the building.

Toilets and bathrooms must be ventilated to the outside.

78.15.1 Every family unit shall have a safe, unobstructed means of egress leading to a safe and open space at ground level in case of fire or other emergency. These emergency exits must not require a key to open them from the inside.

78.15.6 There shall be no storage underneath steps and stairwells unless the stairwell is constructed of materials with at least a one-hour fire rating.

78.15.7 Every hallway, corridor, stairway, exit, fire escape door, and other means of egress or exit shall be kept clean and unencumbered at all times and every exit area shall be adequately lit by electricity.

78.15.8 Every fire exit shall be properly marked.

78.16.1 *Space, Use, and Location of Apartments:*
Every family unit shall contain at least 125 square feet for each of the first two occupants, 100 square feet for each of the next two occupants, and 75 square feet for each added occupant.

Thus,

2 people require 250 sq. ft.
3 people require 350 sq. ft.
4 people require 450 sq. ft.
5 people require 525 sq. ft.
6 people require 600 sq. ft.
7 people require 675 sq. ft.
8 people require 750 sq. ft.

78.16.2 In every family unit where people sleep, sleeping rooms must contain at least 70 square feet for the first person, at least 50 square feet for each additional adult, and 35 square feet for each child between the ages of two and twelve.

Thus,

2 adults sleeping in a room = 120 sq. ft.
2 adults and 1 child sleeping in a room = 155 sq. ft.
2 adults and 2 children sleeping in a room = 190 sq. ft.
2 adults and 3 children sleeping in a room = 225 sq. ft.
2 children sleeping in a room = 105 sq. ft.
3 children sleeping in a room = 140 sq. ft.
4 children sleeping in a room = 175 sq. ft.

5 children sleeping in a room = 210 sq. ft.
3 adults sleeping in a room = 170 sq. ft.
4 adults sleeping in a room = 220 sq. ft.
5 adults sleeping in a room = 270 sq. ft.

78.16.3   Every room used exclusively as a bedroom shall have direct access to a toilet without having to pass through any other room used exclusively for sleeping.

78.16.5   Basement apartments must be waterproofed, dry, and with at least the same window and ventilation percentages as required in the code for all other apartments.

Maintenance

78.17   No owner shall rent an apartment or room which is not safe, clean, sanitary, and fit for human occupancy and which does not comply with the particular requirements of this code.

78.17.1   The foundation, exterior walls, and exterior roof shall be substantially watertight and protected against rodents and it shall be kept in sound condition and repair.

78.17.1 (a) and (b)   The foundation shall support the building. Every exterior wall shall be free of holes, breaks, loose or rotting boards, or timbers, and free of other conditions which would admit rain or dampness to the inside.

(c)   The roof shall be tight and have no defect which would admit rain or dampness and drainage shall be adequate to prevent rain water from causing dampness in the walls.

(d)   The dwelling shall be in rat-stopped condition—all holes in the foundation and first floor are to be plugged up with cement, concrete, or sheet steel, and the building adequately protected against other rodents.

(e)   All cornices, moldings, and other exterior projections from the building shall be kept in repair and free from cracks and defects which make them hazardous and dangerous.

Floors, Interior Walls, and Ceiling Maintenance

78.17.2   Every floor, interior wall, and ceiling shall be kept in sound condition and good repair, and, further:

(a)   Every floor shall be free of holes and wide cracks that could admit rodents and cause accidents.

(b)   Every floor shall be free of bad boards or broken or protruding boards.

(c)   Every exterior wall shall be free of holes and large cracks.

(d)   All interior walls, seams, and interior woodwork shall be free of flaking, peeling, chipped, or loose paint, plaster, or structural materials.

(e)   Plaster, paint, and all other surface materials shall be easily cleanable and reasonably smooth, clean, and tight.

(f)   Every toilet and bathroom floor surface shall be *substantially impervious* to water and be capable of being maintained easily and in a clean and sanitary condition.

Lead Paint

Lead paint is essentially prohibited in all dwelling units. If the owner or landlord does not remove lead-based paint and repaint with an acceptable paint within fourteen days of the time that the health department or the building department notifies the owner, the city has the right to come in and do the repaint job and bill the landlord for the costs. Lead paint poisons small children.

Windows, Doors and Hatchways, Maintenance

78.17.3   Every window, exterior door, and basement hatchway shall be substantially tight and shall be kept in good condition and repair.

(a)   Every window shall be fully supplied with panes without holes and cracks.

(b)   Every window sash (window frame) shall be in good condition and reasonably tight.

(c)   Every window other than fixed window shall be opened easily and shall be held in place with the normal window counterbalance and chain hardware, or other internal mechanisms.

(d)   Every exterior door, hinge, and *latch* (lock) shall be in good condition.

(e)   Every exterior door when closed shall fit reasonably within its frame.

(f) and (g)   All doors, windows, and hatchways shall be watertight, windtight and insect- rodent-tight from the exterior.

(h)   All doors which are used as exits shall be capable of opening from the inside easily and without a key.

Screens

78.17.4 (a)   Every basement window which can be opened shall have a heavy wire mesh screen to keep out rodents.

(b)   "From April 15 to November 15 of each year, every door opening directly from any family unit to the outdoors and every window or other outside opening used for ventilation purposes shall be supplied with a screen of not less than 16 gauge mesh per inch and every screen door shall have a self-closing device in good working condition. However, no such screens shall be required for a family unit on a floor above the fourth floor unless required by the Department of Buildings when unusual circumstances of insects prevail." The landlord is required to supply these screens.

Stairways and Porch Maintenance

78.17.5 Every stairway inside and outside the dwelling and every porch shall be kept in safe condition and sound repair.

(a) Every flight of stairs and every porch floor shall be free of holes, grooves, and cracks which are large enough to constitute a possible accident hazard.

(b) and (c) Stairs with more than two steps must have handrailings in good, well-maintained condition.

(d) No flight of stairs shall have settled more than one inch out of its intended position or shall have pulled away from its supporting or adjacent structure.

(e) No flight of steps shall have rotting, loose, or deteriorating supports.

78.17.6 Cellars and basements shall be maintained in a safe and sanitary condition. They shall have dry floors, proper sewer traps, proper sewer drains, no junk or other fire, health, or safety hazards about.

78.17.7 All the chimney stacks and flues shall be safe and maintained without leaks.

78.17.8 No accumulations of stagnant water will be permitted anywhere on the property.

Occupants' Responsibilities

78.18.1 (a) Keep own dwelling in clean, sanitary, and safe condition.

(b) Keep all plumbing and other fixtures in clean and sanitary condition and take care not to destroy landlord-owned equipment.

(d) An occupant is required to exterminate insects, rodents, and pests only if they are present in that one unit alone. The landlord must take care of exterminating the entire building if insects, rodents, and pests are in more than one apartment.

(e) All occupants must place their garbage and refuse in the proper containers as supplied by their landlord (normally this means the trash receptacles at the back of the building, outside). The refuse must not be placed in any hallway, stairwell, or vestibule landing.

(f) While the landlord is required to supply screens between April 15 and November 15 of each summer season, the occupants may be required to hang and remove the screens if the landlord does not provide such service.

(g) The occupant must not store materials which are dangerous, hazardous, or insect- or rodent-infested.

Landlord's Responsibilities

78.18.2 The landlord must comply with all requirements imposed upon him in this chapter.

(b) The landlord must maintain, in a clean, sanitary, and safe condition, the shared or public areas of the dwelling or premises and maintain and repair any equipment of a type specified in this code which he supplies or is required to supply, including all stoves, refrigerators plumbing fixtures, and heating devices.

(c) The landlord must exterminate any insects, rodents, or other pests in any one apartment if it is the landlord's fault that the infestation occurred. He also must exterminate in any dwelling units and in all dwelling units in the building if the problem exists in two or more units regardless of the cause of the infestation.

(d) The landlord must supply and maintain refuse disposal facilities and have refuse collected by a city or private scavenger at least once a week.

78.18.3 Even if the owner or landlord of a building imposes certain obligations on the occupants such as supplying their own heating equipment or providing for their own extermination, and if the occupants fail to perform and provide proper heating or extermination for themselves, the city holds the owner responsible and requires him to provide proper heat and to clean up any rodent or roach problems.

80 Essentially, gas water heaters and all gas and oil furnaces need permits to be installed and require proper venting to the outside.

Ventilation (Chapter 81)

Essentially, all rooms must have an adequate supply of fresh air. Windows, skylights, and transoms must be large enough when they are opened to let in fresh air and let stale air out, that is, approximately 5% of the total floor space. If mechanical systems are used (such as fans and venting systems), they should move the air in and out as efficiently as the windows. If there are vent holes, they must vent to the roof and must not leak water, such as vents from kitchens and from bathrooms. In the case of mechanical or vent hole openings, they should be large enough to move air in such a way as not to create drafts. Bathrooms must be vented in such a way that air is not circulated back inside the building.

Kitchens (small, less than 125 sq. ft.): If ventilation or window space is less than 5%, that is, less than a six-square-foot opening to outside, then an exhaust fan is required to move the air at 1.5 cubic feet per minute per square foot of floor area. If the kitchen is larger than 125 square feet, at least 5% of the total floor space must be available in open window space, open transoms, and vents. If not, then a mechanical vent fan is required to move the air at at least 1.5 cubic feet of air per minute per square foot of floor area.

Bathrooms: Bathrooms must have a ventilation opening equal to 5% of the floor area of the room. If there is no natural ventilation, then mechanical ventilation is required in the form of an exhaust fan which will move the air at at least 1.5 cubic feet per minute per square foot of floor space. Air supplies coming through ventilation must be clean and dust free.

81.7 Enclosed toilets without access to normal ventilation must have mechanical ventilation.

81.25 Every ventilating system, either natural or mechanical, shall be kept in good repair and in operation so as to ensure the required ventilation of all rooms and spaces to be ventilated during all hours of human occupancy. This means the windows must be able to open and close and all ventilation fans must be in operating condition.

Plumbing

82.3 No person shall construct, add to, or alter any parts of any plumbing system without examination and permit from the water and building departments.

82.11 The owner must protect all pipes in his building from freezing during the winter.

82.11.1 In every existing building all plumbing facilities, piping, fixtures, appurtenances, and appliances shall be maintained in good operating condition and repair. The landlord is required by law to maintain the toilet, the tubs, the showers, and the sinks so they work properly. He is also required to maintain water pressure.

82.14 When odd or defective plumbing is remodeled or replaced or additional fixtures installed, including sewers, the entire system shall be made to conform to the modernized requirements contained within chapter 82.

82.15 Minor repairs to fix leaks do not require permits, but major repairs to the plumbing system do require permits.

82.16 Every plumbing fixture which is rarely used so that there is a danger that the seal on the drain trap would be lost, shall be removed and the outlets securely closed.

82.17 All plumbing work within buildings in the city of Chicago shall be performed by a licensed and bonded plumbing contractor or a journeyman plumber under the direction of a licensed and bonded plumbing contractor.

82.98 Each plumbing fixture shall be separately trapped except for double laundry tubs and combination sink and dishwashers.

82.100   All sewer traps must be accessible to repairs.

82.102   The size of every clean-out opening for drains, such as bath-tub drains shall be of a size and thickness for the standard drain pipes required to drain the appliance, and the clean-out cap or plug shall be made of heavy, red brass not less than ⅛-inch thick, and provided with a heavy raised nut or recessed socket in order that the pressure of sewage draining through the pipes shall not blow a cap off of the trap clean-out.

82.107   Where backflow is a problem, all drains shall be provided with a suitable backwater value to stop the backflow.

82.111   Used fixtures must be free of cracks and chips, must be enamel or hard natural stone and must be sanitized to the satisfaction of the Health Department.

82.117   Toilets shall, at each flushing, be supplied with a sufficient quantity of water to remove all waste matter and properly cleanse the internal surfaces exposed to the atmosphere. The same pipes that feed sinks and drinking fountains shall not also feed toilets.

82.128.1   A bathroom shall not be vented to any other room except the outside.

82.141   All plumbing and pipe seals shall be of the flange-to-flange screw type with soft metal seals. No rubber, leather, putty, plaster, or plastic compound shall be applied to make the joints tight.

The Water Supply and Distribution System

83.2   The Water Department may give owners of buildings an order to fix water supply problems or water can be cut off.

83.6   City water may be shut off by the city if alterations or major repairs are done to the water system in the building without a permit.

83.7   Only master plumbers—licensed and bonded by the city—can work on the water pipes.

83.9   Most work on the water system (except emergency repairs) requires a permit.

83.22   The service pipe is the water pipe from the water main in the street to the dwelling itself. Each service pipe shall be of a sufficient size to permit the continuous and ample flow of water to supply adequately all floors at any given time. The minimum service pipe size is one inch in internal diameter.

83.27   In any building where consumption of water requires a larger service than can be supplied by the existing tap or connection, a new tap or connection shall be made from city mains of the size required. (If there is not enough water pressure in your building your landlord is required to make the necessary larger pipe connections with the city.)

83.46   Where required because of low water pressure, wherever the problem exists in the building and the service pipe supplying the water is two inches or less and the pressure of the water supply is insufficient to furnish an adequate supply, an automatic compression pressure increasing device or a high-level holding tank may be installed.

83.47   All plumbing fixtures shall be provided with a sufficient supply of water for flushing to maintain them in sanitary condition. Every fixture shall be designed to be flushed quickly and at each flushing to remove all waste material.

83.51   All water supply pipes and control valves shall be of sufficient size and capacity to supply water to all fixtures. The pipes must be such that a drop in pressure on a top floor of the building during times of water usage in the rest of the building is not so great as to make the water flow on the top floor inadequate.

83.6   Water pumps that make noise through the water system or cause water hammers are prohibited.

Enforcement of Electrical Standards

86.13   Without a permit it is unlawful to alter or change electrical wiring. A permit is required to bring wiring in a building up to code standards.

86.14   It is unlawful to overfuse any electrical circuit.

86.16   It is unlawful for any person to engage in the business of electrical contracting without first being registered as a contractor within the state of Illinois.

86.20–26   A supervising electrician shall be on the job. He is certified by the city after the successful completion of an examination.

86.27   No electrical equipment shall be installed or altered without a permit.

86.47–54   Management and owners must obtain electrical permits on a monthly basis for regular routine changes and work. A certified supervising electrician must be appointed. This means that a janitor or regular repairman employed by the owner must be certified by the city as the man responsible for electrical repairs in the building.

87.110.12   All live electrical parts or wires must be enclosed.

87.210.15 (a)   The number of circuits for lighting and appliances shall be sufficient for the actual load to be served.

(b)   Wall outlet circuits and ceiling lighting circuits shall be separated from each other. Normally no lighting circuit shall be connected to a receptacle circuit.

87.210.21   Fourteen-gauge wire is the minimum required in all wiring in the city of Chicago.

87.210.24   A receptacle or wall outlet is required every six feet along each wall of every room.

87.210.25   Essentially, in a kitchen with a refrigerator, a 20-amp circuit, separate from the rest of the house circuits, is required.

If you keep blowing fuses your apartment is underwired and is in violation of the city code. Landlords are required to provide enough circuits and enough power to run most normal modern electrical appliances.

Fire Extinguishers

91.47   Fire extinguishers are required in all multiple-dwelling buildings with a floor area of more than 3000 square feet of space regardless of the number of stories involved. The extinguishers shall be located on each floor within 75 feet of all units that are on that floor.

91.52.1   There is a fine of $10 to $200 for each day of each offense.

The landlord is required to maintain the fire extinguishers in a fully charged and operating condition at all times.

If you believe that you have code violations in your building, call the building department and make a complaint. The building department is required to respond to your request for an inspection and they are also obligated to send you a written response to the complaints that you have made. You must, however, ask for a written reply. The number to call is 744-3420. Also see Appendix B for other numbers.

APPENDIX H

Illinois Revised Statutes as They Relate to Tenants and Renting

The Illinois Revised Statutes contain some enumerated tenants' rights. Chapter 80 contains the landlords/tenants laws. The following is a brief summary of its important points:

80.2   Hold-over renters (staying longer than the term of the lease without renewing the lease) remaining without permission are obligated to pay rent at *double* the rent in the lease. (Make sure you get written permission to hold over or you can get socked for a fortune.)

80.4   The *landlord* may enter your apartment and eject you if you owe rent for six or more months and the landlord has obtained a court order to evict you. (The Sheriff can do the same job a lot sooner if you are evicted by the courts.)

80.5   The landlord may cancel a long lease (a year-to-year lease after the first year) by giving the tenant a sixty-day notice of cancellation.

80.6   On a weekly or monthly rent agreement (usually a verbal lease where the rent is paid once a week or once a month and the lease is "renewed" for a like period of time), the landlord can cancel the agreement by giving you a seven-day or thirty-day written notice (seven days for a week-by-week rental, thirty days for a month-to-month rental). No reason is required.

80.8   The demand for rent is the key to all rent laws and almost all landlord/tenant problems, as well as the hammer which prevents tenants from exercising their rights to complain. If rents are in arrears, the landlord can give the tenant a written five-day notice to pay up all back rent or move out. If the tenant does not pay, the landlord can go to court and get an eviction order, which automatically breaks the lease. If you won't leave, the landlord will send the Sheriff out to take the doors off your apartment and move your possessions to the street.

80.9   Notice to quit. If the tenant breaks or defaults on the terms of the lease (a very easy thing because of the bugbear nature of leases), the landlord may give the tenant ten days to vacate by sending him a letter ordering him out. If you won't leave, then the landlord goes to court, you are found guilty of forcible entry and detainer, and the Sheriff takes your door off and, well, you know the rest.

80.10   Delivery of the notices mentioned above can be in person to anyone living in the apartment over ten years of age, via registered mail, or by nailing the notice to the door.

80.12   Even if you receive no notice at all, when the term of your lease is up, you must leave or be hooked for double rents (mentioned in 80.2), possibly for another period equal to the length of your present lease.

80.16–80.27   The landlord may seize a tenant's property only in lieu of rents not paid. (Section 80.4 states that he must wait six months to enter the apartment, however, before he can seize the property.) He must file a "distress warrant" with the courts before he can seize the property. He cannot take personal property such as clothing. The landlord must serve the warrant on the tenant (if the tenant can be found) and the tenant may appear in court to explain why he refused to pay the rents. If the judge finds in favor of the landlord (a good guess) the landlord can sell the property, keep what rent is due, and give the remainder (if any) back to the tenant. This property seizing takes place only when the landlord can get into your apartment and only when you have not been evicted by the Sheriff months earlier. But this does happen.

80.34   The tenant has the right to remove *all removable* fixtures which the tenant owns and controls from a property (as long as there is no distress warrant against them).

80.37   It is unlawful to refuse to rent an apartment because the applicant has children less than 14 years of age.

80.43   If a landlord grants a rent concession, he must write "rent concession" and the amount of the concession directly on the lease. This protects you against the verbal promise and later sharp jab to your bank account.

80.62   Rent credit. If the landlord fails to pay the water, gas, or electrical bills for your building, provided he has promised as part of the lease to pay them, and if the nonpayment of those bills means the utilities will be shut off, you as a tenant may pay them and deduct that amount from your rent.

80.71   Tenants Complaint of Violations of Government Regulations, a 1963 act (complaints about building code violations or some other type of cheating covered by state law):

"Termination of, or refusal to renew, lease prohibitions—validity of provision in lease.

"It is declared to be against the public policy of the State for a landlord to terminate or refuse to renew a lease or tenancy of property used as a residence on the ground that the tenant has complained to any governmental authority of bonafide violations of any applicable building code, health ordinance, or similar regulation. Any provision in any lease, or any agreement or understanding purporting to permit the landlord to terminate or refuse to renew a lease or tenancy for such reason is void."

This is an antiretaliation act. One needs to prove retaliation with your sworn recollection of statements by your landlord, witnesses, submission of a letter from the landlord telling you that "you'll be sorry if you keep this up" or "it isn't nice to call the city." With such evidence, if you go to court you might prove your case, collect actual damages, and perhaps be able to stay where you are.

80.91 *Liability:* The landlord is liable for damages arising out of injury to person and property if it can be proved that the landlord was negligent. Anything in a lease to the contrary is unenforceable. You cannot sign away your Constitutional rights, and the landlord cannot take them from you.

80.101 *Security deposits:* A lessor of a residential property containing ten or more units ... must supply an itemized list of damages within thirty days after you vacate your apartment. He has to supply the paid receipts of actual repairs or repair estimates (if not completed). If, within a maximum of sixty days after you have moved out, he cannot show the paid receipts for all work done (he must have completed the work and paid for it), then he owes you *all* of the security deposit (not just the residue).

The other part of tenants' rights and dealings with landlords is the question of "forcible entry and detainer." This is legal phrasing for illegally entering or remaining in an apartment. Rent or eviction court is really Forcible Detainer Court. The landlord claims that you owe him rent or you broke your lease, or the lease is over and he wants you out. The judge finds that you have forcibly stayed and orders you to leave. The law spends some time defining what illegal acts your landlord is prohibited from doing as it relates to his coming into your apartment. You do have rights!

Illinois Revised Statutes, Chapter 57: Forcible Entry and Detainers

57.1 Whoever enters into your apartment must enter in a "peaceable manner." For instance, your landlord cannot force his way into your place to demand the rent.

57.2 *Forcible entry* (definition of nonpeaceful means of entering): Entering at any time without your permission or a court order, or peaceable entry but then refusing to leave when asked.

57.3 You must be given at least thirty-days written notice to vacate a premises (such as when the building is to be converted to a condominium).

As a tenant you are neither permitted to enter an empty or unoccupied apartment (except for official business, such as accompanying a building inspector) nor are you permitted to remain in your apartment after the lease is terminated.

57.4   Normally your landlord cannot enter your apartment to seize property without a court order (see 80.4).

Illinois Municipal Code, Chapter 24, Division 13

31 and 31.1   Tenants in a building and property owners within 500 feet of a building may sue the landlord and owner if there is a suspicion that building code or other related ordinances are in violation.

If it can be established through inspectors' reports or other evidence that violations do exist, you have won your case, prima facie.

The plaintiffs may obtain corrective measures (injunctive relief) through the courts and also recover reasonable lawyer's fees.

Presumably anyone suing under this act would also be protected from retaliatory evictions or other actions.

APPENDIX I

Sample Housing Conditions and Organizing Survey

This is a short-form housing survey. We originally developed a five-page questionnaire but found it was too cumbersome. This sample should be reworked to reflect the specific problems you have. It should state the name of the owner, management company, or name of the building. In addition to surveying conditions, it reveals what rents are, how they have changed, and what type of support you have in your organizing attempts.

(Name and Address of Organization)

Dear Tenant,

For too long _____ Management Company has been making promises to the people who live in the buildings that it owns or manages. And for too long these promises have gone unfulfilled. Each of us has spoken to the company and asked them to fix, finish, install, or replace something. Most of the time these things have just not gotten done. Because we ask alone, individually, we can't bring enough pressure on _____ to get action. Therefore, we the residents of a _____ Company building at _____ are forming a tenants' union to bring pressure on _____. When we do this, things will start getting fixed and the landlord will listen to our problems. We have found that only through organizing together _all_ the tenants in a building can we get things done.

We insist that the building and apartments where we
live be safe, clean, and well repaired. We insist that
we as tenants be respected as people and not treated
like a commercial commodity, pushed around, and robbed
once a month for the rent.

For starters, here is a survey which will enable you
and us to see what problems there are. Will you please
take five minutes and fill it out? Will you join us,
so that all of us can live in decent, clean apartments
with the dignity we deserve?

1. Does your electrical service work properly
    (outlets, switches, lights, fuses)?   YES   NO
2. Do your appliances work properly (stove,
    refrigerator)?   YES   NO
3. Does your plumbing work properly (leaks,
    pressure, hot water)?   YES   NO
4. Do you have all the doors, windows, storm
    windows, screens that you need?   YES   NO
5. Of the ones you have, do all of them work
    properly (close, lock, unbroken)?   YES   NO
6. Are all of your walls and ceilings free of
    loose paint, plaster, holes, leaks?   YES   NO
7. During the winter is your apartment warm
    enough without being too hot?   YES   NO
8. Is your apartment free of roaches and mice? YES   NO
9. Are the public areas of your building kept
    clean and in good repair?   YES   NO
10. Do your building's outside doors and
    mailboxes lock properly?   YES   NO
11. Is there enough lighting in public areas   YES   NO
    at night?
12. Has landlord responded to your complaints
    about building problems promptly
    and courteously?   YES   NO
13. Has landlord kept promises to you about
    repairing and maintaining your building?   YES   NO

14. If you have any other problems than those listed or
    want to detail any of the above, please do (use the
    back if you need more room).

    _____

    _____

    _____

    _____

15. Have you had an unjustified rent raise
    recently?   YES NO
16. How much has your rent been raised in the
    last two years? From $___ to $___.
17. Would you be willing to join a tenants'
    union to pressure the landlord into
    maintaining building properly and keeping
    the rents fair?   YES NO
18. Would you be willing to help organize a
    meeting of other interested tenants in
    your building who want to act and bring
    landlord into line?   YES NO

Name_____

Address_____

Zip_____Phone_____Best time to call_____

Thank you for your help.

_____

Signature (officer of organization)   Date

APPENDIX J

Tenants' Association Organizational Bylaws and Charter

This is the set of bylaws established by our tenants' association. It states our purposes and establishes a written set of procedures. Use this as a sample and starting point for your own group and modify the charter to fit your particular situation.

Length of the term of office should be practical: long enough that someone can learn the ropes and short enough that he or she isn't worn to a frazzle.

In our group, we tried to be egalitarian. We didn't want a "leader" per se, so we called our chief officer the *chairman*. I think it is bad policy to have a few elites in charge of the association. You must spread the work around in order to get continuing support.

If your group is going to incorporate, you must have bylaws and officers, so a charter is a necessary step. If you do not incorporate, a charter is still a good idea.

Our charter was developed by the entire association and put in working, practical form by Jerry Smeltzer and David deVries.

Sample Tenants' Association Charter and Bylaws

I. Name
This organization shall be known as the ——— Tenants' Association, hereafter also known as the Association and/or the TA.

II. Purpose
To organize tenants, occupants, and residents and to collectively and mutually defend tenants' rights, both legally and morally, in all dealings with the landlord, manager, and owner of our building.

To educate ourselves to enable us to survive as tenants with dignity.

To mutually aid and assist all residents for purposes relating to, but not limited to, the health, safety, welfare, security, and comfort of each resident.

To mutually and collectively protect ourselves so we may pursue our daily lives as tenants, without interference or threat from the landlord, manager, or owner.

To assist tenants in other buildings with their own attempts to form their own tenants' groups by providing information and advice, and to join in citywide and statewide tenants' activities.

III. Membership

A. None but actual residents in the building may become members.

B. All residents over fourteen years of age are eligible for voting membership in the Association.

C. Residents may become members by notifying the treasurer of the Association and paying dues.

D. Members may leave the Association by notifying the secretary in writing.

E. Members will be considered resigned from the Association if they fail to pay dues for three months and/or fail to attend meetings or respond to notices of meetings. Members who contact the treasurer for the purpose of informing the secretary of their continued interest will be considered reactivated if they pay their dues.

F. Membership is prohibited to any representative, agent, or direct employee of the landlord, manager, and owner. When rent concessions are granted to residents by the landlord for work performed, the entire membership shall evaluate the relationship between the landlord and those particular residents. If a conflict of interest is determined to exist, then those particular residents will be barred from membership or asked to resign. When no conflict exists, the residents will be admitted and/or their membership continued.

G. All members shall agree to abide by the bylaws of the Association and by the ordinances and rules it shall pass. Payment of dues will constitute acceptance of the bylaws.

IV. Meetings

A. Regular business meetings shall be held on the fourth Monday of every month at 8:30 P.M.

B. Special meetings may be called by any member of the Association through application to the secretary who must notify all members of the purpose, time, and place of the meeting.

C. The secretary shall call all meetings to order.

D. A quorum for any meeting shall be more than half of all members in good standing.

E. Meetings shall be held within the building.

F. Order of Business:

    Call to order
    Reading of previous meeting's minutes
    Reports of committees and officers

Treasurer's report
Unfinished business
New business
Nominations and elections
Good and welfare
Adjournment

G. The chairman shall at all times keep the meeting in order. He/she shall have the authority to rule any member out of order if the member becomes unruly, speaks out of turn, or interrupts another member.

H. To pass any motion, action, or ordinance a majority of all those present and voting is needed. Under no circumstances shall any motion, ordinance, or action pass if it receives less than 25% of the total number of members of the Association

I. Proxy votes will be acceptable if the absent member previously submits a written notice to the secretary and states what that member's vote will be. No other proxy or absentee votes will be allowed.

J. Motions defeated may be reintroduced once in the same meeting.

K. *Robert's Rules of Order* may be employed if required.

V. Officers

A. Secretary/Treasurer

The Secretary's duties shall include retaining copies of all records, correspondence, and minutes; carrying out all correspondence and making minutes of all meetings; sending out notices of all meetings; notifying members of all pertinent events and activities; calling meetings to order; counting written ballots with the chairman; admitting residents to membership; keeping membership rolls; formally writing up all approved legislation; acting in the stead of the chairman when the chairman is absent.

As Treasurer he/she shall retain all financial records; keep books; issue receipts; collect dues; collect other funds; make deposits and issue checks; pay all bills and approved demands.

B. Chairman

The Chairman of the Association shall preside over all meetings of the Association; appoint committees and receive committee reports; approve all correspondence; act as spokesman for the Association; negotiate, represent, and defend Association policies, actions, and members to the landlord, manager, and owner; oversee the daily operations or problems of the Association.

C. All officers shall be elected for a period of six months.

D. No more than one member from the same dwelling unit shall hold office simultaneously.

E. An officer shall not succeed himself more than once (two consecutive terms only) nor shall any person hold a position as an officer for more than three consecutive terms combined.

F. An officer may be recalled from office at a special meeting called for that purpose. It shall require a two-thirds quorum to impeach the officer and a majority vote of that quorum to remove the officer.

G. New elections will be held immediately to replace the officer recalled.

VI. Dues and Finances

A. The sources of revenue for the Association shall be regular monthly dues from the membership; proceeds from special benefits; special assessments; the interim collection of rents; and other sources.

B. All funds will be placed in the regular operations account of the Association with the exception of rent monies.

C. All rent monies shall be placed in a separate account. These monies will be used to pay the landlord rents due and owing; or pay qualified workmen and suppliers to make necessary and required repairs and to supply necessary and required materials; or pay the courts, as so ordered; or refund member's rents as required.

D. Three signatures will be required to release funds from the banking accounts. The Treasurer will sign and obtain two cosignatures from among the membership.

E. Expenditures of funds will be made with the general knowledge and approval of the membership.

F. Dues shall be paid to the Association Treasurer.

G. The Treasurer shall also collect the rents from all members as required and when necessary.

H. An amended dues structure will be allowed for students and other members not fully employed. The structure will be determined by the membership at large.

VII. Amendments to the Bylaws

These Bylaws may be amended by a majority vote conforming to Chapter IV, Section I after notification to all members of intent to change the Bylaws.

VIII. Ratification

These Bylaws will be ratified when 51% of all residents eligible for membership vote for ratification at a special meeting called for that purpose, and affix their signatures herein.

APPENDIX K

Collective Bargaining Agreement and Contract

This is a contract between the tenants' association and the owner or manager of a building. It grants recognition and rights. This is what every building ought to have to protect tenants. The struggle to get such an agreement signed is long and difficult, but it is well worth it.

You must attach to the back of a general agreement a specific list of demands, repair schedules, concessions, arrangements, and so on. Consult your community group or a lawyer to make sure you have everything you need in the agreement before offering the contract to the building management.

Good luck friends, and congratulations.

The credit for this contract goes to David deVries, an association member who researched and prepared the first draft.

Date_____

COLLECTIVE BARGAINING AGREEMENT AND CONTRACT

between

_____ and _____

Agent   Tenants' Association
Chicago, Illinois   Chicago, Illinois

Definitions:

LANDLORD: _____ Management Co. located at _____ and authorized representatives and agents, and their assignees.

TENANTS' ASSOCIATION: The sole agent for the tenants, residents, and occupants of the (above) building and their designated and authorized representatives, agents, and assignees.

BUILDING: The multiple-dwelling unit building described as located at _____, Chicago, Illinois, County of Cook, ss.

I. Recognition of Association:

A. The LANDLORD hereby recognizes the TENANTS' ASSOCIATION as the sole representative of the tenants, residents, and occupants in regard to all matters pertaining to the maintenance, upkeep, security, safety, and general condition of the building and property on which the building is situated.

B. The LANDLORD shall have the right to negotiate with individual tenants on such matters as length and condition of lease and amount of rent.

C. The TENANTS' ASSOCIATION reserves the right to enter into negotiations with the LANDLORD on behalf of an individual tenant if said tenant so requests the ASSOCIATION'S representation.

D. (1) The LANDLORD hereby recognizes the right of the TENANTS' ASSOCIATION to recruit tenants and potential tenants into the ASSOCIATION and the LANDLORD shall not deny the ASSOCIATION access to tenants and potential tenants. (2) The LANDLORD shall advise all potential tenants of the existence of the ASSOCIATION prior to the signing of any lease and shall indicate how the ASSOCIATION may be contacted. (3) LANDLORD shall advise ASSOCIATION of all new tenants within fifteen days of move-in.

II. Continuity

A. This AGREEMENT and CONTRACT shall remain in force regardless of the person, persons, company, corporation, or trust which/who shall own and/or manage this BUILDING.

B. This AGREEMENT shall remain in force indefinitely subject to renegotiation.

III. Renegotiation

A. Either party shall have the right to request renegotiation of this AGREEMENT.

IV. Good Faith

A. It is agreed by both parties that they will bargain in good faith regarding, but not limited to, section I of this AGREEMENT.

B. Agreements reached by the parties to this CONTRACT shall be written and authorized representatives of both parties will affix their signatures to such documents.

C. It shall constitute a breach of good faith, and a breach of this AGREEMENT, for the LANDLORD to offer special concessions or other inducements or threats to an individual tenant in an attempt to disrupt or destroy the TENANTS' ASSOCIATION or discourage the tenant from participating in the activities of the ASSOCIATION.

D. It shall constitute a breach of good faith, and a breach of this AGREEMENT, for the LANDLORD to discriminate against a tenant by reason of that tenant's membership in the TENANTS' ASSOCIATION or his participation therein as regards renewal of lease, amount of rent, and all other matters.

E. It shall be a breach of good faith, and a breach of this CONTRACT, to render an unfavorable reference for a tenant because of his/her participation in the TENANTS' ASSOCIATION or his/her membership therein.

F. It shall constitute a breach of good faith, and a breach of this CONTRACT, to evict a tenant, occupant, or resident of the building for ASSOCIATION membership, activity, or participation, including taking part in such actions as lawful picketing of LANDLORD, other lawful actions against the landlord, or rent strikes.

G. It shall constitute a breach of good faith, and a breach of this CONTRACT, for the LANDLORD to include in any lease with any individual tenant or possible tenant in the above BUILDING any part or portion of a lease which is contradictory or in conflict with this agreement.

H. It shall constitute a breach of good faith, and a breach of this CONTRACT, for the LANDLORD to: (1) prohibit the ASSOCIATION from distributing written materials to all residents concerning ASSOCIATION ACTIVITIES: (2) prohibit ASSOCIATION representatives from contacting residents within the physical confines of the BUILDING or property; (3) prohibit the ASSOCIATION from holding meetings on the premises; and (4) prohibit the ASSOCIATION from erecting bulletin or notice boards in public areas of the premises or placing notices in public places.

V. Payment of Rents

A. Payment of rents to Management are absolutely dependent upon the LANDLORD'S performance of each and every covenant of this AGREEMENT, and all other agreements and attachments hereto. The LANDLORD covenants and warrants that the above BUILDING is habitable and in substantial compliance with the building, electrical, water, fire and plumbing codes of the city of Chicago, and all other codes, regulations, ordinances, laws, and court decisions which in any way apply. The LANDLORD further covenants and warrants that he will maintain the BUILDING in a habitable condition for the length of each and every lease.

B. Failure to maintain each and every dwelling unit, all public and common areas, and all other parts of the BUILDING in a safe, well-repaired, secure, sanitary, and lawful manner strikes at the very essence of this AGREEMENT.

C. Failure by the LANDLORD to properly perform his duties under this clause is good and sufficient reason for all rents to be withheld until such time as compliance is demonstrated.

D. The TENANTS' ASSOCIATION may take any other action it deems necessary to protect the health, safety, and welfare of its membership including hiring outside contractors to perform urgent or necessary tasks and pay for the same from withheld rents, provided that no such act shall be done until after the LANDLORD is duly notified and fails to take satisfactory action promptly.

VI. Grievance Procedure

A. Authorized representatives of both parties shall meet jointly not less than once every two weeks on a regular basis to present, negotiate, and resolve grievances arising out of this AGREEMENT, its attachments, and other agreements and arrangements reached under this AGREEMENT.

B. Emergency meetings of the above joint grievance committee may be called on 24-hour notice by any member of the grievance committee. Such meetings shall be called in writing and the notice shall state the specific reason for the emergency meeting. Notice must be delivered to the chief representative of each party.

C. All grievances shall be presented in writing.

D. All settlements and resolutions shall be in writing and signed by representatives of both parties.

E. The grievance committee will establish a priority of grievances: (1) Class I grievances shall be considered the most urgent with immediate resolution required; (2) Class II will be considered serious grievances with prompt attention required; (3) Class III grievances will be considered minor situations which require correction within a reasonable time; (4) Class IV grievances relate to long-term problems and need considerable time to correct.

F. The joint grievance committee shall be authorized to negotiate final settlements.

G. Arbitration and fact-finding shall be employed if the joint committee cannot adequately resolve a grievance. A mutually acceptable and neutral fact-finder and arbitrator shall be approved by the joint committee. Binding arbitration shall be employed upon approval of the joint committee.

H. Upon failure to resolve a complaint by negotiation, arbitration, or performance, the TENANTS' ASSOCIATION may take any action it deems necessary to protect the health, safety, security, and welfare of its membership including: (1) withholding rents; (2) hiring outside contractors to perform urgent or necessary tasks and pay for the same from withheld rents and/or deduct the amount of the payments from future rents; and (3) taking action at law.

LANDLORD shall be notified in writing prior to any such actions.

VII. Contract

Upon the signing by both parties to this agreement, this COLLECTIVE BARGAINING AGREEMENT shall become a binding and legal CONTRACT between the two parties, and shall be made a part of each and every lease signed between Management and TENANTS' ASSOCIATION members, now and in the future. Further, that where conflict exists between this AGREEMENT (and its attachments) and the lease, only this AGREEMENT shall survive, and the other shall be considered null and void.

SIGNATURES:

Tenants' Association	Management Co./Landlord
_____	_____
Date	Date
_____	_____
Date	Date
_____	_____
Date	Date

APPENDIX L

Sample Letter of Complaints from Tenants to Landlords

Letters of complaints and requests to the landlord must contain specific information about each apartment and each individual complaint. It must also contain deadlines for completion of work requested.

Copies should go to the landlord, all tenants, the city building department, and your lawyer. Not all of your demands must relate to code violations, however, the city will not respond to the whole list—only those things which break the building code.

Signatures of all those making the complaints must be attached to the letter, unless a viable tenants' association exists and has officers authorized to sign the letter and represent the tenants to the management.

The following sample letter is only a short excerpt from a long letter covering several hundred detailed complaints.

```
                                        July 16, 19__

___(Agent)
Management Company
(Address)
Chicago, IL


Dear ___:                    NOTICE

We, the tenants and residents of (address), Chicago,
Illinois, hereby put you on notice that if certain
conditions in and around the building we currently
reside in are not corrected by such dates as specified,
we the tenants and residents of this building will
withhold any and all rents and place them in a special
```

holding account, until such conditions are corrected to
the satisfaction of the tenants and residents, and the
satisfaction of all official agencies having jurisdic-
tion over the building specified. Then dispositions of
such withheld rents will be reconsidered by us, the
residents and tenants of this building, and such funds
will be disposed of as we all decide, in accordance
with prevailing laws.

Please correct the following problems BEFORE August 1,
19__:

I. At (address)
1. Apartment 1 Front:
    Install window-locks on all windows.
    Install deadbolts on all exterior/external doors.

2. Apartment 3 Front:
    Install glass diffusers, covers, and domes to all
      electrical fixtures.
    Secure, stabilize, and refinish all window frames.
    Repair all windows to operate properly including
      free movement and counterbalance chains.
    Complete installation of front window, plaster,
      wood trim, and paint.

3. Apartment 3 Rear:
    Secure all window frames to prevent them from
      falling out of walls.
    Repair water pipes to stop leaks under kitchen
      sinks.
    Repair window frames on porch to stop rain from
      leaking in.

II. At (address)
1. Apartment 1 Rear:
    Supply new, working refrigerator as promised at
      time lease was signed.

Repair kitchen windows and supply proper ventilation
to kitchen.
Supply proper, new, working cooking stove as
promised at time lease was signed.

Please correct the following problems WITHIN 24 HOURS
OF RECEIPT AND NO LATER THAN 3 P.M., JULY 19, 197_:

Restore all cooking gas and repair all gas leaks.
Supply and install all necessary hook-ups to:

___ Apartment 3 Front.
___ Apartments 1 Front/1Rear.

Please consider the further conditions:
No power, gas, or water shut-offs are to be made
without 24-hour prior written notice to all
residents.
Major failures of power, gas, or water must be
repaired within 24 hours after receipt of notice
by tenant or tenants.
All repairs and maintenance of electrical, gas, and
plumbing systems to be repaired and maintained by
licensed journeymen only.
Except in case of emergency, all residents involved
will be notified in writing 3 days (72 hours) in
advance of repair, maintenance, or extermination
visits. Under no circumstances, except
emergencies, will anyone, except the tenant or
resident, be admitted to an apartment without
prior arrangement, notification, and permission
of the tenant or resident.
All workmen will completely clean up after they
have finished each day, and restore apartment
to its proper state, including plastering holes,
repainting, cleaning of walls and floors, and
replacing of furniture in proper place.

Failure to respond to our legitimate request will
result in a complete inspection of this building by
city officials and others; failure to take action on
your part may also result in other civil and criminal
legal actions as prescribed by law.

We reserve the right to update and change our requests.

We, the undersigned, without pressure or coercion or
threat, hereby declare our approval of these above-
mentioned demands, and give our total support to the
Tenants' Association in its joint venture to correct
the above-mentioned failures and problems, and we
hereby affix our sign and seal on this sixteenth day of
July, nineteen hundred and _____ in Chicago, Illinois.

<u>Signed</u>:

APPENDIX M

The Last Month "Instead of Rent" Letter

This is a sample of a letter you can send to your landlord instead of your last month's rent if you believe you will not get your security deposit back and do not want to go into small claims court later. Send this letter thirty-one days before the end of your lease. Send it certified (return receipt) and keep a copy for your files.

Dear Landlord:

    The lease to my apartment terminates 31 days from now on (date) and I will not be renewing the lease. You are currently holding a security deposit of $_____ paid to your company on (date or dates), plus interest.

    You have my permission to apply $_____ of that security deposit to my last month's rent. Any surplus may be applied towards damages (if any) and all remainder should be returned to me (along with all receipts of work performed) within thirty days of the termination of the lease.

                    Sincerely,

While not precisely "legal," this method of security deposit recovery is effective. It is not worth the landlord's time or trouble to evict you during the last month of the lease, plus he has no standing to sue because he, indeed, has his money already.

Index